Working with
Sexually Abusive
Adolescents

Working with Children and Adolescents

Series editor: Masud S. Hoghughi

Over the course of this century there has been an increasing tendency to base social intervention on evidence of relevance and efficacy. This has been boosted in our own times by the financial demands on governments and greater 'consumer' awareness of their right to high quality service. This is particularly noticeable in health and social services, where demand for 'evidence-based' practice seems to be at its keenest.

Writers and publishers, aware of this demand, are seeking to meet it in a variety of ways and this series aims to be a significant contribution to that process. The books are commissioned from practitioner–academics who are able to cross-translate theory and practice. Authors are encouraged to tackle subjects on which there is not a great amount of information readily available. The perspectives adopted take account of evident diversities across the national and cultural boundaries. Above all, they aim to provide a sound theoretical basis, allied with applied information, to improve coherent practice.

The topics are mainly concerned with 'problem' areas affecting young people, since these are of greatest concern and, unless skilfully dealt with, can result in the blighting of young people's futures. Each book will cover the major theoretical issues, bringing together the relevant information and presenting it in a form suitable for practitioners. The books should also contribute to the continuing development of other relevant disciplines. The information provided in these books will facilitate coherent and high quality practice and thus contribute to young people's welfare.

WORKING WITH SEXUALLY ABUSIVE ADOLESCENTS

Edited by
Masud S. Hoghughi
with Surya R. Bhate
and Finlay Graham

SAGE Publications
London • Thousand Oaks • New Delhi

First published 1997

 SAGE Publications Ltd
6 Bonhill Street
London EC2A 4PU

SAGE Publications Inc.
2455 Teller Road
Thousand Oaks, California 91320

SAGE Publications India Pvt Ltd
32, M-Block Market
Greater Kailash – I
New Delhi 110 048

*RJ
506
548
W67
1997*

British Library Cataloguing in Publication data

A catalogue record for this book is available
from the British Library

ISBN 0 8039 7758 1
ISBN 0 8039 7759 X (pbk)

Library of Congress catalog record available

Typeset by Mayhew Typesetting, Rhayader, Powys
Printed in Great Britain by Biddles Ltd, Guildford, Surrey

Contents

Notes on Contributors

Surya R. Bhate is a Consultant Forensic Adolescent Psychiatrist in the Kolvin Unit, Newcastle City Health (NHS) Trust and Senior Lecturer in Adolescent Psychiatry at the University of Newcastle.

Kevin J. Epps is Principal Clinical and Forensic Psychologist at the Glenthorne Youth Treatment Centre, Birmingham.

Dawn Fisher is a Consultant Clinical Psychologist at Llanarth Court Psychiatric Hospital, Llanarth, nr Raglan, Gwent, NP5 2YD.

Finlay Graham is a Consultant Forensic Adolescent Psychologist in the Kolvin Unit, Newcastle City Health (NHS) Trust.

Julie Hird is a Consultant Clinical Psychologist at Ashworth Hospital and Lecturer in Forensic Clinical Psychology at the University of Liverpool.

Masud S. Hoghughi is a Consultant Clinical Psychologist in the Young People's Unit, Newcastle City Health (NHS) Trust, Newcastle General Hospital, Honorary Professor of Psychology at the University of Hull and Senior Research Fellow at the University of Durham.

Gail McGregor is a Consultant Clinical Psychologist in the Regional Forensic Psychiatry Service, Bamburgh Clinic, Newcastle City Health (NHS) Trust, St Nicholas Hospital.

Adrian Needs is a Senior Psychologist at HM Prison Service College, Wakefield, West Yorkshire.

Graeme Richardson is a Clinical Psychologist in the Regional Forensic Psychiatry Service, Kolvin Unit, Newcastle City Health (NHS) Trust, Newcastle General Hospital.

John L. Taylor is a Consultant Clinical Psychologist with the Northgate and Prudhoe NHS Trust, Northgate Hospital, Northumberland and Associate Teacher in Clinical Psychology at the University of Newcastle.

Preface

Adolescent sexual abusers have been around probably since the beginnings of human society. However, it is only in the past two or three decades that they have begun to be identified as a specific source of threat, demanding specialised intervention. The statistics quoted in this book and elsewhere attest to the rise in the number of adolescent sex offenders, not least because families and social agencies are now more conscious of the long term damage resulting from abuse and hence readier to report abusers.

This book was conceived when all three editors were involved in Aycliffe Centre for Children as Director, Consultant Psychiatrist and Consultant Psychologist respectively. At that time Aycliffe was the largest specialised centre for the assessment and treatment of seriously disordered adolescents in the United Kingdom. Because of its empirical orientation, it had already identified adolescent abusers as a distinct group of disordered young people who required specialised intervention. Accordingly, it developed a wholly separate facility for dealing with them. Out of that practice a national training course evolved, and from discussions about the syllabus for that course, the need for up to date material and hence, this book.

At the time of conceiving this work, apart from the book by Ryan and Lane, it was the only one aimed specifically at the adolescent sexual abuser. Since embarking on it, Barbaree, Marshall and Hudson's justly famous book has come out, as have chapters in a number of others. However, we believe ours remains the only one which is concerned with detailed practice from UK and European viewpoints which are legislatively and professionally quite different from those of North America. Our debt to others' work is amply illustrated in the extensive bibliography at the end of the book.

We believe this book complements rather than displaces others. It is written by people who are daily practitioners with abusers. The orientation of the chapters is, therefore, towards scrutiny of the theoretical material from the standpoint of practical utility. Every chapter could have been significantly expanded.

This work has been in gestation for some time. Apart from the contending pressures on all the authors who are busy clinicians, it also coincided with significant changes in the personal circumstances of the first editor. Colleagues at the Regional Adolescent Forensic Psychiatry Service (Kolvin Unit) provided a haven in which most of the work on this book was carried out. Lionel Joyce, Chief Executive of Newcastle City Health (NHS) Trust, was most generous in recognising the potential of this collaborative enterprise and enabling it to happen. The fact that the Unit is also the setting for some of the best work with adolescent abusers in the United Kingdom helped shape the structure and focus of the book.

The editors are grateful to Ziyad Marar of Sage for his forbearance and understanding of delays while the book was being prepared. Doreen Kipling has been a compassionate and competent midwife to this book, as to so many others. We hope this collective effort will provide a stepping stone to further, more detailed and practically useful work to be published on this deserving and anxiety-provoking group.

Masud S. Hoghughi
Surya R. Bhate
Finlay Graham

1

Sexual Abuse by Adolescents

Masud Hoghughi

Personal safety and protection are fundamental concerns of any society. At its extreme, threat to individuals undermines the wider society and its survival. From the earliest days, therefore, the harshest social sanctions have been reserved for those people who infringe socially accepted boundaries of personal safety. At its core sexual abuse is a threat to personal safety but is also overlain with other considerations which take it beyond physical hurt.

Sexual matters have, over the millennia, acquired particular moral connotations, arising from the early Judaeo-Christian preoccupation with 'legitimate lineage' and with any form of violation which puts this in jeopardy. More recently the rapid changes in sexual norms, open advocacy of lowering the age of consent to sex, awareness of paedophile attitudes and the discovery of widespread sexual abuse of children by adults have given these concerns special urgency. Although the 'discovery' of this problem is relatively recent, highlighted in the United Kingdom by the Cleveland affair, such abuse has a long history. From the 1960s onwards, with 'flower power', a rise in anti-authority attitudes and the formulation of feminist ideologies pointing to abusive power relationships that have resulted from male dominance of social structures, we have become aware of many factors which generate and sustain sexual abuse. Children, as the most powerless and least vocal, are now probably the most abused section of the population, particularly when they suffer from additional disadvantages, such as poverty or intellectual and sensory handicaps.

Evidence has also come to the fore that sexual abuse of children has grave consequences both immediately and in the long term. This 'victim perspective' raises significant political and social issues about how far society is able to protect its most vulnerable members. It also highlights an inescapable consequence of society's overwhelming preoccupation with sex which shapes individual attitudes and creates an atmosphere in which abusive behaviour flourishes.

Sexual abuse and sexual offending

Anti-social acts such as sexual abuse, like other behaviour, can be differentiated according to characteristics of the perpetrators, the victims and the acts themselves. There is general consensus that penetrative and coercive sexual acts are among the most unacceptable forms of anti-social behaviour. As with all other 'problems', an act of *judgement* is involved in interpreting the behaviour as 'unacceptable' (Hoghughi 1992). This, in turn, invokes questions of *what* has been done, *where*, *how*, with what *intent*, by *whom* and a range of other issues. Every one of these opens up a mass of complex jurisprudential, social and psychological issues, almost none of which have been satisfactorily settled.

This point crucially affects our discourse about sexually abusive adolescents, how we identify them, what we do with them, to what purpose and in what contexts. These uncertainties and variabilities about defining the very basic building blocks of sexual abuse render statistics about abusive young people and judgements of what should be done with them uncertain.

What is sexually abusive behaviour by adolescents?

In common with others, we use the term 'adolescent' to cover all children and young people between the ages of 8 and 21 years, although more commonly the reference is to the ages 12–18.

Before we judge an adolescent as 'abusive', we need to have some idea of what constitutes normal sexual behaviour. Normal sexual development is poorly understood and clear milestones with age-related sexual behaviours in rapidly changing societies have yet to be identified. Nevertheless, there is the beginning of some consensus in the definition of abusive behaviour which justifies intervention.

'Abuse' can be parsimoniously defined as a 'sexual act with another person who does not or cannot give informed consent'. It is a negative term, indicating any act intended or perceived as damaging or demeaning, according to the victim or a *concerned outsider*. The act can emanate from any source (parent, stranger or another child) and range in quality from mild to serious, whether or not it involves physical injury.

As with crimes in general, there are always problems in determining intent of the perpetrator or consequence of the act for the victim, particularly when intent is denied or abuse seems opportunistic. Although it is sensible to examine intent closely and establish it, if possible, greater weight should be given to the consequences of the act for the victim, whether physical or psychological, in determining its gravity. Consequences would encompass thoughts, feelings and/or physical impact, in the short, medium or long term, contemporaneously experienced or subsequently recalled and judged as abusive.

According to this view, if a sexual act between two people is regarded by one of them as 'abusive', then phenomenologically it is. All we need is for the victim or someone on her behalf to say it was. In this view, intention of the perpetrator or 'objective damage' is irrelevant. However, as allegations of sexual abuse have significant consequences for the perpetrator, the matter is frequently subjected to legal examination of evidence.

This is where abusive acts overlap with 'sexual offending'. The only feature that separates the two is that offending behaviour is publicly categorised as falling within a specific legal definition, warranting intervention by official agencies and perhaps demanding judicial response. Sexual offending is a form of 'discovered sexual abuse' which is deemed to be serious enough to warrant official response. So all offences are a form of sexual abuse, but not the other way round. As we shall see later, there is probably more sexual abuse than ever comes to light and much of that, even when clearly offending, is not treated as such.

In this book, by concerning ourselves with sexual abuse rather than offending we cover the full range of sexual acts which are deemed inappropriate between adolescents and others, whether these are legally adjudicated or not. There is, at present, no research evidence to suggest that, apart from their legal contexts, the behaviours and the perpetrator/victim characteristics that underlie offending and abuse are any different. General evidence concerning other forms of overt and hidden delinquency further support this view (Hoghughi 1983).

Legal issues

Legal concern with sexual offending goes back a long way. Until recently sexual offending was a variant of offences against the person. In the UK, sexual offences are currently dealt with under a variety of Acts of Parliament which categorise them as rape, buggery, unlawful sexual intercourse, indecency or abduction. They are regarded as significantly more serious than property offences. The gravity of an individual sexual offence is judged by its impact on the victim, the circumstances surrounding it and the attitudes and personality of the perpetrator. The penalties available for sexual offences by young people range from supervision to long detention in custody, depending on the age of the offender and the gravity of the offence.

The relationship between age and acknowledgement of offending is complex. In UK law, children under the age of 10 are not deemed to have the necessary intellectual and social equipment to form intent for committing offences. Between the ages of 10 and 12 they may have the ability to form intent but this has to be proved by the prosecution. Over the age of 12, they are exposed to the same tests of legal competence and responsibility as adults. In this respect, Britain has a lower age of criminal responsibility than most other European countries.

However, even with this tight age limit, until recently young people under the age of 14 were not regarded as capable of committing forcible rape. A number of prominent and much-publicised cases altered this picture. In 1992 the Home Office circulated evidence to show that a significant number of rapes (although a small proportion of the total number) were committed by young people under the age of 14. Accordingly, recent legal changes make it possible to prosecute children over the age of 10 for sexual offences.

Clinicians and social workers have been aware for a long time that very young children are capable of sexually abusive behaviour, even where there may be doubts about their understanding and intentionality. There are, however, few such doubts about teenagers, increasing numbers and proportions of whom engage in sexual activity with their peers. Teenage pregnancy is one outcome of what must be regarded as consensual and, therefore, non-abusive sex between young people.

Equally, we know from clinical practice that in disorganised social and family environments where children are not properly supervised, much 'groomed' or coercive sex takes place. This does not come to light, often because of the prevailing subculture of the environment, where predatory behaviour against person and property is an accepted part of life. When it does surface, families and official agencies are often disinclined to litigate because of mutual suspicion and the unpleasant consequences of getting caught up with the law.

Incidence and prevalence

All statistics suffer from the dual error of containing some items that should not be included and excluding others that should. As our comments on the reasons for under-reporting will show, this is a serious problem with statistics of sexual abuse, particularly when young people are involved. However, there seems to be some emerging consensus about the extent and seriousness of sexual victimisation.

Many studies of clinical populations contain information about the extent of sexual victimisation (e.g. Coons and Milstein 1986, Friedman and Harrison 1984). But since these are biased samples which do not give any idea of the extent of the problem in the whole population, it is more sensible to look at the statistics of incidence and prevalence to gain some idea of the level of sexual abuse. *Incidence* refers to numbers of new cases identified over a specific period. *Prevalence*, on the other hand, is identified on the basis of retrospective information gained from a variety of samples, to give some idea of the *cumulative* extent of the problem in the whole population. In both cases, there are very few studies of adolescent abusers and their victims. The latest available statistics for England and Wales (Home Office 1994) are shown in Table 1.1.

Criminal statistics concerning juveniles and published annually by the Home Office set out only general categories (see Tables 1.2–1.4).

Table 1.1   *Offenders found guilty at all courts or cautioned for indictable sexual offences, by offence: England and Wales, 1993*

Offence	Offenders found guilty or cautioned
Buggery	245
Indecent assault on a male	667
Indecency between males	862
Rape	482
Indecent assault on a female	3,471
Unlawful sexual intercourse with girl under 13	143
Unlawful sexual intercourse with girl under 16	723
Incest	127
Procuration	180
Abduction	43
Bigamy	42
Soliciting by a man	330
Gross indecency with a child	304
Total sexual offences	7,619

Source: Home Office 1994

There is some controversy about whether juvenile crime varies in step with the general level of crime, although most commentators *in general* believe that it does. If this is the case, then Table 1.5, for offenders of all ages, may give some indication of change in the level of detected sexual offences by juveniles.

The British Crime Survey (Home Office 1988) estimates that only about 10% of rape cases are reported, although this percentage is increasing due to changes in quality of police and judicial response and shifts in public attitude. Our own recent work in North-East England suggests that only between 10 and 15% of all *known* sexually abusive and offending adolescents are officially dealt with or reported for further legal and professional intervention. In general, these and following data indicate that sexual offences by young people are steadily increasing and that around 30% of all sexual crimes are committed by males under the age of 21.

Other data give a more rounded picture of the extent of sexually abusive behaviour by adolescents. A study of child sexual abuse in Northern Ireland (Royal Belfast Hospital for Sick Children 1990) showed an incidence of 0.9 per 1,000 of the population, although the authors believed a figure double that

Table 1.2   *Offenders found guilty at all courts, by type of offence, sex and age group, England and Wales, 1993*

Number of offenders (thousands)

Type of indictable offence	Males			Females		
	Aged 10 and under 14	Aged 14 and under 18	Aged 18 and under 21	Aged 10 and under 14	Aged 14 and under 18	Aged 18 and under 21
Violence against the person	0.3	4.0	6.3	0.1	0.8	0.6
Sexual offences	0.0	0.3	0.3	0.0	0.0	0.0
Burglary	0.6	7.8	10.2	0.0	0.3	0.3
Robbery	0.1	1.2	1.1	0.0	0.1	0.1
Theft and handling stolen goods	1.0	11.3	19.7	0.1	1.8	3.8
Fraud and forgery	0.0	0.3	1.6	0.0	0.1	0.6
Criminal damage	0.2	1.3	1.7	0.0	0.2	0.1
Drug offences	0.0	0.7	3.8	0.0	0.0	0.3
Other (excluding motoring offences)	0.1	2.1	7.0	0.0	0.2	0.6
Motoring offences	0.0	0.3	1.4	0.0	0.0	0.0
Total	2.3	29.3	53.1	0.2	3.5	6.4

Source: Home Office 1994

Table 1.3 *Sexual offenders found guilty at all courts or cautioned, by sex and age group, England and Wales, 1993*

All sexual offences	Males			Females		
	Aged 10 and under 14	Aged 14 and under 18	Aged 18 and under 21	Aged 10 and under 14	Aged 14 and under 18	Aged 18 and under 21
Number of offenders (thousands)	2.1	1.2	0.7	0.0	0.0	0.0
Percentages	1.0	2.0	1.0	0.0	0.0	0.0

Source: Home Office 1994

Table 1.4 *Magistrates' courts in England and Wales 1993: proceedings for sexual offences*

	10–14	14–18	18–21
Male			
Indecent assault on a female	68	349	266
Rape	0	120	147
(Total female	1	4	6)

(1.83 per 1,000 of the population) to be a more accurate figure. These are in a similar range to a number of American studies: NAPN (1988), Sarafino (1979), Bagley (1984, 1985) and Russell (1984)

Many people, when given the opportunity, report having been sexually abused as children. Given the pervasive social preoccupation with sex, time spent together with age mates and younger children and hence opportunities for sexual behaviour and the relative 'invisibility' of adolescents compared with adults, a significant proportion of these victims would have been abused by teenagers. This is confirmed by studies which show that teenagers (about 20–25%) would be happy to commit rape (and presumably even more less grave abusive acts) if they could be sure of not being caught or punished (Briere and Runtz 1989, Malamuth 1986). American studies show a disproportionate number of male rapists (somewhere between 27 and 50%) to be in the under 21 age group (Amir 1971, Macdonald 1971, Mulvihill et al. 1969), though these figures differ from those of Britain (Wright 1980).

Rapaport and Burkhart (1984) show that about a third of college students questioned had engaged in sexually coercive acts, and 50% of Muchlenard and Linton's (1987) college male sample had perpetrated abusive acts. These are admitted because the youngsters have a value system which regards 'date rape' as acceptable. The findings are concordant with others that show between a third and half of rape victims to be adolescents (Amir 1971, Hayman et al. 1968, Hursch 1977, Krasner et al. 1976, Svalastoga 1962).

As even this brief exposition has shown, the estimates of incidence and prevalence of sexual abuse by youngsters are both high and an underestimate. Given the secrecy that normally surrounds sexual behaviour even among consenting adults, it could not be otherwise. In the case of juveniles, there

Table 1.5   *Notifiable offences recorded by the police: summary of key figures, England and Wales*

Number of sexual offences (thousands)

	1983	1984	1985	1986	1987	1988	1989	1990	1991	1992	1993
Rape	1.3	1.4	1.8	2.3	2.5	2.9	3.3	3.4	4.0	4.1	4.6
Indecent assault on a female	10.8	10.8	11.4	11.8	13.3	14.1	15.4	15.8	15.8	16.2	17.4
Other sexual offences	8.2	8.0	8.2	8.6	9.3	9.6	11.1	9.9	9.6	9.2	9.3

Percentage change from previous year

	1984	1985	1986	1987	1988	1989	1990	1991	1992	1993	Average annual percentage change (1983–93)
Rape	+7	−29	−34	+8	−16	+16	+3	+19	+2	+11	−13.2
Indecent assault on a female	0	+5	+4	+13	+6	+9	+3	0	+3	+7	+4.8
Other sexual offences	−4	−3	+4	+9	+2	+16	+11	−3	−5	+2	+13

are many more reasons for being cautious about reported incidents (Hoghughi and Richardson 1990a). These include:

- disorganised and chaotic families in which abuse of or by a child is not noticed;
- suspicion of police and official agencies and the tendency not to involve them unless stakes are very high;
- experiences of parents as abuser or abused, which lead them to underplay importance of sexual abuse;
- child victim's inability to articulate the abuse;
- victim's fear of parental reactions;
- victim's concern for reputation among peers and in the neighbourhood;
- unwillingness of offender to self refer because of feeling that nothing wrong has been done;
- age of perpetrator and tendency by parents and official agencies to underplay anti-social acts;
- 'boys will be boys' ideas and hope that the youngsters will grow out of such behaviour and not repeat it;
- fear that official intervention might exacerbate perpetrator's condition and add to his problems;
- fear of consequences for victim and victim's family if they report it and are dragged into the law enforcement system;
- absence of any clear guidelines about what to do with the abuser and uncertainty about outcomes, even if a treatment facility could be found;
- confusion in public services and legal system about balance of public protection and diversion from the criminal justice system in the case of adolescent perpetrators.

Characteristics of abusers

With increasing research on adolescent abusers, a cumulative picture is gradually emerging of their main characteristics. In considering these, however, it is important to recognise that the 'averages' reported hide wide variations in individual profiles. Although general conclusions may be drawn, work with individuals has to be based on accurate *individual* assessments.

Age

Most adolescent sexual abusers tend to be between 14 and 15 years old. However, abusers as young as 8 (Kahn and Chambers 1991) and as old as 19 (Becker et al. 1986b) are reported. In a recent study of 100 English adolescent abusers, Richardson and colleagues (1995a) report a mean age of 15, with an age range of 11–18 years. There is some hint that adolescent rapists are older than child molesters, as might be expected given the greater physical force and daring needed for physical assault.

Socio-economic status

In general, adolescent abusers do not appear significantly different from their otherwise delinquent peers. If anything, they tend to come from somewhat less disorganised and criminal families (Fagan and Wexler 1988) and to have engaged in less delinquency. Nevertheless, as might be expected from those who commit such grossly deviant acts, studies show a consistently high level of family and parental pathology including unstable family backgrounds, parental separations, violence, experience of physical abuse and neglect and only about a third of adolescents living with both parents (Awad et al. 1984, Bagley 1992, Becker et al. 1986a, Fehrenbach et al. 1986, Lewis et al. 1979). These are similar to the findings of Beckett et al. (1994) with a group of Manchester adolescents.

It is interesting that child molesters appear to come from less disorganised and deprived families (Awad and Saunders 1989, Hoghughi and Richardson 1990b, Vinogradov et al. 1988). As we shall see later, differences seem to be emerging between molesters and rapists. In the most recent study Richardson et al. (1995a) found 73% of their sample of 100 English abusers to come from the Registrar General's social class V, 17% from class IV and 10% from the remaining classes. They also found that over 50% of their youngsters had no contact with the natural father and came from families where parents had separated with a history of parental violence towards the children.

Although in most respects the English sample were like their North American 'model adolescent sex offenders' (Ryan and Lane 1991a), they were likely to be of lower socio-economic status and higher Caucasian origin. They were also more likely to come from broken homes, to have been taken into residential care and to have had more school and anti-social behaviour problems (Richardson et al. 1995a).

Intellectual and educational features

As with delinquents in general, abusive adolescents are unlikely to be intellectually very bright or verbally very articulate (Hoghughi and Richardson 1990b). They are likely to have significant difficulties at school and to be poor achievers (Fehrenbach et al. 1986, Kahn and Chambers 1991, Saunders and Awad 1988).

Becker et al. (1993) found that although a much larger proportion of their sex offenders than ordinary delinquents regarded themselves as having learning difficulties (50% against 19%), their general intelligence level was similar. Richardson et al. (1995a) found that almost two-thirds of their sample were chronic truants, 44% 'statemented' under the 1981 Education Act and 78% presented behaviour problems at school.

Social development

With growing recognition of the range of skills required in making and maintaining social relationships, much research has shown that anti-social adolescents have a wide range of social skills deficits (e.g. Hoghughi 1996, Hollin 1989). It is not, therefore, surprising that adolescent abusers are shown repeatedly to have difficulties in this area (Awad et al. 1984, Fehrenbach et al. 1986, Nangle and Hansen 1993). Even amongst a group of seriously disordered, anti-social youngsters, abusive adolescents show particular difficulties in self presentation, assertiveness, sympathy and sensitivity skills (Hoghughi and Richardson 1990b).

Becker et al. (1993) found similarly that their sexual abusers showed a higher degree of withdrawal and social anxiety than non-sexual offenders. Many more reported being bullied at school and having few friends or social contacts. Related to this, only 50% of the group had had girlfriends compared with 81% of 'normal' delinquents. A minority of these had experienced consensual sex compared with nearly 60% of delinquent youngsters. As yet another difference between child molesters and the group who assaulted adults, Awad and Saunders (1991) found that two-thirds of child molesters were lonely and isolated individuals compared with-one third of the assaulters.

Clinical state

Previous research has shown anti-social children to suffer from a wide range of clinical symptoms (Hoghughi 1996, Hollin 1989). The same applies to abusive adolescents, both molesters and assaulters (Bagley 1992, Becker et al. 1986a). Richardson et al. (1995a) found that 72% of their youngsters had had 'severe' childhood problems, 69% were physically aggressive, 61% were beyond parental control and had committed a wide range of offences, including a remarkable 30% who had set fires.

Kavoussi et al. (1988) using the *DSM-IIIR* (American Psychiatric Association 1987) found conduct disorder as the most common clinical feature of their adolescent sex offenders. Bagley's (1992) sample of sex offenders suffered from more hyperactivity, anxiety, depression, suicidal ideas and poor self concept than his ordinary young offenders. By contrast Richardson et al. (1995a) found that none of their sample of 100 English adolescent abusers was or had been suffering from mental disorder, although many had the conduct problems associated with persistent anti-social acts.

Experience of prior victimisation

This is one of the most significant features of sexually abusive adolescents, apparently marking them out from ordinary delinquents. As awareness of issues of sexual abuse has grown, so researchers have paid more attention to this feature, which is now seen to apply to a substantial proportion (though probably still a minority) of adolescent abusers (Groth 1978). Indeed 'theories' and 'models' of sexual abusiveness have been developed (Becker et al. 1986a, Becker et al. 1993, Ryan et al. 1987) which posit experience of abuse as victim as a significant precursor of becoming a perpetrator. There is considerable variation in estimates of victimised adolescent perpetrators. Bagley (1992) found a significant difference between sexual abusers and other young offenders in experience of victimisation. On the other hand Benoit and Kennedy (1992) did not discover such a difference.

Other research focused on the *amount* and kind of victim-isation rather than whether it has occurred. Becker and her colleagues (Becker et al. 1988, Becker and Stein 1991), estimate that about 30% claim prior abuse. Others such as Awad and Saunders (1991) estimate over 21% whilst Pierce and Pierce (1990) estimate 48% and Kahn and Lafond (1988) almost 60%. Richardson et al. (1995a) found externally corroborated evidence that 41% of their sample of abusive boys had themselves been sexually abused, with about half of these subjected to penetrative acts. Awad and Saunders' research (1989, 1991) suggests that the incidence of prior victimisation may be greater among molesters than assaulters, thus lending support to a 'social learning' or modelling perspective in child molestation cases.

The overall conclusion from the ever growing data on the characteristics of abusers is that they are probably more like non-specialised young offenders than different from them. It seems safest to assume that the same conditions that generate and maintain more serious forms and intensity of 'normal' delinquency pertain to sexual offending. Within this large group, there are probable systematic differences but we do not yet have enough information to be certain what they are.

Characteristics of abuse

Researchers have found it useful to distinguish three forms of abuse or offending: (1) non-contact abuse, which includes exhibitionism, voyeurism and obscene phone calls; (2) sexual molestation, which covers the full range of abusive acts against a child; and (3) sexual assault, which covers rape or attempted rape of a peer or adult, most often female (Becker et al. 1993, Murphy et al. 1992)

Numbers

There is general agreement that by the time an adolescent abuser comes to the notice of social agencies, he has probably committed many abusive acts. These range from a few to hundreds (Awad and Saunders 1989, 1991, Becker et al. 1986a, Blaske et al. 1989, Hoghughi and Richardson 1990a, Richardson et al. 1995a). O'Brien (1989) found that his 170 offenders had committed a total of 1,636 criminal sexual acts against 461 victims. In the Richardson et al. study (1995a) the 100 English abusers had committed a total of 1,281 acts against 469 children. Personal clinical experience suggests that in some cases where a relatively bright offender operates in a disorganised environment, there can be almost *daily* victims over many years until he is caught, often accidentally.

Forms of abuse

We must assume that our knowledge of variations in abusive acts is a function of the research instruments. The same can be said of the variations in the incidence of penetrative acts as against fondling and non-contact abusive acts. Fehrenbach et al. (1986) found that 23% of non-incarcerated adolescents had committed rape and 59% fondling.

In a mixed sample of custodial and community cases Kahn and Chambers (1991) reported vaginal penetration in 33% of cases. Wasserman and Kappel (1985), on the other hand, recorded that 60% of the cases involved some penetration, 52% of which were penile. They also observed that penetrative acts increased with the offender's age. In the Richardson et al. study (1995a), the proportion of penetrative acts was 66%, all penile, with the majority targeting the vagina, about 20% the anus and a yet smaller group both.

Age of victim

The victims' ages vary widely. Non-contact offences (such as obscene phone calls and exhibitionism) are primarily directed at female peers and adults (Fehrenbach et al. 1986, Saunders et al. 1986). There is some uncertainty in the research evidence on the age of victims of contact abuse, which seems to be a function of reporting and sampling rather than the reality of abusive acts. Becker et al. (1986a), Fehrenbach et al. (1986) and Wasserman and Kappel (1985) all report that the majority of contact offences are against young children. On the other hand, Saunders et al. (1986) found that 67% of rapes were against female peers. British findings with both institutionalised and community-based youngsters would support a younger age of most victims of abuse, penetrative or not (Hoghughi and

Richardson 1990a, Richardson et al. 1995a, Ussher and Dewberry 1995).

Gaining compliance

Because sexual abuse is a 'person'-directed act, research shows that both child molesters and rapists use verbal threats and physical coercion to overcome victim resistance. Awad and Saunders (1991) and Becker et al. (1986a) confirmed this, whilst showing that use of physical force to overcome resistance increased with the age of the victim. Richardson et al. (1995a) showed that 68% of their perpetrators had used physical force as the primary means of subduing victims. In the majority of cases, verbal and physical intimidation had also been used. Only a minority used inducements, their positions of authority (e.g. babysitter/elder sibling) and verbal persuasion to gain compliance.

Victims' gender

There is general agreement that the majority of reported and detected abusive acts are against females (Fehrenbach et al. 1986, Hoghughi and Richardson 1990b, Richardson et al. 1995a, Wasserman and Kappel 1985). However, the younger the victims, the greater the likelihood that they will be male (Awad and Saunders 1991, Davies and Leitenberg 1987, Richardson et al. 1995a). In the majority of instances, the perpetrator knows the victim (Marshall et al. 1986, 1988), though rapists are more likely to go for victims who are older and unknown to them (Awad and Saunders 1991, Davies and Leitenberg 1987, Fitzpatrick and Fitzgerald 1991).

Typologies of abusive adolescents

Although each adolescent abuser is unique, as a group they have many similarities. To designate and recognise 'types' of adolescent abusers is potentially an efficient way of dealing with them, particularly if relevant treatments can be developed. This is the core of all clinical classifications, of which diagnostic systems are an example (Hobbs 1975, Hoghughi 1992).

The most obvious bases of these are background, personality, social functioning, clinical presentation and abuse characteristics. O'Brien and Bera (1986), for example, describe six types of adolescent abuser – naive experimenter; under-socialised child molester; the sexual aggressive; the sexual compulsive; the disturbed compulsive and the group influenced. Becker (1988) distinguishes between specialised deviant perpetrators and those for whom sexual abuse is part of a wider picture of generalised delinquency.

O'Brien (1989) compared a group of sibling abusers with a variety of others on family and background factors. He found sibling abusers to come from the most seriously disordered families, where they themselves were likely to have been abused by a family member. They also had a longer history of sexual offending and had committed more penetrative acts. The picture is likely to become more complex as our knowledge increases (White and Koss 1993).

Knight and his colleagues have made sustained effort to develop taxonomies of juvenile sex offenders (Knight et al. 1989, Knight and Prentky 1990, 1993, Knight 1992). They have utilised typologies derived from clinical evaluation of adult child molesters with and without adolescent sex offending histories. They report factors which discriminate well among groups of adolescent sex offenders, showing that adolescent child molesters had more often experienced sexual abuse as children than other groups. Juvenile rapists came more frequently than others from families in which deviant or abusive practices against other family members prevailed (see also Hsu and Starzynski 1990).

Richardson and colleagues (1995b) studied a sample of 100 abusive male adolescents between the ages of 11 and 18. Their results show victim choice to be the most revealing criterion for distinguishing four groups of perpetrators. These comprised (1) an incest group; (2) a child group, who had abused unrelated children or those from the extended family; (3) a peer/adult group, who had assaulted age mates or older females; and (4) an abused group, who had victims from at least two groups.

Space restrictions do not permit a detailed critique of these attempted typologies. On the positive side, they indicate the vigour of research activity, generate hypotheses which refine prognostic thinking about perpetrators and may lead to differential diagnostic and therapeutic methods which will promote work in this area.

On the other hand, it does not seem to be adequately appreciated that discovering differential characteristics is not the same as creating reliable and valid typologies. The types derived are closely determined by the data on which they are based, which, as we have seen, are seriously deficient. Furthermore, different statistical methods yield different 'types' from the same data. It is questionable whether at this stage of development of the field, typologies help rather than hinder practical and effective work with abusers, since the similarities of the youngsters, *as sex offenders*, vastly outweigh their differences (Hoghughi 1983)

In general terms, we can already claim to know much about adolescent abusers. This knowledge is rapidly increasing in reliability, extent, finesse and utility. However, apart from the abuse itself, we are nowhere near being able to identify systematically many features that differentiate abusive adolescents from others. In any case, in such a high profile area as sexual abuse, with its grave consequences for both perpetrators and victims, only detailed *individual* assessment rather than recourse to diagnostic or typological information is likely to lead to therapeutically effective work.

2

Theories of Adolescent Sexual Abuse

Masud Hoghughi & Graeme Richardson

Most researchers and practitioners operate by some organising principle – or theory – when working with sexual abusers. Because not every stage of an intervention can be explicitly stated, they have to use assumptions which guide information gathering and interpretation. Since the earliest days of interest in this area, commentators have used prevalent theoretical orientations, such as sociology or dynamic psychology, to understand abusive behaviour. Increasingly, however, theoretical discourse has focused on explaining abuse in specialised terms. A brief overview of these terms may be helpful in indicating the current status of theorising in this area.

In philosophy of science, a theory is an 'organising principle' which sets out the order, relationship, complexity, weight and impact of elements of an area of discourse (Kuhn 1970). There are different scales of theories dealing with issues on a macro to micro basis, often intermixed with 'paradigms' or 'ways of seeing things'. We are not yet in a position to claim that there are *any* theories of sexual abuse in the sense that the term 'theory' is used in, for example, physics. There is nothing like the empirical basis, established by replicated research within appropriate research designs, that would allow us even to be sure of our basic facts. What we have instead are emerging clusters of issues and findings which are *broadly* agreed by workers in the field. These provide a basis for further exploration which, if the workers are self critical and rigorous, add refinement to existing findings and throw light on issues that perplex us.

Sexual abuse is a form of 'deviant behaviour', so laws and theories of 'normal' behaviour are applicable to it. Furthermore, until we can support contrary claims with good evidence,

theories of sexual abuse must fit into our current understanding of how both normal and *other* deviant behaviours are
generated and sustained. Philosophically we cannot have a
theory of sexually abusive behaviour by adolescents which is
unique to such behaviour, until we have exhausted the application of other knowledge about both normal and abnormal
behaviour.

Feminism

This approach, in its many forms, addresses some of the issues
which are the concern of sociology. These include social
structures in which individuals are alienated from mainstream
norms; in which they exercise and are subject to unequal
power; suffer poverty and deprivation; operate within poor
kinship networks and loose social organisations; are exposed to
deviant experiences and practices in the course of growing up
and hence develop a propensity to seek sexual gratification
without concern for its consequences. The crux of feminist
views is that sexually abusive behaviour is a fundamentally
male behaviour (e.g. Dale et al. 1986, MacLeod and Saraga
1991). Male dominated society renders women and children
powerless and portrays them as possible and desirable sexual
victims, through both media projections and extensive availability of pornography. Boys grow up to see themselves as
'macho' and 'superior'. Those with particularly serious problems of identity then seek 'easy' or coercive sex with children
and women.

This core view has acquired many layers of sophisticated
argument, which question the 'construction of facts' about
sexual abuse; explore dominant ideologies; analyse different
theories from a feminist perspective; and examine practice
issues with victims. It is argued that the whole public process of
enquiring into and analysing sexual abuse takes place in legal,
medical, or official structures which shift focus from the 'real
underlying causes' and turn sexual abuse into a 'problem' like
any other to be diagnosed and treated. These structures
constrain analysis of issues and, therefore, the range of possible
and desirable responses to sexual victimisation. Locating the
problem in a family, or in individual or situational factors,
pushes workers wrongly to search for recognisable signs and

symptoms, risk factors, and ways of reducing them, as they would do in any other 'pathology'.

The most recent writings in this area emphasise the special 'meaning' of sexual abuse, the fact that the male gender in many guises continues to influence policy and practice in the field, blurring focus of responsibility for abuse and the tendency of clinical writings, including key texts, to implicate the mother in cases of intrafamilial abuse. These are traced to the traditional gender stereotype of dominant males having their way with weaker women, this characteristic being extended to anyone who is weaker, including other males and, of course, children.

Clearly, feminism is a powerful and increasingly pervasive perspective in what is after all an area that particularly touches women and children. Through direct or empathetic experience, women are better able to articulate the impact of sexual abuse than men, however learned the latter may be. They, after all, know the vulnerability of women like no other. The most important impact of feminism has been to force focus on gender issues as permeating all aspects of society, especially sexually abusive acts (Mackinnon 1987, Vander Hey 1992).

On the other hand, the feminist perspective does not offer a theory which is predictive or capable of being tested in the normal manner. Like psychoanalysis, it suffuses all discussions of sexual abuse. It is more often concerned with polemic (which is necessary but not sufficient) than with scientific scrutiny or progress. More importantly, feminism does not generate practicable methods and techniques of intervention and cannot, therefore, help the practitioner (Gonsiorek et al. 1994).

Family systems perspective

Discussion of the feminist view leads naturally to a consideration of the family, both as the major influence on the abuser and the arena in which much adolescent abuse of younger siblings, children in the community or during 'babysitting' occurs.

This perspective throws light on the family experiences which shape and sustain abusive behaviour. Considerable effort has been devoted to identifying features of families in which abuse takes place, given impetus by the advance of 'systems theory' in the assessment and treatment of a wide range of disordered behaviour (e.g. Fishman 1988). There is ample evidence that the majority of identified adolescent abusers come from unstable and disturbed family backgrounds. We know from many studies that those adolescents with a *generalised* propensity to anti-social acts may have a genetic or constitutional predisposition to disordered behaviour (Hoghughi 1996, Hollin 1989).

Even more widely documented are the facts of adolescents' socioeconomic disadvantage: their poor education and unsatisfactory experiences of parental care, control, expression of affection and support. These disadvantages are often underlined by family instability (Awad et al. 1984, Bagley 1992, Fehrenbach et al. 1986, Hoghughi and Richardson 1990a), family violence (Lewis et al. 1979, Skuse 1995) and particularly by poor attachment bonds (Marshall et al. 1993). Other studies have drawn attention to young people's exposure to sexual deviance among their relatives and their witnessing of sexual activities between parents (Awad and Saunders 1991, Smith 1988). Most commentators have been struck by the abnormally high numbers of abusive adolescents who have themselves been abused in the family (see Chapter 1). Finkelhor's (1984, 1986) 'four factor model' includes family variables as a major (though implicit) factor in the aetiology of sexually abusive behaviour.

Two types of family have been particularly highlighted as conducing to sexual abusiveness: (1) where the pattern of family interactions is rigid, with inappropriately high parental expectations, severe punishments, poor communications and excessively strict rules about sexuality; (2) chaotic family patterns, where boundary setting is inadequate, parents' and children's relationships are poorly defined, there are frequent crises and where feelings are inadequately discussed. Both of these result in inadequate or deviant attachment patterns with serious consequences for the adolescent's ability to form intimate relationships (O'Brien and Bera 1986, Marshall et al. 1990, Loeber 1990). In general, we cannot understand individual behaviour in isolation from its context and the major influences on it, of which family environment is the most important. Its quality has a seminal and continuing impact on individual behaviour. However, other than in specific instances of exposure to inappropriate sexual experiences, the family's role is all-encompassing and diffuse rather than focal.

We need an understanding of abusers' family dynamics as one (albeit very important) element among many others. But, even in cases of exposure to sexual victimisation, we need a range of other explanatory concepts and mechanisms to make sense of why one abused youngster becomes an abuser, but not another. Understanding family structures by itself will not suffice (Vander Hey 1992). Here, it is perhaps worth regarding *parenting* as the critical process variable in whether or not children turn into sexual abusers. Parenting is concerned with the three major objectives of caring for, controlling and developing children.

Care is about ensuring the child's physical, emotional and social survival and well-being. *Control* concerns the setting and enforcement of boundaries of acceptable and desirable behaviour, reflecting both society's and parents' standards. *Development* is aimed at ensuring that the child's potential in all functional areas is fostered and promoted (Hoghughi 1993). To the extent that children are not protected against abuse, pornography, exposure to deviant models and adverse experiences, the care requirement is not met. When they first begin to express attitudes and behaviour patterns which are deviant generally, or specifically in regard to sex, they require a definition and enforcement of boundaries that brings them back into line. When this is not done appropriately or adequately, their behaviour is likely to escalate. There is some evidence that experience of aggression may be a key variable differentiating abusive adolescents from others (Skuse 1995). Poor development of potential of abusers is just one adversity which marks their lives and does not appear to be centrally implicated in abusive behaviour.

We should remember that families themselves operate in a social context. Given the profile of the majority of families of abusers, we recognise that they are themselves inadequately cared for, controlled and developed. Many parents may have experienced abuse and, therefore have confused or ambivalent attitudes to their children's sexual or predatory behaviour. They have scant chance of adequately parenting their own children, particularly at the margins of society from which most of the sexually abusive adolescents come (Hoghughi 1996).

The dynamic perspective

Psychodynamic theory has been more concerned with the 'fact' and consequences of 'incest' than with the perpetration of sexual abuse, particularly by adolescents. Freud's own writings were profoundly influenced by his disbelieving and shocked reaction to accounts of abuse in his female patients. These were largely from the same social and religious milieu as Freud himself and spoke of abuse by their own kith and kin. Thus they implicated men like himself in large scale abusiveness. The implication was so shocking that Freud denied their truth and interpreted them as deviant fantasy (Gay 1988, Summit 1988).

This face saving reinterpretation was perpetuated for a long time by psychologists and psychiatrists, in subtle ways underplaying the harm done by incest and suggesting the child's complicity in the act (Bender and Blau 1937). Even the most zealous dynamic therapists have had to accommodate recent views of sexual abuse. Because even dynamic theories are not infinitely elastic, they now play down the traditional dynamic formulations. Contemporary dynamic practitioners focus on interpreting the 'facts' of a child's development and relationships in order to make sense of his abusive behaviour. The full range of dynamic concepts, including defence mechanisms, are used in this context. Sometimes these provide a different and useful perspective on a youngster's behaviour, particularly when this encourages therapeutic tolerance, as a prelude to treatment (Breer 1987).

The dynamic approach operates on the basis of concepts, methods, and practices which are as pervasive as they are resistant to empirical scrutiny. 'Explanatory' terms are often used with freedom and detachment from supportive empirical evidence. Complex accounts of early developmental experiences in dynamic terms are, in their retrospective nature and absence of epidemiological support, of limited value. However, psychodynamic views are now so much part of the culture that little is achieved by pointing to their questionable empirical status.

Psychological perspectives

Psychology is an experimental science, aiming to provide reliable and valid information regarding all aspects of behaviour.

As the subject deals with the whole spectrum of behaviour from its physiological bases, through motivation, cognition and affect, to learning and maintenance processes, it is difficult to speak of one psychological perspective. Depending on the particular focus, there may be wide variations reflecting the breadth of the subject matter.

Functional analysis

This is a general approach adopted by psychologists in analysing and explaining the interdependent elements of 'causation', triggering and maintenance of behaviour (Samson and McDonnell 1990). It is theoretically open-ended and can be used within any of the perspectives mentioned in this chapter.

Essentially, the approach identifies *antecedents*, major features of the *behaviour* itself and its *consequences* (the ABC). Antecedents concern background, personality factors and predisposition (such as poor inhibition against rule breaking), contextual pressures (e.g. watching a pornographic film), facilitation (e.g. babysitting alone) and trigger factors (such as the child wanting to play). Antecedents can include unobservable data, such as genetic predisposition, thoughts and feelings. Behaviour can be evaluated in terms of time, location, victim choice, method and other variables. Consequences can be analysed in broad terms of a 'good–bad' balance sheet for the abuser, including physical, material, social and psychological gains and losses. The net balance is seen as contributing to the learning history of the abuser and affecting probability of perpetrating such behaviour again.

'Diathesis-stressor' paradigm

A more abstract but useful approach deriving from clinical psychology is through the 'diathesis-stressor paradigm' (Davison and Neale 1990). This is perhaps the most important current approach used by psychologists in considering all forms of abnormal behaviour. The essential idea is that all abnormal behaviour is the outcome of the *interaction* of personal vulnerability factors and external stressors. This view appears to underlie the most rigorous approaches to developing models of sexually abusive behaviour in adolescents (Marshall and Eccles 1993).

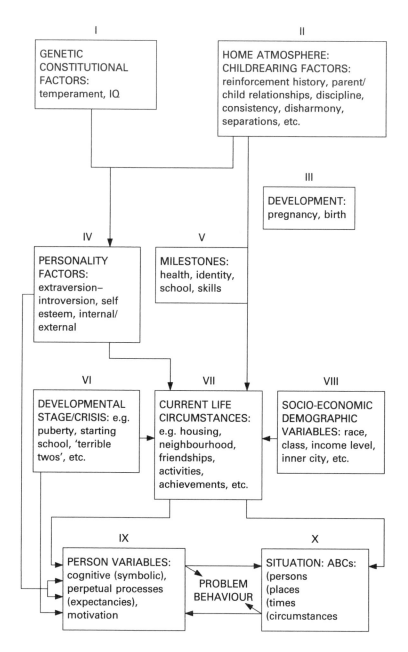

Figure 2.1   *The 10-factor clinical formation of causation (adapted from Clarke 1977 by Herbert 1991)*

Personal vulnerability may include anything from the 'wrong' genes to having been sexually abused. The diathesis or vulnerability can be set out in detail according to any number of different classifications, though poor parenting and inadequate emotional bonds seem to be particularly important factors. Stressors encompass any event which makes a negative impact on the person – such as being angry, drunk or sexually aroused. In later chapters, major elements of both vulnerability factors and stressors will be elaborated. These must be assessed if we are to make sense of how abuse occurred and what should be done to reduce the risk of its recurrence.

Counsel of perfection would demand that *each* factor should be considered and elaborated in detail. Indeed, this seems to be the objective of a number of programmes, most notably that of the Northwest Treatment Associates (Silver, reproduced in Salter 1988). Yet in the rush and press of day to day work, such detailed work is more often an aspiration than reality. Although all workers want to do their best, they need something more convenient than innumerable headings and lengthy expositions allow.

As an aid to this, it may be useful to classify the factors leading to the sexual abuse, within the diathesis-stressor framework as set out in Figure 2.1 (Clarke 1977, Herbert 1991). *All* these factors are implicated in sexually abusive behaviour of adolescents. They have to be considered in all attempts at assessment and treatment, even if there is no information on a set of variables or it is not regarded as critical in an individual case.

This way of looking at relevant factors has the advantages of comprehensiveness and simplicity. A further feature is that it utilises the same sets of factors as are employed in the explanation of any *other* abnormal or criminal act. When even the 'facts' of sexually abusive behaviour are open to question and their interpretation as 'criminal' or 'aggressive' as opposed to 'sexual' is subject to controversy, this may be at present the most useful approach.

Developmental theory

A core element of psychologists' approach to abusive behaviour is consideration of developmental issues. Much is known about adolescent social and sexual development (e.g. Bancroft 1989, Kimmel and Weiner 1985). Evidence suggests that in the last 30 years there have been real changes in sexual behaviour and attitudes among adolescents (Brooks-Gunn and Furstenberg 1989, Schofield 1965, Sorensen 1973). Most adolescents are sexually experienced by age 19, including over half who have had sexual intercourse. Adolescents have to learn to respond to internal physical changes, as well as stimulation by peers and others. As with any other activity, such learning will be affected by their confidence and competence in dealing with the world, themselves resulting from the interaction of genetic, constitutional and parenting experiences.

Deviant socialisation experiences, including sexual victimisation and poor parenting, block and distort acquisition of necessary competencies for normal sexual development and may nudge the adolescent towards seeking and exploring opportunities for deviant behaviour. Marshall and Eccles (1993) particularly identify the failure to develop secure attachment bonds to parents as a major vulnerability factor in abusive adolescents. They recognise, however, that although such a developmental perspective may account for an adolescent's disposition, it has to be fitted within a multi-faceted theory that accounts for how deviant sexual 'scripts' are developed and reinforced through masturbatory fantasies and response to abusive preferences.

Learning theory

This is the overarching theoretical approach adopted by psychologists to understanding and explaining abusive behaviour. Learning is now regarded as the core process by which physical development is shaped to produce the sort of people we become. A 'learning' approach to development and maintenance of sexually abusive behaviour has been adopted by a number of commentators, though some have emphasised particular learning mechanisms (e.g. McGuire et al. 1965).

Three learning processes are identified, all of which are implicated in learning to become an abuser.

Classical conditioning is based on *pairing* of events and experiences. If a child has been sexually abused by an adult male over a long enough period, he is likely to see 'being a male' largely in terms of such behaviour. Depending on the balance of physical and emotional sensations associated with the abuse, his reaction is likely to be somewhere along the spectrum from the fearful and avoidant to the excited and demanding. This process is regarded as crucial to the development of emotional reactions whose origins we cannot always identify. It is now regarded as a major mechanism in turning an abused child victim into an adolescent abuser, though the reasoning has major empirical gaps. Classical Pavlovian conditioning is also seen as accounting for one of the core processes by which deviant fantasy becomes paired with and leads to abusive behaviour (McGuire et al. 1965, Marshall and Eccles 1993).

Operant conditioning is the mechanism by which we learn to manipulate our environment and satisfy our needs, wants and desires. It is based on recognising, through trial and error, that our acts have good or bad consequences. Over a period of time we learn to identify what will help us get what we want and avoid what will not. Since in real life there is usually a 'down side' or price attached to anything that is desirable, it is the widest, *relative balance* of 'good and bad', the 'aversive' and 'rewarding' rather than absolute values which lead to learning and repeating an anti-social act (Hoghughi 1996). Thus a youngster may learn that children give him less trouble as sexual outlets than adolescent girls of the same age.

Social learning is concerned primarily with learning from other people's example. As children grow up in social and family groups, so they acquire considerable knowledge and skills not through direct experience but vicariously, through hearing from and seeing other people. Hearing stories of sexual exploits, seeing other youngsters or parents engaging in sexual behaviour and watching pornographic films may well inculcate in them thoughts and feelings as well as teach actual ways of carrying out sexual acts. The 'learnt' balance sheet will determine whether and how the propensity to abuse will be activated when the opportunity arises (Bandura 1977, Hoghughi 1996).

Sexually abusive behaviour involves all three forms of learning probably at all times, though the prominence of each form may vary depending on the segment of activity. Sexual arousal in the presence of a potential sexual victim may well involve classical conditioning; grooming and stalking would involve instrumentally learned ploys; and execution of abuse would either be based on operant conditioning or on learning from others' example. Facilitators and inhibitors of sexual abuse, whether they are internal (such as conscience) or external (such as fear of punishment) acquire their force from a youngster's past exposure to these in his 'good–bad' balance sheet of experiences. Youngsters with a propensity to child molestation do not stalk or groom children in full public view, because they have learned to be wary of being seen to do so.

Though such detailed analysis of the learning involved in abusive behaviour is not very common, nevertheless the majority of those who work with abusers utilise its concepts explicitly or implicitly. This has been the case particularly since the move away from mechanistic views of human learning, overlapping with the greater emphasis on cognitive and affective factors in shaping behaviour, as in Abel et al. (1975), Ryan (1989) and Weissberg (1982).

The merits of this approach are that it is based on rigorous and wide ranging empirical evidence; it is economical; its concepts and methods are open to scrutiny and its validity is judged by appropriate and extensive usage. All treatments of sexually abusive adolescents include large elements (or whole programmes) based on it.

Other models

Workers in any field soon begin, however implicitly, to structure their findings to make sense of the phenomena. The approaches derive from general theoretical disciplines applied to abusive behaviour. However, there are a number of others which are more specific to it.

Although more concerned with child sexual abuse, Finkelhor's 'four factor model', appropriately adapted, helps make sense of other forms of abuse (Finkelhor et al. 1986). It encompasses (1) 'emotional congruence' – to account for why an adolescent is sexually drawn to a child; (2) 'sexual arousal to children', looking at patterns of development associated with regarding children as appropriate sexual objects; (3) 'blockage', exploring why age mates are not exclusively utilised as sexual partners; and (4) 'disinhibitions', concerning conditions which normally prevent even a person aroused by children from carrying out an abusive act. Finkelhor does not regard this conceptualisation as a 'theory' and accepts that each factor may be the end product of different processes of socialisation. The fact that extending this model to other forms of abusive behaviour by adolescents may raise other questions, and application of the model to individuals may not always be productive, does not reduce its importance as a good conceptual map of child sexual abuse.

Ryan (1989) is concerned with explaining how victims become abusers. She places particular emphasis on experience of abuse and its role in creating deviant memories and perceptions which in turn affect how an abused person interprets opportunities for sexual exploitation, the linkage creating a 'dysfunctional response cycle'.

She explores this through identifying a child's experience of abuse and resulting feelings of helplessness, lack of 'empathic nurturing', loss of or betrayal by parents, as well as the trauma of physical, sexual and emotional abuse. An adolescent with such a history is likely to experience the same feelings when found in a situation which is reminiscent of his own abuse. This results in development of the adolescent's self concept as 'poor me', accompanied by bad feeling and sense of self as a victim. Ryan then brings together much of what is known about characteristics of abusers to create a plausible linkage between their history and triggers for the commission of subsequent abusive acts (Ryan et al. 1987).

Ryan uses this background to identify the major issues to be covered in treatment of abusive adolescents. These include guilt and accountability, power and control, anger and retaliation, fantasies and reinforcement, secrets, confidentiality and empathy. She believes that traditional therapeutic approaches, which ignore parallels in the experience of being abused and abusing, are likely to be inadequate in preventing recurrence of abusive acts. Although her account is speculative and based on a series of untested hypotheses, it merits serious consideration in identifying the role of experience as victim in generating subsequent abusive behaviour.

Becker and Kaplan (1988) provide a model of deviant sexual behaviour. Although they recognise that theirs is not an empirically validated model, nevertheless they regard it as helpful in making sense of varieties of abusive adolescents. They suggest that, following the first sexual offence, there are three paths adolescent abusers may follow: (1) the 'dead end path' in which they do not commit further abusive acts. These youngsters are likely to have suffered the most serious conse-quences following an abusive act but for whom the act may have been casual, opportunistic, copycat and devoid of force; (2) the 'delinquency path' in which the abusive act is part of a wider pattern of anti-social acts; (3) the 'sexual interest pattern path' in which the adolescent develops a preference for abusive sex.

The latter are likely to find the experience pleasurable, not suffer any serious consequences, derive further pleasure and reinforcement through masturbatory activities and fantasies and be deficient in the ability to relate to age mates. This model is helpful in identifying reasons why some adolescents become persistent abusers, although it has to be augmented by other analyses to provide a basis for adequate assessment and intervention.

O'Brien and Bera (1986) suggest a general model for relating social and individual factors to the abuse cycle in abusive adolescents. Individual factors include family issues, having been a sexual and physical victim, poor socialisation, organic issues, exposure to pornography and poor self education. Social factors include rigid gender roles, patriarchy,'erotophobia' and homophobia. These two sets of factors interact to affect the motivational mainsprings of adolescent behaviour, such as need for affection, intimacy, power, control and, therefore, arousal patterns.

Because of this motivational background, situational oppor-tunities are interpreted as fit for abusive acts, internal inhibi-tors are overcome, victim resistance is circumvented, the act takes place, resulting in reduced need or increased pleasure, to be subsequently reinforced by fantasy and masturbation and justified by the adolescent through a range of distorting mechanisms. This seems a reasonable chain of events but is best regarded as a model for individual assessment and treatment of the type that is covered in Chapter 9, on relapse prevention.

As suggested by this overview, we have as yet no serious 'theories' either deriving from a discipline or specifically related to sexually abusive acts, 'single factor' or 'multi-factorial', which explain or predict sexually abusive behaviour as uniquely different from other deviant acts. However accurate and detailed our individual assessments may be, we are not yet sufficiently sure of how our 'facts' relate to the whole population of abusive adolescents or particular groups within them to account for the differences and similarities. Practitioners must take account of the full set of factors as set out in Figure 2.1 in order to account for the abusive act. Hypothesis-driven work is necessary for research and development but should not be confused with giving clients the best service.

It still remains a moot point whether sexually abusive acts are fundamentally different from other deviant acts, other than through orientation to specific opportunities. Despite the zeal to promote particular theories, the evidence available would suggest that we are best advised to regard sexually abusive behaviour as a variant of deviant acts against the person until we have good evidence to the contrary.

3
Managing Risk

Kevin J. Epps

Managing the care and treatment of sexually abusive adolescents entails predicting their likely future behaviour in an effort to prevent further episodes of abuse. Decisions about management generally consider the amount of supervision the young person requires in various settings and whether he should remain at home or be removed to alternative accommodation, perhaps even to a secure setting.

Prediction is concerned with assessing the probability of a future occurrence and is hotly debated within the psychological literature (Blackburn 1993). In recent years, research has indicated that there may well be circumstances in which practitioners can validly assess the 'dangerousness' of particular individuals, even though the validity of such assessments remains untested. This is certainly the case with respect to sexually abusive adolescents. The strategies and techniques for risk assessment, such as those proposed by Loss and Ross (1988) and Smith and Monastersky (1986), are at an early stage of development and should be used with caution.

Research into recidivism and treatment outcome with abusive adolescents is surprisingly sparse. However, it appears that their overall recidivism rates are substantially lower than those of adults. Unfortunately, most of the few studies that have been conducted suffer from methodological inadequacies (Debelle et al. 1993). There have been no rigorously controlled studies and the length of follow-up has been relatively short. Marshall et al. (1992a) suggest that follow-up periods of less than four to five years are unsatisfactory. Research into adult sex offenders indicates that child molesters and those offenders who select only male victims appear to be at particular risk, followed by offenders who target any extra-familial girl. Enduring sexual preference for children, especially boys, seems to be associated with a high rate of reoffending. The finding that most sexually abusive adolescent boys offend against girls, usually acquaintances or relatives, rather than against boys, may help to explain the relatively low rates of sexual reoffending (about 10%) reported in follow-up research.

Given the private nature of sexual acts, the reasons for under-reporting mentioned in Chapter 1, and the very poor attrition rate for all juvenile offenders, the low recidivism rates are likely to be a gross underestimate. Also, the research to date does not tell us which clinical and behavioural factors are associated with sexual reoffending, and the extent to which these vary from case to case. Indeed Kahn and Chambers (1991) conclude that 'surprisingly few variables were found to have a significant relationship to reoffending'. This begs the question: how can we justifiably predict abusive behaviour in adolescent sex offenders, given our lack of knowledge about factors associated with it?

Monahan (1984, 1988) points out that, more than other mental health practitioners, workers with abusers have a special responsibility to prevent further victimisation. Thus, practitioners have to accept that their decisions may determine others' exposure to risk. This awareness may explain why most social workers and probation officers request help in making risk assessments.

Risk and dangerousness

It is important to distinguish between these concepts. At its simplest, 'risk' can be defined as the probability of a future event or behaviour. There are two main parts to this definition: estimation of probability, and the act itself. Two main methods have been used – actuarial and clinical.

The *actuarial* method is concerned with collecting statistical data about the likelihood of particular behaviours and using this to inform decisions. To be reliable, the method depends on analysis of large amounts of information, often not available in relation to recidivist adolescent sexual abusers. Further, even if information were available, it is difficult to know to what extent a particular individual is representative of the population studied.

Clinical assessment concerns gathering information necessary for making informed decisions about an individual, developed largely in psychiatry and clinical psychology. This method relies heavily on individual clinical judgement, and is therefore open to bias. It is inevitably influenced by the personal history of clinicians, experience of similar cases and theoretical orientation. Several studies have found that often clinicians are no better than lay people in making risk judgements. Some researchers have advocated the use of a combination of actuarial and clinical methods to enhance the accuracy of clinical predictions (Meehl 1954, 1986).

In considering the abusive act, it is not always clear what constitutes sexually abusive behaviour. This poses problems of determining cut-off points about seriousness of risk. The Criminal Justice Act 1991 lists a number of factors that should be considered when assessing the seriousness of an offence. These include the:

- nature of the offence
- characteristics of the victim (e.g. age, intellectual ability)
- intention and motive
- role in the offence
- attitude to the offence.

In contrast to the term 'risk', 'dangerousness' does not refer to an event or behaviour, but is an attribution to a person or event by an observer. It does not specify the kind of behaviour, likelihood of its occurrence in particular situations, or the interaction of individual and environment which leads to abuse. The equation proposed by Scott (1977) serves as a useful reminder: Offender + victim + circumstances = offence.

In the light of the above, assessment of risk should ideally aim to:

- combine information about the individual (*clinical information*), with
- information about statistical base rates (*actuarial information*), with
- information about situational factors contributing to the behaviour (*environmental information*), with
- opinions about the potential harm caused by certain behaviours (*seriousness*), to produce:

- decisions and specific recommendations that can be justified and defended (*clinically defensible decisions*).

A model for risk management

Adolescents live in a variety of systems, such as family, school and peer group, that fundamentally affect their lives and are affected by them. Family bonding and organisation seem to be particularly important in the development of abusive behaviour. Research suggests that the families of adolescent sexual offenders are characterised by high rates of conflict, disorganisation and dysfunction. Although evidence is sparse, uncontrolled studies also suggest that adolescent sexual offenders have difficulty maintaining close interpersonal relations and are isolated from peers. In risk management, it is important to take these systemic effects into account and:

- decide whether you can (have the time and resources to) carry out the assessment;
- evaluate the urgency of referral, in relation to risk to abuser and victim(s);
- convene a Child Protection Team discussion to determine urgency, if need be;
- decide whether the adolescent should be removed from the context of abuse.

Table 3.1, adapted from Ross and Loss (1991), sets out important areas for decision making at this stage.

Some abusive adolescents are deemed 'high risk' by social workers and probation officers because of the quality of the discovered abuse and other social and psychological features of the adolescent, as summarised in Tables 3.2 and 3.3.

The quantity and quality of information varies enormously from case to case. Some sexually abusive adolescents have had extensive involvement with statutory agencies. Numerous assessments have been conducted, including specialist involvement from psychiatrists and psychologists, resulting in more rapid and confident evaluation of risk (Vizard et al. 1996). In other cases the team may be starting with a 'blank sheet' with little or no information to use as a basis for decision making. If parents and adolescent co-operate in supplying adequate

Table 3.1 *Risk assessment*

Assessment area	Type of information
Extent and seriousness of abuse behaviour	• Use of force, physical coercion, threats, especially extent of aggression/violence • Length and progression of history of sexually abusive behaviour • Number of victims • Frequency of abusive behaviour • Extent to which abuse was opportunistic or planned
Individual characteristics	• General degree of behavioural self control • History of absconding • Extent of substance use/abuse • Attitude to sexually abusive behaviour • Acceptance of responsibility • Attitude to victims • Willingness and ability to co-operate with suggested management strategies
Family characteristics	• Level of parental or other care-giver supervision • Parental attitude to victims • Parental attitude to abusive behaviour • Willingness and ability to co-operate with suggested management strategies
Situational characteristics	• Degree of unsupervised access to potential victims

information regarding the areas listed in Table 3.1, decision making can be speedy and confident. The more the assessment team meets with hostility, denial and resistance, the more it is likely to feel anxious and uncertain and hence recommend serious management interventions to eliminate the possibility of further abuse. This can sometimes exacerbate feelings of hostility and resentment, making further assessment more difficult.

This is more likely if the adolescent denies all or some acts. Some abusers deny part of the abusive behaviour. Motives for denial may come to light during intervention, such as embarrassment or shame regarding certain behaviours. The youngsters will need reassurance, which is a delicate task since

Table 3.2   *'High risk' offender characteristics*

- Long history of anti-social behaviour, such as bullying
- An extensive, varied criminal history
- Impulsive, unpredictable anti-social behaviour
- Educational failure
- Academic underachievement
- Long standing peer and relationship problems
- Resistance and hostility to authority figures
- History of excessive substance abuse (i.e. drugs, alcohol, solvents)
- Inappropriate and disinhibited sexual behaviour (e.g. exhibitionism) in a range of situations and settings
- Failure to regulate sexual behaviour in the presence of other children and adults
- A strong compulsive element of sexually inappropriate behaviour
- Preoccupation with specific sexual acts (e.g. anal sex)
- Preoccupation with acts of violence towards children and peers
- Use of hard core pornography
- Evidence of violent sexual fantasy, demonstrated through speech, play, writing and drawing
- Lack of concern for victims of sexual and physical abuse
- Lack of concern for own welfare
- Denial of all, or part of, sexually abusive history
- Failure of previous management and treatment interventions to prevent further anti-social behaviour and sexually abusive acts
- Unwillingness to engage in attempts to prevent risk of further abuse
- Unwillingness to consider behaviour change

Table 3.3   *'High risk' offence characteristics*

- Sexual abuse against more than one victim
- Sexual abuse in a range of situations and settings
- The selection of victims with particular physical characteristics (e.g. blonde hair)
- The selection of victims with particular behavioural characteristics (e.g. those who appear vulnerable, such as children with learning difficulties)
- Sexual abuse against boys and girls
- Sexual abuse against children of various ages
- The use of threats, coercion and/or force during abusive acts
- The use of force and violence in excess of that required to perpetrate abusive acts
- The threat, or use, of a weapon
- The use of a variety of sexual acts during abuse
- Penetrative sexual abuse
- Attempts to degrade or humiliate victims (e.g. forcing the victim to eat faeces)

disclosure may entail legal consequences. Whilst the adolescent must be faced or confronted with denial and the contrary evidence, adopting a 'confrontational', 'brow-beating' approach will almost certainly intensify resistance and denial. With abusers, assessment of denial will form an important part of initial risk assessment. Its significance will be greater in the case of 'high risk' adolescents, whose characteristics are shown in Tables 3.2 and 3.3.

Risk estimation

When available information has been collected, it will be necessary to summarise and interpret assessment findings. This is probably the most difficult part of the assessment process. This involves developing a hypothesis, specifying the factors that appear to play an important role in helping to trigger and maintain sexually abusive behaviour.

There will always be more than one interpretation and one hypothesis. The aim is to select the most probable hypothesis, which best summarises assessment findings. The term 'clinically defensible' has been coined to describe this notion (Pollock et al. 1989). It is impossible to predict the behaviour of any individual with a high degree of accuracy, no matter how thorough and comprehensive the risk assessment, not least because much detail will be missing (Loeber and Dishion 1983). The formulation simply tries to make the best sense of the available information to allow defensible decisions. Thus, the formulation can change in response to new information.

Formulation should lead to clear management strategies and therapeutic interventions to reduce risk. The model of risk assessment outlined in Figure 3.1 suggests areas that can be targeted for intervention, such as the young person (to achieve greater self control, take more responsibility for his behaviour and deal more effectively with stress); the family (to improve supervision and encourage a sense of shared responsibility); the peer group (to reduce their influence over the young person); the environment (to reduce the opportunity of contact with potential victims); and potential victims (helping them to avoid the abuser and take evasive action). The management programme constructed for the adolescent should flow directly from the formulation.

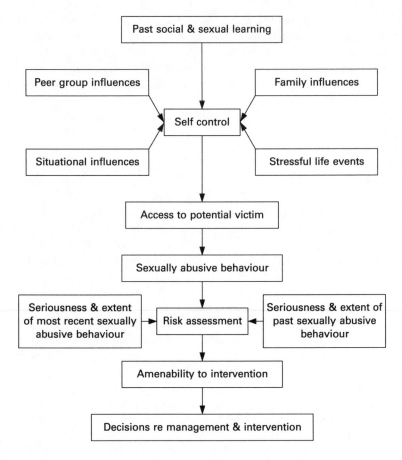

Figure 3.1   *A systems approach to risk assessment*

Containing and managing risk

A recent review of research on juvenile delinquency concludes that it is unreasonable to expect any 'one off' intervention to have a long lasting effect against future anti-social behaviour by adolescents (Mulvey et al. 1993). Services need to be reoriented with a view to providing long term support and help.

Managing risk is a complex process. It involves: (1) managing the abuser, with particular emphasis on his attitudes and behaviour in high risk situations; (2) managing the environment, evaluating changes in the risk formation as a result of environmental and situational changes, especially the degree of supervision; and (3) gathering information about access to potential victims.

Managing the abuser

Attempting to contain the risk presented by the offender forms part of the process of relapse prevention discussed in Chapter 9. The strength of this approach lies in its emphasis on helping the abuser to recognise and understand the psychological and situational variables that put him at risk of repeating the act. Through this process it becomes easier to assess risk of reoffending: workers may gain access to the abuser's internal psychological world of thoughts and feelings and their relationship to abuse. Pithers (1990) describes the process of helping abusers to recognise the situations that put them at risk as the 'internal management' of relapse prevention.

External management, on the other hand, refers to provision of supervisory monitoring and control. This entails efforts from both abuser and those responsible for supervision. External management is especially important for abusers who are less able or willing to participate in internal management strategies, which is frequently the case with adolescent abusers. Close supervisory contact and monitoring may be necessary to prevent the abuser from entering high risk situations. Clearly, effective communication between various agencies responsible for the welfare, education and supervision of adolescent abusers is essential. Abel (1987), referring to his programme for adult offenders, describes a strategy called the 'surveillance group'. Four or five people who are in regular contact with the offender (e.g. family, relatives, friends), meet initially with the programme therapists to construct a list of risky and provocative situations for the offender. They subsequently monitor the offender's behaviour and provide regular. reports to the therapists.

Managing the environment: situational control

Sexually abusive adolescents are, broadly speaking, managed and treated in two kinds of environment: (1) in residential settings, administered by justice, health and social services agencies, some of which offer secure accommodation; (2) in the community, living as part of their family, or with foster or community parents, or in specially staffed and resourced living accommodation.

In exceptional cases, where the adolescent is considered to be a serious risk to others, and cannot be safely managed in available community or residential provision, secure accommodation may be sought. This requires a court application by the local authority under the 1989 Children Act. Often this arises because the adolescent is attempting to, or succeeds in, abusing other young people in his current placement and/or absconds, thereby placing himself and others at risk. Sometimes the application for secure accommodation does not arise directly from the sexually abusive behaviour, but from other behaviour, such as violence to residential staff or persistent non-sexual offending.

Occasionally, secure accommodation may not be immediately available, or the local authority may agree to develop an alternative resource in an attempt to manage the young person in the community. Sometimes there are no other options: secure accommodation cannot be used beyond the age of 18. Some adolescents leaving secure accommodation at this age may still pose significant risks, and cannot be subject to continued detention, even under the 1983 Mental Health Act. In these circumstances some local authorities have been known to develop and resource a special community placement for a single youngster, staffed round the clock by residential social workers. Clearly this is not a long term solution. It can be an isolating experience for the young person, creating problems in the provision of education, therapeutic intervention and access to peers.

Residential settings   Sexually aggressive and abusive adolescents have always existed in residential units for difficult and delinquent young people. Indeed, such units accommodate some of the most violent and sexually aggressive adolescents in the country. It is only over the last few years, however, that abusive adolescents have been singled out for special attention, following widespread recognition of sexual abuse and the development of community programmes for them. Some facilities have even taken the initiative to develop specialist units for sexually abusive adolescents. Most residential units however, have continued to work with mixed populations of young people, while developing assessment and intervention programmes aimed specifically at sexually abusive adolescents. Epps (1991, 1994a) draws attention to some of the difficulties of working with this group of young people in secure conditions. One of the few advantages of working in a residential context is that it allows for greater control over the environmental and situational variables that contribute to sexually abusive behaviour.

Building design and structure   The design and structure of a building should facilitate the task of observing, supervising and managing young people. This is especially important when caring for sexually abusive adolescents, given the potential for abuse in a residential setting. A building which makes effective supervision difficult places young people, and staff, at risk. Single-storey buildings, built around a central point, like the hub of a wheel, facilitate supervision. In contrast, multi-storey buildings that are long and narrow, especially those with many small rooms or recesses, hinder supervision. Some of the effects of poor building design can be offset through the use of closed-circuit television cameras and two-way radios: these are especially necessary in secure conditions though they raise some ethical issues. Purpose-built secure facilities should be reserved only for the highest risk, most difficult and violent young people. Two forms of security can be identified: external and internal.

External security refers to the restrictions applied outside the building, which may include high perimeter fences and surveillance cameras. External security measures can enhance the quality of life for residents, allowing youngsters to have more unrestricted freedom within the unit. Fewer staff are also needed for supervision, thereby allowing facilities to be used more frequently. Internal security includes the use of closed-circuit television and specially designed doors and windows. These features are essential in parts of the building where young people may remain unobserved for relatively long periods of time, such as bedrooms.

Staffing and supervision   It is important within residential facilities to ensure that young people are appropriately supervised, thereby reducing the risks of bullying, violence, sexual intimidation or assault. Staffing levels should never be allowed to drop below generally agreed levels. It is useful to identify and operationally define different levels of supervision, each suited to particular circumstances. Young people who are assessed to be at high risk of sexually abusing other residents, for example, may need constant supervision. Supervision levels may also need to be adjusted according to time of day or in response to situational factors, for example when young people are in bathrooms.

Peer group characteristics Residential facilities should have a written admission policy, specifying criteria for admission. This allows managers to control the mix and stability of the peer group, and avoid admitting young people who cannot be managed safely within the group. For example, young people who are assessed to be at risk of sexually abusing or intimidating other boys or girls should only be admitted if staffing levels allow adequate supervision and control of the group. There may be times when a combination of events, such as staff sickness and one or two extraordinarily demanding young people, necessitates a temporary halt to admissions so as to maintain safety and stability.

Before young people are accepted for admission, as much information as possible should be collected about their behaviour in other settings, allowing for a preliminary assessment of risk. If possible, the youngster should be interviewed before admission.

Behaviour management and control Residential units also allow for a greater degree of supervision and behaviour management. Procedures for managing and responding to behaviour should be clear and explicit, understood easily by staff and young people. In addition to preventing harm to residents and staff, they should also make explicit the boundaries of acceptable behaviour, and the consequences that follow unacceptable sexual and other behaviour. The aim is to develop a living environment that is safe and stable.

Communication and decision making Good communication and effective systems of decision making are needed if information is to be disseminated across the staff team for quick and appropriate response. Effective procedures for making decisions about case management are vital when changes occur

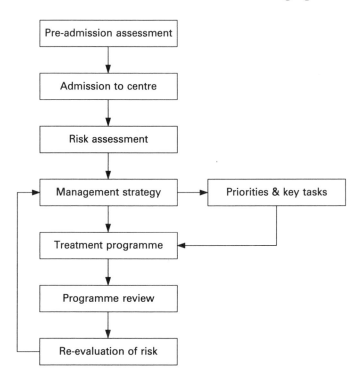

Figure 3.2 *Model for risk assessment and management at Glenthorne Centre (Epps 1994b)*

that affect risk formulation, such as a reduction in security or the level of supervision, for example when a sexually abusive youngster is moved from secure to open conditions. A balance has to be struck between protection of the community and the rehabilitation of the young person. Premature release from security can result in youngsters failing to cope, increasing the risk of absconding and perhaps reoffending. Epps (1994b) describes one approach to this problem in the operation of a risk management system, as summarised in Figure 3.2.

Family settings Some sexually abusive adolescents are never removed from the family, continuing to live at home or as part of a foster family, throughout the process of intervention. The main concern must always be the protection of possible victims. It is important not only to assess the degree of risk that the abuser poses to other members of his family and

Table 3.4   *Assessment of family functioning*

History of sexually abusive behaviour in other family members
Reaction of family members to disclosure of abuse
Level of child supervision
Choice of alternative caretakers or babysitters
Sleeping arrangements
Emotional/physical care and stimulation
Sexual behaviour within the family
Attitude to outside helpers and statutory agencies

community, but also to be aware of changes in family structure and functioning that may alter the risk.

To do this, it is necessary to look at the strengths and weaknesses in the way the family functions. It is also vital to examine ways in which the family contributes, overtly or covertly, to the development and maintenance of sexually abusive behaviour. Most instances of child sexual abuse involve perpetrators who are known to the child and interactions which are to some extent predictable and preventable. The assessment should include all family members and, where appropriate, extended family. Assessment of family risk should be informed by different kinds of information, as shown in Table 3.4. If risk of further abuse is to be minimised, parents or other adult caregivers must do two things: supervise and observe the abuser; and supervise and protect potential victims. This applies equally to children outside the family (e.g. visiting and neighbouring children) as to those living within it. Two factors will affect the quality of supervision: the ability and willingness of parents to supervise. Ability to supervise can be undermined by illness, whether physical or mental, intellectual limitations, and competing demands on time and availability. Thus, parents who recognise the seriousness of the problem, and are willing to supervise, may find themselves unable to do so if they become ill or are forced to work longer hours. Other parents, however, may be in a good position to supervise, but be unwilling to do so, perhaps because they do not believe the abuse has occurred, or do not think that it is serious. Clearly an unsupervised adolescent abuser sharing a house with potential victims is at greater risk of abusing again.

Parents also need to communicate with each other about their movements and daily routines and be aware of how these affect their ability to provide adequate supervision. Potential victims need to feel able to talk about their concerns and anxieties and feel able to report incidents of attempted or actual abuse.

Situations in which children enter a reconstituted family, or are fostered or adopted, create particular risks. Children may be unfamiliar with unwritten rules regarding sexual boundaries, and may misinterpret or misunderstand sexual behaviour. For example, one 15-year-old boy alternated between spending time with his father and his new partner, and his mother and her new partner who also had another child, a 6-year-old girl. Since living with her new partner, his mother had taken to walking around the house naked, even inviting her son to sit on her lap when she was naked. He later reported feeling sexually excited, but also very confused and compromised. Shortly after this incident he crept into the bedroom of his stepsister and fondled her. Gradually his sexually abusive behaviour escalated, culminating in the attempted rape of his half-sister, for which he was arrested and convicted. Although he eventually accepted responsibility for his offending behaviour, the behaviour of his mother clearly played a contributory role.

Access to potential victims: teaching children self-protection

Children are sexually abused in different settings, usually by boys well known to them, such as brothers or family friends, but sometimes by complete strangers. The type of relationship between the perpetrator and the victim will influence the way in which the child is engaged in sexual activity. Thus, a perpetrator who has regular contact with victims has the opportunity to persuade and groom them, introducing them to sexual behaviour gradually, while gaining their trust and confidence. This type of approach is frequently used by adult paedophiles and occasionally by experienced adolescent abusers, especially those who have themselves been groomed and abused by adults.

Some perpetrators, however, have no regular contact with children, or have made a conscious decision not to abuse children known to them, perhaps through fear of being caught. These abusers are more likely to prey on unfamiliar children, having no desire to engage victims in a longer term relationship. Findings from community surveys show that boys are more likely than girls to be sexually abused outside the home, especially boys from low income families who have also been subjected to physical abuse.

These stranger assaults are more likely to be accompanied by the use of threats, physical coercion and violence in an effort to force the child to participate in sexual activity. It is also likely that perpetrators of stranger assaults abuse in an opportunistic way, not planning the act, using excessive force in their desperation to engage the victim with little thought of the consequences. There is some evidence to suggest that abusers of children are more likely to be reported to the police if they are strangers than if they are known to the victim.

West (1991) recognises that some children are particularly vulnerable to abuse, especially those who have previously been abused. Victims of childhood sexual abuse sometimes exhibit sexualised and 'seductive' behaviours (Yates 1982), making them vulnerable to further abuse by adolescents and adults with a proclivity for sexually abusing children. Finkelhor (1988) refers to this effect as 'traumatic sexualisation', caused by premature and inappropriate sexual learning. Sexually abused children are often rewarded by their perpetrators with material goods such as sweets and money, and may come to view sex as a way of manipulating people. According to Finkelhor (1988), children who have been abused under conditions of danger, threat and violence are especially likely to be traumatised.

Young children are usually unaware of the distorted way in which perpetrators interpret their behaviour and are oblivious to the fact that they may be placing themselves at further risk. The justification used by one adolescent offender to abuse his 7-year-old sister is illustrated by the following interview extract:

> 'she led me on; she was sitting opposite me with her knees raised to her chest, so that I could see her knickers. She was doing this to tease me. Anyway, I know she's had sex before, with a man. She knew what she was doing. She was asking for sex. She enjoyed it – you ask her yourself!'

Preventive management

Broadly speaking, two types of sexual abuse prevention programmes can be identified: those aimed at all children (primary prevention) and those targeted towards 'at risk' children including children who have already been abused (secondary and tertiary prevention). Elliott (1992) regards the latter as suggesting that abused children are somehow responsible for their abuse or for being unable to stop it. She suggests that programmes should be aimed at all children, not just the abused.

Primary prevention programmes assume that all children are potentially at risk and will therefore benefit from self-protection strategies. Programmes usually provide classroom-based instruction for children of all ages on how to protect themselves from sexual assault and what to do if they experience actual or threatened abuse. Children are taught a variety of techniques, including: how to distinguish between 'good' and 'bad' touching; how to be assertive, ranging from repeatedly saying 'no' to the use of self defence techniques; and the importance of not keeping secrets. Most programmes aim to reduce the risk of abuse by changing the children's behaviour. By teaching them to avoid risky situations, to avoid inappropriate touching, to say 'no' (if possible) when anyone tries to do something which makes them frightened or confused, not to keep secrets, and to seek adult help, it may be possible to help children avoid abuse.

Research suggests that boys exposed to preventive programmes perceive themselves as less likely to be abused, perhaps because they feel better able to control potentially abusive situations. However, doubts have been expressed about the ability of such programmes to prevent sexual abuse. Outcome research in this area as well as comparative merits of different management ploys is lacking and must be a priority for the future.

4

Assessment

*Finlay Graham, Graeme Richardson and
Surya Bhate*

Health, probation and social services are asked with accelerating frequency to assess adolescents who are accused of or have been convicted of sexual abuse or offending. In the North-East of England, roughly 80% of such requested assessments are for adolescents who have not been convicted. Adequate assessment is rightly seen as an essential prerequisite to treatment. Several texts, predominantly North American in origin, describe and discuss issues associated with this assessment task (e.g. Gil and Johnson 1993, Perry and Orchard 1992). This chapter attempts to combine knowledge of the North American experience with that of working with sexually abusive adolescents in the United Kingdom to present a practicable framework of comprehensive assessment (see also Oster et al. 1988).

Assessment of sexually abusive adolescents involves the same kind of history-taking and information-gathering process as in any other comprehensive clinical assessment. What makes the task difficult, however, is the unwillingness of the adolescents to disclose deeply personal and sensitive information about their sexual behaviour. This is especially relevant when the alleged acts are *sub judice* and disclosure of full details of the behaviours may compromise the individual's defence. Another difficult issue is the previous sexual abuse experienced by the perpetrators. Adolescent males, for reasons associated with their self-image, are reluctant to disclose abuse. Adolescents are expected to describe verbally their sexual feelings and behaviours in an interview where they are in a less powerful position, and to do so to a level of detail which would even tax many adults. It is, therefore, difficult to achieve a worthwhile assessment quickly. Time is needed to establish rapport, a sense of safety for the adolescent, a common language and a context in which sensitive issues can be discussed (Groth and Loredo 1981).

When working with abusive youngsters, it is easy to overlook the question of individual rights. Quite simply, young people have the right to withhold information which might affect their defence against allegations of criminal misconduct. The North American approach to this issue is generally more coercive and gung-ho than the European and, more specifically, the British. Here, because of legislation and anxiety about directive approaches, a tentative approach often has to be adopted.

Hypothesis-driven assessment

Practitioners with abusive adolescents should be aware of the theories outlined earlier but recognise that different cases will be distinguished by different combinations of factors. Heterogeneity of sexually abusive adolescents (e.g. Barbaree and Cortoni 1993) coupled with the absence of adequate theories of causation suggests a 'whole' person approach to assessment, although in reality all information gathering has to be selective. Selection necessarily involves ruling out some factors based on a combination of research evidence and clinical experience. The outcome of this selection process may differ from one case to another, as we shall see later.

In general, it is reasonable to assume that sexually abusive behaviour in adolescence is unlikely to be driven by mental illness (Kavoussi et al. 1988, Richardson et al. 1995a); it is not, on the whole, the adolescent's sole area of difficulty (Richardson et al. 1995b); it is not associated with a particular personality type (Schlank 1995) and there is little evidence that it is linked to a preoccupation with a deviant arousal pattern (Marshall and Eccles 1993). As seen in Chapter 1, evidence shows that inadequate parenting, prior sexual abuse, exposure to inappropriate sexual role models, opportunity, learning by outcomes, low self esteem, poor social competence and cognitive distortions are all implicated in the aetiology of abusive behaviour in adolescents.

In our view, the most supportable hypothesis is that the sexually abusive behaviour is learned. Normal principles of learning, such as positive and negative reinforcement, would account for the continuation of such behaviour, whatever may have precipitated the first incident. Identification and under-standing of learning processes, therefore, become the target of assessment, with 'causes' remaining conjectural. Assessment should change tack, in line with the emerging profile of the individual.

Purpose of assessment

Assessment has several purposes, of which the most prominent are:

- identification of abnormal/anti-social/deviant patterns of thought, feeling and behaviour;
- identification and understanding of the learning experiences and processes which might have led to such behaviours and their maintenance;
- identification of particular situational contexts in which abuse has occurred;
- evaluating likelihood of repeat behaviours;
- ascertaining the adolescent's motivation to accept help towards more effective control of his behaviour;
- eliciting information necessary for the formulation of an intervention/treatment strategy.

Process of assessment

Assessment of sexually abusive adolescents takes much time, and treatment often cannot be withheld while assessment is continuing. The two processes are interlinked and any attempt at rigid separation is counterproductive. However, care must be exercised to ensure that detailed treatment is not commenced prior to an adequate formulation.

The assessment process is facilitated if parents, general practitioner, social worker and school are involved, in addition to the adolescent himself. Parents can make an invaluable contribution to unravelling the adolescent's learning history. In the case of adolescents under 16, parents may need to be consulted regarding the content of proposed treatment programmes and will be invaluable in augmenting it. Younger adolescents should not be provided with sexual information beyond that which they already possess without parents' agreement.

In relation to assessments for courts, the purpose at the pre-trial stage should be addressed carefully. Reports requested by the Crown Prosecution Service, defence solicitor or the court are prepared to a specific brief. Under these conditions, whatever the youngster says may be reported and he should be informed of this fact. Confidentiality within a *therapeutic* interview is different, and should be explained. The decision to use information obtained in a therapeutic interview presents a more complex dilemma for the clinician, particularly when withholding it may put others at risk of victimisation. The issue becomes further complicated when an individual is referred initially for assessment or treatment but subsequently a request for a court report is made. In these circumstances, consultation with a fellow professional or head of service is advisable. Assessment undertaken following completion of the criminal justice process is usually free from such difficulties and can proceed in the normal way.

Engaging with the sexually abusive adolescent

Experience in working with abusive adolescents indicates they are usually best seen with their parent(s) at the initial interview. They should be reassured that their sexual behaviour will not be discussed at this joint session. This point needs to be made in the appointment letter to reduce some of the anxiety associated with being seen. The purpose of the assessment should be explained. It is generally helpful to state that many adolescents experience similar problems and have been assisted by the work of the clinic. Reassurance should be given that only the minimum necessary details of the sexually abusive behaviour will be sought to gain an understanding of its origin and dynamics. Attempt should be made not to embarrass, and the interviewer must be aware of how difficult it is to discuss intimate details.

Motivation should be discussed in depth using motivational interviewing techniques before progressing to assessment. Our experience would suggest that many abusive adolescents are only superficially interested in modifying their behaviour. Their compliance is often driven by parental pressure or fear of external sanctions. They co-operate on the surface, only to give up or heavily resist when the exploration or modification becomes painful. It takes time and patience to explain what the service has to offer the young person and to debate the pros and cons of the offer being accepted or rejected, as part of the process of negotiating an intervention 'deal'.

Initially the young person is unlikely to want to participate or to consider himself in need of therapy, and he will almost certainly be ignorant of what might be on offer and what engaging in the assessment process will mean for him. He has a right to be informed, to discuss the advantages for himself of the right to choose whether or not to do so. The consequences, if any, of not taking part should be explained and debated in a similarly honest manner. Treatment by coercion should be avoided on both ethical and clinical grounds. Parents should be helped to understand the purpose of their involvement. Critically, they must understand the need for, and agree to give, their support for the assessment process.

It is helpful to start the assessment with general issues and progress gradually towards sexually abusive behaviour. Engagement is influenced greatly by the pace and content of interviewing. If there is one issue which destroys the attempt to engage, it is a blinkered and relentless pressure to have the young person disclose full details of his sexual misbehaviours. This might well be legitimate in an interrogative interview conducted by the police under appropriate safeguards. But clinical assessment is designed to assess treatability. Our interest as therapists should focus primarily on antecedents and consequences. As rapport and trust develop, more information will be spontaneously disclosed.

Assessments of sexually abusive behaviour can also become intense, with resulting stress on both parties. Useful ploys for relieving pressure include interspersing questions with general chats about subjects of interest to the youngster; or psychometric testing which the adolescent can complete in private, or simple breaks for refreshments.

Assessors should accept that offender self reports are usually unreliable. Only when there is exceptional rapport and trust will frankness prevail. It is, therefore, necessary to augment the information given by the youngster with that obtained from other sources (e.g. parents, school, police, victim statements, social workers), and multiple interviews with the adolescent must be carried out. Psychometric questionnaires relying on self report provide an alternative source of information with the additional merit that they give normative data to which an individual response profile can be compared.

Denial in the face of direct questions should be expected and the role of denial discussed with the adolescent and his family. They should be helped to understand why from a therapeutic viewpoint its effect is dysfunctional. Denial forms a primary obstacle to assessment and undermines treatment planning. It needs to be challenged although great care should be taken in doing this. Better reasons for telling the truth have to be conveyed.

Content of assessment

The following list encompasses information necessary to reach an adequate formulation of the young person's difficulties and how he might best be helped.

- Current situation – are sexually abusive behaviours being safely contained?
- family history
- parenting style

- sexual knowledge/learning to date

- sexually abused?
- sexual beliefs

- sexually abusive incident(s)/ nature and seriousness of offence
- situation in which sexually abusive incidents occurred
- anger
- sequencing of thoughts, feelings and behaviours in the run-up to the incident, during the incident and in the aftermath of the incident
- perpetration strategy/strategies

- Personal and social functioning

- behaviour in school
- in some cases, intellectual level
- sexual fantasy, deviant sexual arousal, if appropriate
- profile of relationships
- analysis of risk of reoffending
- mental health

- victim statements if available
- social network
- motivation to engage in treatment

The assessment procedures and elements may be summarised as follows:

SUMMARY OF ASSESSMENT PROCEDURES/MEASURES

Use multiple sources of information and adopt a multi-agency, eclectic approach to the assessment

1. Details of incidents of sexually abusive behaviour
   - reports from significant others, e.g. parents
   - witness or victim statements
   - medical evidence
2. Professional reports – psychiatric, social services, psychological, probation, education
3. Clinical interview – semi-structured with youngster and parents to obtain a detailed developmental history
4. Psychometric testing
5. Self monitoring diary
6. Direct observation (institutional settings)
7. History of offending

The task of setting out to collect this considerable body of information is approached most effectively in stages.

Collation of information from other agencies

Request relevant reports from:

- social services
- police, particularly re victim statements
- school
- probation service
- health professionals

Liaison

Discuss the case with colleagues in other disciplines and establish beginnings of joint working practice. If working in a

National Health Service unit, inform general practitioner of involvement.

Criminal justice

Establish the current position with regard to proceedings. Is the matter *sub judice*? Is a court report likely to be requested at a future date? What role will your assessment play in this process? What are the views of the defence solicitor and the police?

Child care situation

Is the youngster under any care, supervision, or wardship orders? Is he registered on the Child Protection Register? Are his immediate needs being met and is the potential to engage in further sexually abusive behaviours safely contained?

Interview with parents and young person

Explain the purpose of the interview, emphasising that sexual misbehaviour is encountered regularly; that the children concerned are not monsters and that worthwhile assistance can be given. Discuss the natural tendency to deny but highlight the dangers of doing so – problems don't get better by denying their existence. Use of analogies is helpful in this context. Emphasise that the entire purpose of the assessment is to identify and meet treatment needs aimed at reducing the risk of recurrence of the abusive behaviour. Discuss likely consequences for the young person if a repetition occurs. Discuss the claim which all youngsters make in this situation: 'it will never happen again'. Discuss the unfortunate regularity with which it does when help is rejected.

Judge the response of parents so far and attempt to motivate them if a positive response is not forthcoming. Parental support is critical and has been shown to be one of the major factors influencing relapse. It is, therefore, worth spending considerable time on this issue. Experience indicates that most parents can be engaged, providing they regard it as in their son's interests and not simply part of an official investigation.

Table 4.1 *A framework for multi-agency assessment*

Risk evaluation	Assessment conducted by whom	Scale of assessment
Low	Social worker	Good family assessment and basic assessment of individual. No specialist procedures
Moderate	Social worker/probation officer + consultancy input from health professionals	Good general assessment including some specialist procedures as indicated
High	Health professionals + social worker/probation officer	Comprehensive assessment involving several specialist procedures

End the initial session with parents by discussing the need for subsequent assessment to be conducted with the young person on his own and agree mutually acceptable arrangements to facilitate this. Clinical and empirical evidence strongly suggests that it is difficult to establish productive rapport with sexually abusive adolescents when their parents are present. Effective engagement with and subsequent comprehensive assessment is more likely to be achieved within an individualised interview. Offer to meet the parents separately to continue assessment, offer educational input and begin family work.

At this point the known facts of the case should be collated and clinical judgement reached on the severity of the case before proceeding further. This can be facilitated by reference to risk assessment schedules, such as those given in *Assessing Risk in Sexually Abusive Young People* (Graham 1995). Although not validated psychometric procedures, these risk assessment checklists do provide a useful adjunct to clinical decision making. Risk assessment is discussed in more detail in Chapter 3.

The scale of subsequent assessment required and the measures needed to complete the task adequately should be related to the level of risk identified to date (see Table 4.1).

The ideal would be for assessments to proceed via an integrated multi-disciplinary team experienced in working with adolescent sexual offenders and their families. This is not as expensive a service as might first appear, if well developed procedures are used by competent staff.

Individualised assessment of functioning

Sexually abusive behaviour occurs within a context which permits the abuse and by a perpetrator who has chosen abusive rather than consenting sexual behaviour. It is, therefore, prudent to address the general features of both the individual abuser and his situation in addition to the factors which are considered to relate directly to the sexually abusive behaviours. Our understanding of the causation of sexually abusive behaviour is sketchy. The most balanced view, based on current empirical knowledge, is that causation is probably multi-factorial (e.g. Becker 1988), so we need a general assessment against which aspects of sexual behaviour can be focally evaluated. This also provides a relatively low-key atmosphere, during which rapport may be more easily established.

Experienced practitioners should have well established schemata appropriate within their own profession for carrying out focal assessments as necessary. For others, it may be helpful to identify some of the more important areas. These include the following.

Social competency   This term is used in a broad sense here to encompass the ability of the individual to develop and maintain social relationships appropriate to his age and situation. In particular, it refers to skills the individual possesses for use in establishing and maintaining social relationships which may form a prelude to 'normal' sexual relationships. Poor social competency is recognised as a contributory factor predisposing toward sexual abusiveness (Knight and Prentky 1993; Marshall et al. 1995).

A wide range of techniques are available for assessing social skills. These include observational assessment, rigorous behavioural monitoring and questionnaires. In relation to the specific problems associated with adolescent sexual abuse, the following issues need to be addressed:

- eye contact
- conversational skills
- relationships with same-age peers
- interpersonal problem-solving ability and whether avoidance is a regular feature
- age appropriateness of play

- age/sex profile of preferred social contacts
- intimacy skills

Relevant measures include Fear of Negative Evaluation (Watson and Friend 1969), *Social Skills Training with Children and Adolescents* (Spence 1978), *Normative Adaptive Behaviour* Checklist (Adams 1984).

Anger This is a negative response to frustration and devaluation. Pierce and Pierce (1990) report a high incidence of physical abuse amongst adolescent sexual offenders. Prior sexual abuse is a recognised factor in the background of approximately 50% of sexually abusive adolescents (e.g. Richardson et al. 1995a, Ryan 1989). Anger can be assessed by identifying triggering events, behavioural and cognitive responses and their consequences. Where violence is present as part of abuse or where motivation appears a confusing mixture of sex and violence, assessment of anger is essential.

Relevant measures include *State-Trait Anger Expression Inventory* (Spielberger 1991) and *Reactions to Provocation* (Novaco 1991).

Low self esteem Along with the associated fear of negative evaluation, this may contribute to a choice to seek younger children for sexual relationships. Routine assessment of self esteem is recommended, through such measures as *Culture Free Self-Esteem Inventory* (Battle 1992).

Intelligence Assessment of intelligence is a specialist area, and assessment should be undertaken by a psychologist. Intellectual level has a major bearing on the type of treatment programme an individual can be expected to engage in and benefit from and may even contribute to the aetiology of the sexually abusive behaviour (Wechsler 1992). Any of the usual measures of intelligence may be used.

Locus of control The degree to which the individual believes his behaviour to be controlled by internal as opposed to external factors merits assessment as it is relevant in planning a relapse prevention programme. The principal beliefs which feature in the individual's internalised control should be explored and potential cognitive distortions identified through the use of such measures as Nowicki and Strickland 1973.

Personality   Sexual abuse does not occur in a vacuum. Understanding the adolescent's temperament and predominant mode(s) of adaptation may help in shedding light on how external stimuli impinge on the individual. Relevant measures include *Millon Adolescent Clinical Inventory* (Millon 1993), *Eysenck Personality Scale Inventory* (Eysenck and Eysenck 1964), *The Psychopathy Checklist* (Hare 1990).

Assertiveness   Some sexually abusive adolescents are inhibited verbally and have great difficulty in expressing their thoughts and feelings. Significant difficulties in this area reduce the youngster's ability to engage with others socially and may lead to withdrawal or aggression, particularly with female peers. Assessment may be made using such a measure as the Assertiveness Scale (Rathus 1973).

Coping skills   An individual's approach when faced with problems is relevant to understanding why he approaches sexual relationships in a particular way. Abusive behaviour might, in some circumstances, even be conceptualised as a dysfunctional coping response and may be evaluated on such instruments as *Adolescent Coping Scale* (Frydenberg and Lewis 1993), *Coping Responses Inventory* (Moos 1993).

Broad review of mental health problems   This should be undertaken on a selective basis as appropriate. Negative thoughts and emotions feature prominently in the early stages of many sexual assault cycles. These may be evaluated using standard measures such as *Beck Anxiety Inventory* (Beck 1990), *Beck Depression Inventory* (Beck 1978a), *Beck Hopelessness Scale* (Beck 1978b), *Suicide Ideation Questionnaire* (Reynolds 1987).

Substance misuse   The degree to which the sexually abusive adolescent misuses drugs, alcohol and solvents, and their involvement as precursors of sexually abusive incidents, should be assessed. Substance misuse has been found to feature in the early stages of many sexual assault cycles. Relevant measures include *Alcohol Use Inventory* (Horn et al. 1990), *Adolescent*

Drinking Index (Harrell and Wirtz 1994), *Substance Abuse Relapse Assessment* (Schonfeld et al. 1993).

Clinical interview

A carefully constructed clinical interview is the most appropriate method for assessing sexually abusive behaviours, although all self-report procedures are fragile. In approaching this task the following may be considered helpful:

- Use a semi-structured approach (as in e.g. Appendix A, p. 74). Be prepared to explore new information.
- Be familiar with information from social services reports, victim statements and other sources beforehand.
- Mention the commonness of problems of sexual behaviour. Sexually abusive behaviour is wrong and hurtful but the individuals are not monsters and they can be helped.
- Discuss confidentiality in detail, depending on whether referral is for official report or not. Global statements such as 'everything said here is confidential' are inaccurate and dishonest.
- Explain the costs of denial and benefits of honesty.
- Remember the enormity of what you are asking.
- Confront and persist but do not get into a confrontation.
- Do not go too fast; it may take several sessions.
- Try to gain an overall understanding of the case and its dynamics, not minute details.
- Work from antecedents and consequences back to behaviour, as descriptions of behaviour are most embarrassing for the adolescent and are also less useful in treatment work.
- Concentrate on thoughts, feelings and behaviours and not on labelling the person.
- Minimise questioning which might be interpreted as judgemental. Structure expectations towards the belief that he is not unique: 'A number of young men find . . .'; 'Tell me about times you've felt like that'.
- Identify cognitive distortions: 'Did you know what you were doing was wrong?'; 'What did you say to yourself to make it OK to have sex with . . .?'
- Summarise what he has said and reflect back. Compare to victim statement. Confront with anomalies.
- Develop trust but do not trust what you hear.

An interview protocol is presented in Appendix A but should only be commenced if sufficient rapport and motivation have been established. A basic motivational interviewing schedule is presented in Appendix B (p. 000).

Specialised assessment of sexually abusive adolescents

The following specialised assessment procedures require careful interpretation, present potential ethical problems, lead to technical and theoretically complex treatment interventions and so should only be used within a specialist and multi-disciplinary team. The procedures should be implemented selectively, as judged appropriate on the basis of the profile emerging from general assessment of the young person.

Deviant sexual arousal The significance of deviant sexual arousal in adolescents is less clear cut than with adults. Sexually abusive adolescents frequently abuse children much younger than themselves. The abusive behaviours, however, appear to be driven more by *opportunity* than by *preoccupation* with a specific focus of deviant arousal. Adolescents tend to show more widespread sexual arousal patterns which include arousal to deviant stimuli within an overall profile which includes arousal by non-deviant stimuli. They tend not to display the degree of compulsion, preoccupation and fixation regarding a particular sexual target or behaviour as adults and seldom fit the diagnosis of any single sexual deviance.

Assessment of deviant arousal may be indicated if (1) a sexually abusive adolescent displays a *repeated* pattern of abusive behaviours against particular (types of) victims; (2) preoccupation is displayed with particular sexual acts or victims; or (3) repetitive deviant masturbatory fantasies are disclosed.

Several methods of assessment are available for this purpose. All present problems of validity and reliability and have varying degrees of ethical difficulty. The techniques, briefly outlined, include the following:

> *Penile plethysmograph* This is a flexible band placed around the subject's penis, the electrical resistance of

which varies as it expands and contracts. The band is connected to a polygraph which records changes in the band's resistance as tumescence changes.

A variety of neutral and sexual stimuli are presented either visually or on audiotapes. Changes in penile tumescence are recorded, so that those which achieve the greatest arousal can be identified. Changes in response pattern can be identified as treatment progresses.

The technology of such assessment is impressive, with modern equipment coming complete with standardised stimuli, computerised scoring and other aids. The technique is undoubtedly a useful research procedure but validity issues remain to be answered satisfactorily. Major ethical and political issues would be involved with using such an assessment method with sexually abusive adolescents. In particular, the use of pornographic sexual stimuli would present difficulties.

Galvanic skin response   The subject's hand is placed on a pad which measures electrical resistance in the skin. Arousal is thought to correlate with increased sweating and as this occurs, skin resistance changes proportionately. As in the penile plethysmograph these changes are recorded on a polygraph and, on modern machines, computer scored. The measure is obviously less direct than on the penile plethysmograph with regard to sexual arousal and as a result has even greater validity problems, since *any* form of arousal, including anxiety, raises the GSR. Ethical problems, however, are lessened and if non-pornographic sexual stimuli are employed then this technique merits consideration for research use with sexually abusive adolescents.

Card sorts and questionnaires   A range of sexual stimuli, including the deviant, are presented verbally. The adolescent has to rate each scenario according to how sexually arousing he finds it. Validity and reliability problems common to all self-report measures are present, i.e. is the subject responding honestly and will he respond differently under other conditions? Unlike the penile plethysmograph and the galvanic skin response, this response is under the subject's conscious control. There are ethical problems in presenting deviant sexual behaviours openly to adolescents (Nichols and Molinder 1984, Becker 1993).

Sexual fantasy The role of fantasy in sexual relationships is poorly understood. 'Normal' fantasy is wide ranging and the break point at which it would be deviant speculative. With some abusers, however, behaviour has been clearly driven by a pre-existing fantasy.

Assessment of sexual fantasy presents major methodological and clinical difficulties. Methodological difficulties are those present in all self-report procedures but exaggerated because of the acutely sensitive nature of the subject matter. Clinically, the very act of describing a sexual fantasy appears to reinforce it.

Various techniques exist for assessing sexual fantasies:

Fantasy log – The adolescent is asked to keep a diary of sexual fantasies experienced.

Questionnaires – Potential sexual encounters are described and the subject is asked how frequently he engages in fantasy about them as, for example, with the *Wilson Sex Fantasy Questionnaire* (1978).

Assessment work through interview.

Physiological response (e.g. PPG) to provided fantasies.

Cognitive distortion This can have a major influence in sustaining sexually abusive thought and behaviour and thus requires the most careful assessment. Cognitive distortions are beliefs which contradict objective evidence and the stance most people would take on the subject. An example would be: 'Sexual activities with young children are not harmful to them and are, in fact, a good way of introducing them to sexual relationships.'

Adherence to this type of cognitive distortion (a) eliminates internal inhibitions against having sex with children, (b) provides a positive justification for doing so and (c) removes any guilt which might be experienced after the event. This phenomenon is covered in detail in the adult sex offender literature, but is less marked in abusive adolescents. Our tentative clinical hypothesis is that cognitive distortion is itself a developmental phenomenon which has not reached its conclusion in adolescence. The most productive area for cognitive distortions among adolescent abusers is discussion of what constitutes consent to sex and perception of passiveness in the victim as permission to continue. A system designed to elicit commonly encountered cognitive distortions within a UK population of sexually abusive adolescents is presented in Appendix C (see Becker 1993).

Victim empathy   The underlying argument for assessing this issue is that abusers have little empathy for their victims and awareness of the harm they do to them. Like cognitive distortions, this serves to facilitate abusive behaviour. Our understanding of this issue with abusers is imprecise. Most crime involves victimisation and most persistent criminals display limited empathy towards their victims. Whether this is different with abusers is questionable. Our current ability to assess victim empathy reflects the uncertainty of the concept but procedures are being developed (Hanson and Scott 1995).

Sexual attitudes   In some cases of abusive behaviour negative sexual attitudes may be a significant predisposing factor. Cases involving rape or indecent assault of a same-age or older female are instances where assessment of sexual attitude might be useful. Appendix D contains a basic sexual attitude questionnaire. Use of a questionnaire of this type should be judged in relation to the adolescent's age, level of sexual knowledge, sexual behaviour and the age/sex of their victims.

Neuropsychological assessment   Recent research into conduct disorders has identified the presence of neuropsychological deficits that may be associated with problem behaviour. These are thought to impair ability to control behaviour. Specialised assessment is required to explore these possibilities (Moffitt 1993).

Psychiatric assessment   Adolescents rarely refer themselves for psychiatric assessment. The content of psychiatric assessment, in the case of those referred for sexually inappropriate and abusive behaviours, overlaps with assessment that may be undertaken by other professionals. The following represent the principal factors which would feature in an adequate psychiatric assessment of a sexually abusive adolescent:

- presence of bodily symptoms, such as headaches, anxiety, palpitations, eating or elimination problems;
- mood – presence of sadness and its persistence; depressive feelings, misery, suicidal ideation and general inability to enjoy life. Disturbance of sleep/appetite, loss of weight and related matters;
- presence of any unusual beliefs or experiences such as hallucinations (auditory or visual);
- history of substance abuse, usually moving from tobacco, alcohol consumption and solvents to amphetamines, Ecstasy, LSD and other illegal substances. Details of usage, frequency and methods of obtaining the substances are helpful;
- details of anti-social behaviour including aggression and truancy (to achieve a general picture of anti-social behaviour);
- information about any sexual or physical abuse they may have experienced;
- any signs or symptoms of post traumatic stress disorder, if previously abused;
- educational functioning, attainment, attitude to school and, where relevant, attitude to work;
- parents' accounts regarding pregnancy, complications at birth, milestones, temperamental characteristics, mother/child relationships, with a particular reference to difficulties in bonding and history of chronic illness;
- the adolescent's mood, ability to concentrate and mannerisms, and in joint sessions, relationships with parents and sibling(s).

Physical or neurological examination of the client is rarely necessary unless there is evidence of facial asymmetry, obvious clumsiness or poor visuomotor co-ordination.

Psychiatric assessments should be comprehensive, multi-axial, and not simply concerned with the presence or absence of mental illness. They will need to include the nature and severity of presenting problems, provoking and ameliorating factors, assessment of educational and social functioning of the child, family factors, developmental details and coexistence of other illnesses. It is as important as it is difficult to avoid duplication of other and possibly more reliable information from other sources.

Case formulation

'Case formulation' is the current psychological approach to identifying the major factors associated with the causation and maintenance of the problem. It is a critical but often overlooked stage between assessment and treatment. It involves collating the information accumulated during the assessment process and analysing it in order to understand and explain the individual's problem. Information provided by other disciplines and agencies should be included. Experience is more critical at this stage than at any other in the assessment process since formulation involves a judgement and not simply a description. In many cases with abusive adolescents, formulation involves identifying priorities and attempting to make some sense out of an assessment which has uncovered a chaotic situation. A major requirement in developing a formulation is to present this to the patient to help him make sense of his difficulties and to progress to treatment.

Our clinical experience confirms the research findings concerning the lack of any single causal factor with regard to the aetiology of sexually abusive behaviour. Apart from the diathesis-stressor approach, none of the others mentioned in the previous chapter adequately encompasses the widely differing formulations which we encounter across individual cases.

As the following box indicates, a number of elements are necessary for treatment planning, of which case formulation is the necessary precursor:

Formulation of the case

1. precipitants of sexually abusive behaviour
2. situation in which abuse occurred
3. family and social context
4. predispositions, learning experiences, personality
5. function of sexually abusive behaviour
   - power
   - learned
   - opportunistic
   - sexual gratification
   - anger expression
   - compulsion
6. skills deficits – cognitive, behavioural, social, coping

---

7. motivation – receptivity to change
   - comfortable with sexually abusive behaviour
   - find behaviour debilitating
   - others find behaviour intolerable
8. treatment targets – psychological and behavioural change
9. preferred treatment modality – individual, group or mixed, involvement of family
10. preferred treatment orientation – behavioural, cognitive, dynamic
11. treatment evaluation – behaviour, psychometric, self report
12. multi-disciplinary/multi-agency working

From assessment to treatment

An assessment is the necessary precursor to treatment; the translation of one to the other is an important step. This requires careful and sensitive negotiation with the adolescent, family, or carers and the referring agency. Many adolescents appear prepared to comply with the assessment phase, but are reluctant to proceed to treatment. The critical task is convincing the adolescent and his family of the benefits of continuing to attend for treatment. This task is more difficult and delicate when there is no court-ordered mandate for treatment, and the adolescent is effectively a voluntary client.

Following completion of the assessment a meeting should be held involving the adolescent, his family or carers, social worker and the referring agency. If appropriate, the adolescent should be praised for completing the assessment phase and for addressing difficult and often distressing issues. He is encouraged to remain involved and to begin to address critical issues identified during the assessment. The potential benefits of participating in treatment are emphasised, along with the potential risks of not continuing with treatment.

The adolescent's motivation to continue into treatment is reviewed, practical issues regarding attending appointments are discussed and questions about further intervention resolved. To encourage participation in further work, it may be helpful to focus on some of the more personally distressing issues identified during the assessment, such as chronic feelings of anger and disturbing memories associated with the adolescent's own experience of abuse. The adolescent can also be encouraged to address more pervasive difficulties, such as interpersonal and social skills deficits which, if not treated, may have adverse effects on his general development.

An assessment based on co-operation by the adolescent will already have started the process of therapeutic change. Having ascertained general difficulties as well as factors specifically associated with abusive behaviour, the assessor is in a position to offer help which may well be accepted, particularly if parents/carers support it and it helps avert the threat of more unpleasant legal and other consequences.

The tendency to utilise a uniform treatment programme usually run on a group basis does not fit comfortably with the marked heterogeneity of abusive adolescents nor with the multiplicity of situational and personal factors which appear to have contributed to the development of the behaviours. The difficulties are that:

- multi-factorial aetiology is minimised;
- individual issues are minimised;
- the purpose of assessment is reduced to classification as abuser/not abuser. If abuser then entry to uniform programme follows;
- certainty about what is right and needed is often displayed in such programmes;
- treatment content tends to be based on dogma/belief rather than on objective formulation of individual assessment information;
- treatment practice tends to be focused on groups whilst the practical, clinical difficulties of delivering such treatment in a community context involving voluntary attendance is seldom acknowledged.

We do not claim that structured group work has no part to play in the treatment of abusive adolescents, but that this needs to be developed as one, and only one, element of a treatment approach. Individualised work should be the major component: in our experience there are many issues which simply cannot be addressed adequately in groups. Equally there are other issues which are more effectively addressed in group work. An

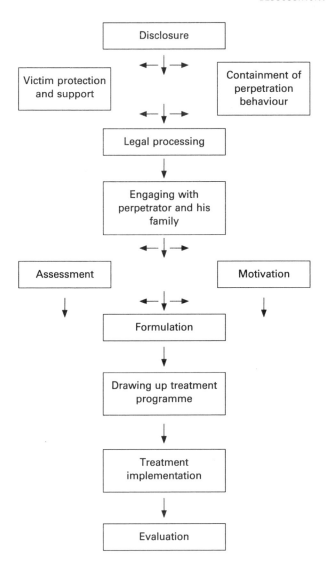

Figure 4.1   *Overall intervention process*

individualised package based upon the formulation should be constructed to include selected elements of individual and group therapy. In our practice, the balance is tilted to individual and family work with outpatients and towards structured group work in residential programmes. Individualised assessment serves no purpose if treatment has already been predetermined and pre-packaged for all abusers.

Summary of assessment issues

1. Is there a problem?
   Whose problem is it? } MOTIVATION
   Do you want to change?

2. What did you do? } BEHAVIOUR
   What are you doing?

3. Why did you do it? } UNDERSTANDING
   Why are you doing it?

4. Will it happen again? } RISK
   Will it get worse?

5. What can we do to help
   you change?
   What do we need to do to } INTERVENTION
   reduce the risk of you doing
   it again?

6. How have you changed? OUTCOME

Appendix A : individual clinical interview protocol

To be used as a follow-on to assessment of general functioning, to establish rapport when legal proceedings are complete and where confidentiality issues have been discussed. Comments to the youngster are set in boxes.

General sexual development

1. Did you get sex education classes?
2. How many girlfriends have you gone out with?
3. Could sexual things be talked about comfortably in your family?

> 'I need to find out what you know and don't know about sex before we go on. Can we do this by a short quiz?'

4. Biological knowledge quiz game. Ensure appropriateness of age and circumstances; tailor accordingly. Consider using anatomically correct dolls for younger perpetrators.

female sex organ	☐	male sex organ	☐
mechanics of intercourse	☐	ejaculation	☐
masturbation	☐	menstruation	☐
erection	☐	anus	☐
homosexuality	☐	condom	☐
oral sex	☐	pregnancy	☐
sexual fantasy	☐	sexual arousal/urges	☐

* PROVIDE INFORMATION ON NORMAL SEXUAL BEHAVIOUR (after consultation with parents if appropriate). Tell the adolescent that it is normal for young men

– to have sexual fantasies
– to get aroused
– to masturbate
– to want to have sexual experiences
– to have a range of sexual fantasies and urges

> 'These are all normal parts of growing up.'

* MOTIVATION – why is it important that we get answers to the following questions?

– To help you understand?
– To help you avoid getting into further trouble?
– To help identify any worries or concerns you have?
– To help identify any areas you may need help with?

> 'Please answer these questions as honestly as you can –
> we're not trying to embarrass you or get you into trouble,
> nor are we judging you. It is to try to help you understand
> what happened more fully and help you avoid further
> trouble.'

5. What was your first sexual experience?. . . . .
6. What age were you? . . . .
7. Have you ever seen two people having sex? . . . .
    What did you see?. . . . .
    Who?. . . . .   When? . . . .
8. Have you ever seen sexual magazines?
    When?. . . . .   What?. . . . .
    Where did you get them from? . . . .
    With whom? . . . .
9. Have you ever seen sexual videos?
    When?. . . . .   What?. . . . .
    With whom? . . . .
    Home made? . . . .
    Violent? . . . .
10. Have you ever been touched in a way that you did not
    want to be touched? . . . .
    By whom?. . . . .   When? . . . .
11. Have you ever been pressurised into sexual behaviour?
    When?. . . . . What? . . . . By whom? . . . .
12. What age were you when you started to masturbate? . . .
13. How often do you masturbate now?. . . . .
14. What have your relationships with girlfriends involved so
    far?. . . . .

Antecedents of the sexually abusive incident

(Only if the boy accepts he did something that has brought him
to attention.)

Reminder: • Process
           • Experience – won't shock
           • Confidentiality
           • Honesty – treatment

> 'You've done well so far.'

1. Where did the incident take place?................
   What time was it?...............................
2. Was anyone else around when it happened?..........
3. Had anything unusual happened that day? Had anything made you feel sexy?............................
4. Would you usually be at this place at this time?.......
5. Had you been taking drugs/alcohol/solvents?.........
6. How were you feeling just before?..................
   ....
7. What thoughts were going through your head just before?.......................................
8. Had you fantasised about doing this?...............
9. Had anything happened to get you sexually aroused just before the offence?
   What?...
   Who?..
10. Had you been thinking about doing this for some time before you did it?..............................
11. If you did not plan the behaviour why did it happen?......................................
    ....
12. Was the victim known to you?...................
13. Do you think the victim was sexually attracted to you?..
14. How often had you engaged in sexual behaviour with the victim previously?...........................
15. Describe your victim
    Age?................   Sex?.................
    Relationship with you?.........................

Offence behaviour

1. Did you set things up in any practical way?..........
2. How did you select your victim?..................
3. Was the victim resistant?......................
4. How did you overcome resistance? (Use prompts but try to obtain verbal account from the perpetrator.)
   Threats..............   Friendship.............

Aggression . . . .   Bribes . . . .
Playing games. . . . .
5. How did you show the person that you wanted sex with
them? . . . .
6. What did you do? . . . .

'Now we need to know exactly what you did to your victim.
Talking about this is not easy so again I would ask that you
answer this short questionnaire. Just put a tick against the
things you did.'

Give questionnaire on separate sheet to young person and
allow him to complete it in private.

expose self. . . . .   kiss . . . .
touch over clothes. . . . . . .   touch under clothes. . . . .
touch parts of body   –   breasts. . . . .
                           –   nipples. . . . .
                           –   penis . . . .
                           –   crotch . . . .
                           –   balls . . . .
                           –   vagina . . . .
                           –   anus . . . .
Stick finger in anus/vagina?
Put mouth on what part of the body – breasts/nipples/
crotch?
Suck vagina/penis
Make victim touch you where – nipples/crotch/penis/balls/
anus?
Make victim suck your penis?. . . . .
Make victim stick fingers/penis up your anus?
Put your penis where?
– chest . . . .   crotch area (not in) . . . .
– in vagina . . . .   in mouth . . . .
– anus area (not in) . . . .   in anus . . . .
Insert any object into vagina/anus?

7. Do you think your victim wanted you to do it? Why? . . .
. . . .
8. Did your victim ask you to stop?. . . . . . .   How? . . . . . .
9. How did you get your victim to carry on?. . . . .

10. Did you have an erection?. . . . .
11. Did you ejaculate? . . . .
12. Did you say anything to your victim afterwards so she/he wouldn't tell? What?

(Use prompts but try to obtain a fuller verbal account.)

        threat to hurt him/her. . . . . . threat to kill him/her. . . .
        threat to hurt/kill victim's parents/brother/sister? . . . . .
        threat to victim's parents . . . threat with a weapon?. . .
        tell victim they are bad. . . . .
        won't be friends . . . .
        trouble with police . . . .

13. If you were alone with the victim again would you be tempted to repeat the behaviour? . . . .
14. Do you know anyone similar to the victim who you would be tempted to do the same thing to? . . . .
15. How many times in the past have you done this sort of thing?. . . . .
    For how long have you been doing it?. . . . .
16. With how many different victims?. . . . .
17. What other sexual behaviours have you been involved in?
    . . . .

Consequences of the behaviour

1. What did you enjoy most about the behaviour? . . . .
    What did you not like about the behaviour? . . . .
2. Did you feel like doing it again with the same person/ another person/doing other things to them?
3. Did you masturbate/fantasise about it afterwards?
4. How many times had you done the behaviour before you got caught? . . . .
    For how long? . . . .
5. How were you found out? . . . .
6. What happened when you were found out?
    Parents . . . .
    Victim . . . .
    Victim's parents . . . .
    Social workers . . . .

Police . . . .
Court . . . .
Others . . . .

Attitudes to offence

Review events from previous questions:

> 'What you seem to be saying is . . .'

who . . . .
what . . . .
when . . . .
where . . . .
how . . . .

> 'Have I got that right?'

1. Do you think it was your fault this happened? . . . .
    If no, then whose? . . . .
2. Did you feel at the time that what you were doing was
    wrong? . . . .
3. Did you know it was against the law? . . . .
4. Do you regret doing it? . . . .
5. Do you feel ashamed of what you did? . . . .
6. What do you think should happen to you now? . . . .

Attitudes to victim

1. Where is your victim now? . . . .
2. How do you feel about that? . . . .
3. What do you think about your victim now? . . . .
4. How do you think your victim would feel about your being
    here today? . . . .
5. Do you think about your victim very much? . . . .
6. Do you think you have hurt your victim? If yes, in what
    ways? . . . .
7. Do you think your victim was partly to blame? . . . .
    Why? . . . .

8. Describe your victim's behaviour when he/she first became aware you were going to abuse/attack them. . . . .
9. Describe how you think your victim felt during and just after you abused/attacked them. . . . .
10. Describe your feelings for your victim while you were abusing/attacking them. . . . .
11. Describe your feelings for your victim just after you abused/attacked them. . . . .
12. Describe how you think your victim would have described you during and just after you had abused/attacked them.
. . . .

Expectations

1. What do you think should happen to you now? . . . .
2. Where do you think you should live? . . . .
3. Should you be getting treatment? . . . .
4. What sort of things do you think you need to work on? . . . .

Appendix B: motivational interview (brief)

1. Is this behaviour a problem for you? . . . .
2. Do you want to change this behaviour? . . . .
3. Why should you change?
   Reasons for   Reasons against
   . . . .
4. Who else wants you to change? . . . .
5. Who does not want you to change? . . . .
6. What do you think life will be like for you if you don't change? . . . .
7. Do you want to sexually abuse anyone again? . . . .
8. Are you at risk of reoffending? . . . .
9. How can you stop yourself from sexually abusing/ attacking someone again? . . . .
10. What evidence do you have that you will not do this again?
. . . .
11. Would you take part in treatment if it was offered? . . . .
12. Do you think that you need treatment to help you? . . . . Why? . . . .

Appendix C: assessment of cognitive distortions

Cognitive distortions can occur across a wide range of issues. The objective of assessment is simply to identify whether cognitive distortions are present or not. In our experience, assessment is conducted most effectively on a selective basis, taking into consideration the adolescent's age, profile of sexually abusive behaviour to date and age and sex of victims. The following statements covering a wide range of cognitive distortions are presented *individually on cards* which the adolescent is asked to classify as TRUE or FALSE and place in separate piles. The title of the area of distortion is written on the back of the card either in full or in a coded abbreviation for easy identification subsequently. This can be done in private without the interviewer present if the adolescent prefers. Cards are selected from the overall pool, as appropriate for presentation to a particular adolescent. The results are then used clinically in the sense that any cognitive distortions are recounted, identified in the assessment report and targeted for inclusion in treatment.

Child molestation

'Informed consent'
1. A young child is able to say whether or not he or she wants to have sex with an older person.
2. Young children like to experiment by doing sexual things with older people.

'Vicarious learning'
1. A good way for young children to learn about sex is to watch older people having sex.
2. A good way for young children to learn about sex is through watching pornographic videos.

'Direct learning'
1. It is all right for teenagers to teach children about sex by doing sexual things to them.
2. A good way for a younger child to learn how to masturbate is for a teenager to masturbate them.

'Sexual game play'
1. It is normal for teenagers to play sex games like doctors and nurses with younger children.
2. It is OK for a teenager to play with younger children's sexual parts as long as they think it is just a game.

'Seriousness'
1. It is all right for a teenager to rub his penis against a child so long as he does not put his penis inside the child.
2. It is OK for a teenager to do sexual things with a younger female child but not with a younger male child.

'Harm'
1. Just fondling a younger child's sexual parts cannot do them any harm.
2. A teenager who puts his penis inside a younger child is not doing any real harm if the child enjoys it.

'Reciprocal'
1. A teenager who only makes a child play with his penis is not taking advantage if he does the same to the child's penis.
2. A teenager who only makes a child lick his penis is not taking advantage if he licks the child's vagina afterwards.

'Mutual enjoyment'
1. If younger children do not cry when a teenager is doing sexual things to them it must mean that they like it.
2. If a teenager does sexual things to younger children and they do not tell their parents afterwards then they must have enjoyed it.

'Seduction by a child'
1. If a younger child dresses in clothes that make her look older then it means she is looking for a teenage boyfriend.
2. If a younger child dresses in sexy clothes, like black tights and short skirts, it is normal for a teenage boy to get turned on.

'Curiosity'
1. When younger children stare at a teenager's penis, it means that they want to do sexual things with him.

2. If a child is looking at pornographic videos or pictures and asks 'what are they doing', it is OK for the teenager to show them how it feels.

'Misperceived age signals'
1. Some children act much older than they are and are able to enjoy sex.
2. Some children are so attractive and well developed that they turn on teenagers.

'Affection'
1. Most children like a lot of affection and doing sexual things with someone they like is a way of getting more affection.
2. If a teenager cares for a younger child, a good way of showing it is for him to give sexual pleasure to the child.

'Abuse of authority'
1. Children should do as they are told, and that includes sexual things.
2. If a teenager is babysitting for younger children and he tells them to do sexual things then they should obey.

'Denial'
1. Most children make up stories about older boys and adults doing sexual things to them.
2. Children make up stories about being sexually abused to get back at people they do not like.

Child rape

1. If a teenager is attracted to a younger child it's OK for him to use force to make the child have sex with him.
2. It's all right for a teenager to use force to do sexual things to a younger child so long as he does not punch or kick the child.
3. If a younger child flirts with a teenager and turns him on then it's the child's fault if the teenager forces the child to have sex.
4. Sometimes a child might have to be held down so an older boy can teach them about sex.

5. Sometimes it is necessary to threaten a child to get them to do sexual things because they don't know what they are missing.
6. Sometimes a child might have to be forced to play sexual games with an older boy.
7. If a child does not fight back when a teenager forces the child to have sex this is not rape.
8. If a younger child cries and struggles when a teenager is forcing the child to do sexual things, it's OK for the teenager to use more force.
9. Any healthy child can resist a rape if it really wants to.
10. If a child does not tell anyone after a teenager has forced the child to have sex this is not rape.

Peer female rape

'Date rape'
1. If a teenage girl is flirting and talking about sex with her boyfriend and he tries to have sex with her, it's her fault if he does not let her back out of it.
2. When a teenage girl is alone with a teenage boy she does not know very well, and flirts with him and teases him, she really wants to feel what it's like to be raped.
3. Teenage girls who lead boys on and get them excited then try to change their minds and tell the boy to stop really want sex.
4. When a boy tries to have sex with a teenage girl and she only struggles at first then stops, she must have changed her mind and wanted it to happen.

'Social roles'
1. Teenage girls are usually shy and inexperienced and need to be pushed into sex by the boy.
2. Teenage girls say 'no' to sex because that's what they have been taught to say by their parents, but they have to do it some time, so the boy must make them do it.

'Victim is liar'
1. Most teenage girls who say they have been raped are lying, and only say this so they do not get into trouble with their parents.

2. Teenage girls often report rape because they feel guilty about having sex and feel better by blaming the boy.

'Victim enjoyed it'
1. Teenage girls feel sexual pleasure even when they are forced to have sex.
2. If a teenage girl enjoys sex with a boy even when she is forced into it, it cannot be called rape.

'Harm'
1. When threatened by a stronger boy most teenage girls would agree to have sex and so are not really harmed.
2. If a teenager does not physically injure his girlfriend, forcing her to have sex will not cause her any lasting harm.

Family abuse

1. When brothers and sisters do sexual things to each other it shows they care for each other.
2. When mothers and fathers do sexual things to their children it shows they care for them.
3. A good way for a child to learn about sex is for an older relative to have sex with them.
4. It is good for parents to have sex in front of their children so that the children learn what sex is about.
5. If pornographic videos are being watched in the family home it is OK for children to be in the same room.
6. There is no reason why older relatives should not share baths in the home with younger children.
7. Brothers and sisters sharing beds, even when there is a big age difference between them, is OK.
8. If an older relative gives a younger member of the family sweets or money for doing sexual things then this makes it OK.
9. Parents who encourage their children to play sexual games with each other are not doing anything wrong.
10. There is no reason why other members of the family should not go into the toilet when a younger child is using it.

Indecent exposure

1. Showing off your penis to a female is a good way of turning her on and making her want to have sex.

2. Showing a female your penis in public is a way of showing her that you fancy her.
3. Females like to see a male's penis and will be unable to resist looking at it even in a public place.
4. The very sight of a penis makes women want to expose their own sexual parts in return.
5. When a man can't chat up females the next best thing he can do to show that he is sexually attracted to them is to show his penis.
6. A good way to shock a female is to show her your penis.
7. A good way for a male to become sexually excited is first to expose his penis to a female.
8. Masturbating in public is OK because the added excitement makes it even more pleasurable than normal.
9. Males who expose themselves have a larger than normal penis which females find particularly attractive.
10. Females enjoy watching men masturbate even in public.

Appendix D: sexual attitudes questionnaire

The questionnaire is intended for clinical rather than statistical use and as such no attempt has been made to provide normative data. Any negative sexual attitudes reported on the questionnaire would be targeted for examination in treatment.

1. Men are expected to be stronger and more aggressive than women. It is expected that men sometimes force women to have sex.
2. Men have a higher sex drive than women and this excuses them sometimes forcing women to have sex.
3. Women expect men to take the lead in sex and like to be overpowered by men before sex.
4. If a woman goes out with a man and says 'No' to sex she really means 'Yes' but does not want to appear too easy in case the man thinks she has a bad reputation.
5. Prostitutes will have sex with anyone and so cannot be raped.
6. Some women's fantasies come true when they are raped.
7. Women enjoy sex even when they are forced into it.
8. If a man does not physically injure a woman, forcing her to have sex will not cause any lasting harm.

9. If a woman accepts a lift from a man she does not know very well, it is her fault if she is raped.
10. Women who have sex with a lot of men should not complain when they meet a man who rapes them.
11. Women who dress up deliberately to turn men on, get what they deserve when a man they have turned on forces them to have sex.
12. Some women are just man-haters and deserve to be punished by men.
13. Some women are just 'dirty sluts' and deserve to be used by men for sex.
14. A real man should use his physical strength and force even when having sex with a woman.
15. Some women are only sexually excited when the man plays rough, and forces them into sex.
16. More powerful and aggressive men are better at sex than weaker men.
17. Some women do not report being raped because they really enjoyed what happened to them.
18. Most men who rape women are upset or ill when they do it and are not behaving as they normally would.
19. Women who pick up men are asking to be raped.
20. Forcing women to have sex is something all men want to do, but only some men have the guts to do it.
21. Just because a man rapes a woman once does not mean he has a sexual problem.
22. Most men have to get their anger out by hurting women.
23. Most men when they get angry want to have sex to make themselves feel better.
24. Most men when they have been turned on by a woman are going to have sex one way or another.
25. Men have the right to discipline and punish women.
26. Most women cannot be trusted.
27. Most women need to be kept in their place by a man.
28. If a man did not keep his woman in her place she would think he was a wimp.
29. Sometimes men have to force their woman to have sex to prove their manhood.
30. Some women think they are better than most men and have to be taught a lesson.
31. It makes a man feel good when he's in total control and can do what he wants to a woman.

32. Most men who attack women and have sex with them are only getting their own back for something bad the woman did to the man.

Appendix E: sexual fantasy questionnaire

NB: only to be used in clinically appropriate circumstances, taking account of the young person's age, parental attitude, confidentiality and stage of legal processing.

General experience of sexual fantasy

1.	I have dreams/fantasies	True/False
2.	I cannot stop fantasising about sex	True/False
3.	I like fantasising about sex	True/False
4.	Some of my fantasies upset me	True/False
5.	Sometimes fantasies just pop into my mind	True/False
6.	My fantasies are about people I know	True/False
7.	My fantasies are about make-believe people	True/False
8.	My fantasies are about things I have done	True/False
9.	My fantasies are about things I would like to do	True/False
10.	My fantasies are about things I have seen	True/False
11.	My fantasies are about the things I got into trouble for	True/False
12.	I have no control over my fantasies	True/False
13.	When I have a fantasy I feel I want to do something sexual with other people	True/False
14.	In the past when I had a fantasy I had to do something sexual with other people	True/False
15.	Having a sexual fantasy is wrong	True/False
16.	I am worried about my sexual fantasies	True/False
17.	My fantasies make me do sexual things to other people	True/False
18.	When I have a fantasy I am more likely to do sexual things with other people	True/False
19.	I masturbate at least once a week	True/False
20.	I masturbate every day	True/False
21.	I masturbate more than three times a week	True/False
22.	I never masturbate	True/False

23. When I masturbate I don't think about
    sexual things   True/False
24. When I masturbate I think about sexual
    things   True/False
25. I feel masturbating is wrong   True/False
26. I do not like masturbating   True/False

Specific contents of sexual fantasies experienced

> 'How often do you have sexual thoughts, daydreams or
> fantasies about the things or people described? Read the
> description and circle the frequency which best fits you.'

1. A boy who is younger
    than you   never/monthly/weekly/every day
2. A girl who is younger
    than you   never/monthly/weekly/every day
3. A boy who is about your
    own age   never/monthly/weekly/every day
4. A girl who is about your
    own age   never/monthly/weekly/every day
5. A man who is older than
    you   never/monthly/weekly/every day
6. A woman who is older
    than you   never/monthly/weekly/every day
7. One of your relatives   never/monthly/weekly/every day
8. Your sister or stepsister   never/monthly/weekly/every day
9. Your brother or
    stepbrother   never/monthly/weekly/every day
10. Showing your penis to
    someone   never/monthly/weekly/every day
11. Watching someone
    undress   never/monthly/weekly/every day
12. Watching people
    having sex   never/monthly/weekly/every day
13. Touching a girl's
    private parts   never/monthly/weekly/every day
14. Touching a boy's
    private parts   never/monthly/weekly/every day

15. Touching an older
    woman's breasts   never/monthly/weekly/every day
16. Touching an older
    woman's private parts   never/monthly/weekly/every day
17. Masturbating an older
    man   never/monthly/weekly/every day
18. Masturbating a
    younger boy   never/monthly/weekly/every day
19. Sucking a boy's penis   never/monthly/weekly/every day

5

Psychosocial Treatment

Adrian Needs

The psychosocial domain

Difficulties in social interaction are a feature of many psychological problems. Social difficulties contribute to the development and maintenance of psychological disorders, and quality of prior social adjustment has a marked effect on outcome. Training in self presentation, interaction skills, meeting with members of the opposite sex, anger control and assertiveness form components of many treatment programmes for adolescent abusers. Several descriptive and theoretical accounts in the field of sexual offending have accorded a central significance to problems in social functioning (Groth 1977, Marshall et al. 1993). So far, however, unequivocal evidence of specific deficits and psychosocial treatment has remained elusive. This has characterised the field of social skills as a whole (Furnham 1983) and might suggest that formulations need to be improved rather than abandoned.

Social functioning in adolescent abusers

Descriptive studies of adolescent abusers, quoted throughout this book, show that most are characterised by poor social relations. A high proportion are rather isolated, having difficulties in creating and maintaining friendships, although this may be true of child molesters and exhibitionists more than of rapists. Many adolescent sex offenders have unsatisfactory or limited involvements with the opposite sex and experience problems of assertiveness.

Additional evidence comes from retrospective studies with adult sex offenders. These are important since they point to cumulative difficulties from adolescence onwards. Tingle et al.

(1986) reported that the majority of their rapist sample had few or no friends in adolescence. A typological study of adult offenders who began sexual offending in adolescence indicated that the majority of rapists and child molesters can be assigned to subtypes exhibiting low social competence, as defined, for example, by instability of relationships and employment (Knight and Prentky 1993). Low social competence was found to be more widespread in those who began offending in adolescence than as adults. In fact the prevalence was higher in the former group than has been found in most studies of adolescents. Although measures of social competence employed in various studies are not strictly comparable, social difficulty seems to be associated with persistence of offending. In Fehrenbach et al.'s (1986) adolescent sample, extent of social isolation was linked to severity of sexual offending. It is possible that severe and maladjusted abusers are most likely to persist. In addition, early apprehension and incarceration might have particularly limiting effects on the psychosocial development of already maladjusted individuals.

Studies of social functioning in adolescents who commit other types of offence have often suffered from methodological difficulties, and findings have been mixed (Hollin 1990). The issue of whether adolescent sexual abusers are more likely to show impairment of social functioning compared to other young offenders is complicated by the high proportion of adolescent abusers with a history of non-sexual offences or of other forms of aggressive or anti-social behaviour (Awad and Saunders 1989; Becker et al. 1986a; Fehrenbach et al. 1986). This might suggest that, for some of these offenders, sexual offending occurs in the context of generally disordered or anti-social conduct and other problems. However, as noted by Marshall et al. (1993), not all adolescent abusers in these samples have shown widespread misconduct. Some studies suggest that adolescent abusers are more likely than other adolescent offenders to be socially isolated, to experience social anxiety or alienation from same and opposite-sex peers (Blaske et al. 1989, Fagan and Wexler 1988). Moreover, although adolescent sex offenders are less likely to use physically injurious force than their adult counterparts, Van Ness (1984) found problems in controlling anger to be more than twice as common in a sample of incarcerated adolescent rapists than in a non-sex-offender sample.

There has on the whole been little published work on specific deficiencies, unique to adolescent sex offenders, in the component skills which might underlie competent social performance. Studies of such aspects as conversational skills (Segal and Marshall 1985), assertiveness (Stermac and Quinsey 1986), problem solving and interpreting emotional cues (Lipton et al. 1987) in adult sex offenders are at best promising. Social competence tends to be specific to situations and tasks, including the possibility that difficulties might occur for some only at deeper stages of a relationship. It might be unreasonable to expect anything other than heterogeneity among samples of sex offenders, even when they have committed ostensibly similar offences. This is likely to be as true of adolescents as of adults, despite the uncertain representativeness of incarcerated samples.

A lack of uniformity on standardised tasks does not preclude relevance of social functioning in the individual case; descriptive as opposed to experimental studies imply that there may be many individual cases where it is both complex and highly relevant (e.g. Needs 1988a).

The adolescent period

There are particular reasons for believing that the resolution of social difficulties at the adolescent stage may be crucial to the development of abusers. Adolescence has typically been regarded as a period of elevated social demands and tasks. Exploration of issues such as identity, autonomy, expansion and realignment of social contacts, new roles and feelings takes place against a background of physical changes and expectations of increased responsibility as preparation for adulthood. Social interactions centred around making friends, dating and being part of a peer group play a vital role in socialisation and the achievement of developmental tasks which are essential for future social, emotional and occupational functioning. The influence of peers on behaviour and beliefs is especially powerful at this stage.

Factors such as a history of physical or sexual abuse and neglect, psychiatric or emotional problems and learning difficulties are far from unique to adolescent abusers but are common amongst them (Barbaree et al. 1993, Marshall et al. 1993). Where present, they are likely to have a major disruptive impact on development (Knight and Prentky 1993). An individual whose viewpoints and behaviour have been shaped in such a context is likely to be at a serious disadvantage.

Problems can be exacerbated by additional pressures. These include the tendency for negative and limited styles of thinking and behaving to be reinforced by their outcomes. For example, hostile persons tend to elicit hostility, confirming their initial stance, or reticent individuals by minimal participation fulfil the anticipation that others will show little interest. Avoidance of close relationships, too, can prevent the revision of mental models from the past (Garlick 1991) and weaken the regulatory influence of social interaction upon thought (Rierdan 1980). Strained interactions, the stigma of social awkwardness or failure to provide support and social reference points for peers might elicit rejection or compound existing negative biases and a sense of isolation (La Gaipa and Wood 1981). Gaining support or validation of the self, a major preoccupation of adolescence, can thus be undermined.

Formulations of social (in)competence

Psychosocial interventions have been dominated by variants of 'social skills training', an approach which is fraught with difficulties and is 'not yet supported by compelling evidence of treatment efficacy' (McFall 1990: 311).

It is a short step from judging performance to be more or less 'skilled' to regarding ineffective performance as due to a deficiency in component 'skills'. Most attempts at intervention have concentrated on supplanting maladaptive social functioning with a fresh repertoire of supposedly more adaptive skills. Standard methods such as demonstration, rehearsal and feedback exist for the training of skills. This orientation is consistent with behaviour therapy, particularly work on assertiveness which emphasised the primacy of behaviour over cognition and affect in creating change. In addition the 'skills' metaphor suggests that social behaviour can usefully be regarded – and trained – in the same way as a motor skill such as riding a bicycle.

In this model, the attainment of social goals is mediated by perception of situational cues, decision making regarding appropriate responses, and performing hierarchically organised sequences of overt behaviour. The latter 'output phase' produces changes in the environment which are constantly monitored, leading to further adjustments through a feedback loop. Despite this identification of several points in the sequence at which performance could be impaired, much work in the social skills field has concentrated on the modification of overt behaviour (the 'response acquisition' approach). Other developments have focused on the perceptual or 'response discrimination' phase, or on factors such as anxiety, poor problem solving or maladaptive thinking which can have a disruptive effect on skilled performance. Aspects of this model are echoed in McFall's (1992) division into 'decoding, decision-making and enactment skills' and Liberman et al.'s (1989) 'receiving, processing and sending'.

As previously noted, competence in social interactions is specific to situations and tasks. The assumption of global traits simply obscures this patterning and underlying processes. This is relevant when considering the transfer or generalisation of treatment gains, as noted by Becker et al. (1978) in their attempt to modify the social skills of a teenage rapist. *Acquisition* of skills in training sessions is far less difficult than ensuring clients will *use* them in the actual environment. Furthermore, skills which are not used are unlikely to be maintained. This is not unique to social skills training, and several authors have suggested steps which should be taken to maximise the chances of generalisation (e.g. Glick and Goldstein 1987). Others have argued that conventional approaches, even when expanded beyond a narrow response acquisition approach, are misguided and likely to be futile (e.g. Trower 1984, Winter 1992). Much of the literature on the efficacy of social skills training is consistent with Furnham's (1983) observation that generalisation represents the 'Achilles' heel' in this area. Several studies with young offenders have failed to find consistent and lasting improvements in overt behaviour, cognitive measures or recidivism (Hollin 1990).

Some results have been more encouraging. For example McGurk and Newell (1981) reported sustained improvements and an absence of reoffending (albeit as defined by official records) in a 16-year-old incarcerated sex offender after only eight hours of skills training. Hazel et al. (1982) reported long term maintenance of a range of quite complex social skills (e.g. resisting peer pressure) in a non-incarcerated delinquent sample. Glick and Goldstein (1987) reported indications of generalised treatment gains in nearly half the clients who had undergone their ambitious 'structured learning' approach. Improved ratings of social skills were reported in a sample of four non-incarcerated 'sexual deviants' at 3- and 12-month follow-up assessments by Hayes et al. (1983).

The last three studies used additional procedures (e.g. meetings with the therapist to discuss difficulties) in order to promote generalisation. Promising results have also been reported fairly consistently in the field of anger control, where additional cognitive interventions such as training in the use of self statements or inner speech and the discussion of consequences of maladaptive behaviour are well established (e.g. Goldstein and Keller 1987). Training in 'cognitive skills' is not without problems (Coyne 1982, Dow and Craighead 1984). These have often included an inadequate conceptual basis and a tendency to ignore existing cognitive structure. It is however worth noting that the use of self statements was found to enhance transfer of training to dating situations among a non-offender sample of socially anxious individuals (Glass et al. 1976).

The framework presented here is based on that outlined for use with adolescents by Felner et al. (1990), elaborated by some of the areas of research relevant to social functioning described elsewhere (Needs 1988b). The framework identifies four areas of functioning (cognitive, emotional, behavioural and motivational) and differentiates between three levels (the person-centred, the transactional, and outcomes). These areas are regarded as largely interdependent.

In evaluating the available material, it is evident that procedural advances have been made to promote the generalisation and maintenance of social skills training. Yet concerns which are reflected in behaviour and thinking may still work against change, and interventions which fail to accommodate adequately the 'personal meanings' of social interactions for the adolescent may fail to touch him. This is not confined to behavioural skills training. For example, self statements used in 'self instructional training' may have no meaning in terms of the adolescent's existing cognitive structures and thus make no sense. Acceptability is also likely to be influenced by subculture, especially amongst adolescents. While self statements are important determinants of behaviour and feelings they cannot necessarily be replaced in isolation and as readily as spark plugs in a car (Coyne 1982).

Adolescents with a history of negative social interactions present particular challenges. Suspicion of social interaction, limited views of other people and insecurities regarding self might make acceptance of different viewpoints especially difficult. Models of self which are different from the adolescent's might be rejected by those who are poor at or resistant to apprehending other perspectives. In any case, ability to *utilise* different perspectives and the processes involved in personal change are interdependent (Radley 1974) so that limitations in the former impede the latter. This is particularly relevant in the case of intellectually limited adolescents who live in unsympathetic family and social environments where the opportunity to practise budding new skills may be devalued.

Assessment

Assessment should be directed towards constructing a *profile* of areas where problems do and do not occur. The assessor should also be sensitive to issues of situational specificity and to other contextual features such as the client's interpersonal environment (including subculture), age, developmental level, and learning abilities (Hazel et al. 1982, Stermac and Sheridan 1993). The role of social interaction difficulties in abusing should be provisionally established. As with many target areas, while preliminary appraisal is important, assessment should continue as further information and hypotheses emerge.

Initial assessment should include detailed interviewing concerning social functioning in the recent past, the present and projections and aspirations for the future. In addition to providing information this is part of the process of negotiation of goals, encouraging focus and engaging the individual. Particular attention should be paid to recent examples of social difficulties. As well as raising relevant issues, this information can be useful in constructing role plays during intervention. Emphasis should be on questions such as what, where, when and with whom, as well as areas where the person would like things to be different (Liberman et al. 1989). These authors treat the 'why' question with some disdain. While it can distract or entangle a group, it is also true that 'why' can be used to great advantage outside the group setting without resulting in endless speculation of dubious significance, if a degree of structure is used (Needs 1988a, 1988b, Wright 1970).

A wide net can be cast by the use of self-report instruments such as the Matson Evaluation of Social Skills in Youngsters (Matson et al. 1983), used in the adolescent sex offender programme described by Becker and Kaplan (1993), or the Social Situations Problem Questionnaire (Spence 1980). Norms for many potentially relevant questionnaires which may be appropriate for fairly literate late adolescents (see, for example, Salter 1988) have not been established. Responses to individual questionnaire items can still provide a basis for discussion, as can additional self-report approaches such as open-ended questionnaires and sentence completion tasks (McGuire and Priestley 1985).

Cognitive skills

Sensitivity to interpersonal (e.g. affective) cues can be sampled using video vignettes as stimulus materials (McFall 1990). A range of targets and contexts should be explored: perceptual skills (and biases) vary across type of emotion, person and situation. Questions on such matters (e.g. 'How do you think the other person was feeling?' and 'How did this come across?') can also be used more informally to address cue utilisation, inferences, and empathy after role plays during the course of intervention (Liberman et al. 1989). In a similar fashion, questions regarding aspects of problem-solving such as goals, options, and advantages and disadvantages of particular courses of action can be employed. Other possibilities include descriptions of scenarios to which the individual generates a response (e.g. Freedman et al. 1978).

Although time consuming and complex, repertory grids (e.g. Fransella and Bannister 1977, Stewart and Stewart 1981) can yield much information concerning the discriminations and associations made by a person in the social domain. With sex offenders this can be especially interesting when the construing of women or children is examined. With adolescents, the degree of abstractness or concreteness of the discriminations (or 'constructs') used can raise hypotheses about social experience and developmental level (Adams-Webber 1979).

Emotion

When there is reason to believe (e.g. through interview or case history data) that emotions such as anxiety or anger are involved in an adolescent's behaviour, information can be gained through starting an appropriate diary or log. Supplied headings can ask for details such as situational characteristics, thoughts, behaviour, attempts at coping and outcomes; intensity can be rated on a scale of 0 to 10. A diary can only be used with motivated and literate clients, but can provide useful information on patterning, changes over time and situations which can be explored further.

Whether or not a diary format is used, it is crucial to discover the personal issues and meanings which are at stake for abusive adolescents in social encounters, particularly with possible victims and in situations which precede offending. In the case of anger this should include beliefs about how the world 'should' be and attributions of blame as set out, for example, in the appendices to the previous chapter. In social anxiety, perceived evaluative demands and sources of self-doubt are of relevance. Related and sustaining self statements should be identified, either through listing of thoughts following a real or simulated episode or by questionnaire. This can also take the form of a free-response description during a group session. A more sophisticated adaptation of this approach termed 'cognitive mirroring' – in which clients are videotaped then asked to describe their thoughts in detail at certain breaks in the film – has also been described (Reid 1979). Identifying inner speech prior to an interactional task is an additional possibility.

Behaviour

Direct observations of behaviour in which appropriately trained staff complete rating scales (preferably across a range of settings) is possible in institutional settings. Like most assessment techniques, these can be used either to identify apparent deficits or as parts of evaluation following treatment. Relevant issues to be considered here include comprehensiveness, relevance and independence of items and the scaling of responses.

Most behavioural assessments have used role plays in which typically the individual is asked to make conversation with (or otherwise respond to) a confederate. One option is to give a series of such tasks with varied stimulus characteristics. Some can be standardised, others can be designed to reflect known areas of social difficulty in the adolescent's life. It is also possible to construct naturalistic situations, with added twists to the episode to see how the adolescent responds.

Whilst the validity of assessments in contrived situations is questionable, other assessment techniques are not entirely free from such concerns. The relevance of frequency counts of 'molecular behaviours' such as eye contact is also uncertain. Ratings of overall impressions and inferential or amalgamated elements (such as empathy or giving explanations) should not be sacrificed in favour of measures which have the appearance of being scientific but in reality are just easier to collect. Ratings should of course be made by more than one trained observer, and definitions of target behaviour and styles should be specific and detailed. In addition, if the assessor is interested in anything like a 'pure' measure of behavioural skills (i.e. 'enactment' or 'sending') then the effects of deficits in perception or processing should be minimised to the extent of giving the individual clear instructions (even incentives) for enacting the required behaviour. It is salutary to know that even habitually unassertive women students were capable of enacting assertive responses when under strong instructional demands to do so (Rodriguez et al. 1980).

Motivation

This is a critical issue when negotiating programme goals, and if problems in co-operation or a failure to improve become evident. Repertory grids can be used to draw comparisons between individuals in the adolescent's life selected as representing aspects of social competence. 'Macho' film stars are often nominated by adolescent abusers. Grids can also highlight constructs of particular significance (for example one individual had a well-developed interest in being a 'rebel') or suggest concerns involved in a pattern of unstable relationships (Needs 1988a).

A form of assessment which is directly concerned with the clarification of ambivalence over change is the 'ABC' technique

(Tschudi 1977). Also derived from personal construct psychology, the information provided by this structured form of questioning is less rich and diverse than that provided by a grid but it has the advantage of being much more economical of time. Here a possible target state (e.g. 'being more interested in other people') is stated along with its contrast (e.g. 'keeping yourself to yourself'). The advantages of the target (e.g. 'being liked; takes mind off problems') and the disadvantages of the contrast (e.g. 'feeling lonely; bored') are explored, and then the disadvantages of the target (e.g. 'others might let you down; feeling false') and the advantages of the contrast (e.g. 'feel more secure; others don't make demands'): the latter level identifies misgivings which might need to be addressed before the possible target can be adopted as a goal.

Transactional level

Assessment here is concerned with the reciprocal impact of individual and environment. It typically involves interviewing the adolescent and observers. While relevant to social functioning generally, this can be crucial in the exploration of escalating sequences involved in anger (Toch 1969). An examination of the individual's interpersonal and subcultural environment should also be included (Baum et al. 1986, Gresham 1985).

Outcome level

Psychometric instruments exist for the assessment of adolescent self esteem (e.g. Harter 1988, Rosenberg 1965) and locus of control (Nowicki and Strickland 1973). At this level it is also worthwhile to assess loneliness, since it may have a particular significance in relation to sexual offending (Marshall 1989). The original form of the UCLA Loneliness Scale (Russell et al. 1978) seems to be linked to 'reticence'. The latter encompasses several facets of an avoidant and inhibited style and low general well-being; it also shows some relationships with rather alienated styles of thinking about social situations and relationships (Needs 1988b). The original version of the scale, despite its imperfections, seems to be more 'user friendly' to adolescents than the later version described by Russell et al. (1980).

Repertory grid-based information concerning self and other people is also relevant at this level, as is 'self-characterisation' (Fransella and Bannister 1977). Green and Yeo (1982) described an imaginative use of this technique within a group where adolescents were encouraged to write character sketches of themselves, themselves as they would like to be, and themselves as seen by others. The technique can encourage insight into self definition by disentanglement from habitual perspectives (although for this reason it can seem strange at first) and can be used to identify constructs which can be adapted for experiments with different 'roles'. The fact that everyone in the group (including the therapist) completed the task may have contributed to the apparent success of the technique in the group. Systematic use of self characterisation with adolescents is illustrated by Jackson (1988).

Intervention

General issues

Intervention can take place individually, in groups (e.g. four to eight with two group leaders), or a combination of the two. The arguments are familiar. Sessions with a single client permit an exclusive focus allowing flexibility, development of personalised rapport and a relatively seamless join with individually administered assessment techniques. Groups, on the other hand, are often more cost effective. They furnish a ready pool of participants for role play and the opportunity for learning from group members. Presence of others with similar problems can reduce feelings of subjective isolation and provide a more credible source of feedback than the therapist alone. A combination of the two approaches is used when assessment, review or follow-up sessions are held outside the group.

Group interventions vary depending on whether they use a set curriculum of skills or whether sessions are constructed primarily around the specific problems of individuals (including issues arising from homework assignments). Several authors have reported a combination of both (e.g. Liberman et al. 1989). Where a set curriculum is used, situations selected for role plays should still be based on the real life circumstances of adolescents (Glick and Goldstein 1987).

The most widely used techniques for training behavioural skills are modelling (demonstration) and instruction, rehearsal with coaching (in role plays) and feedback (including social reinforcement). These are most likely to be effective in combination (Twentyman and Zimering 1979), although with exclusive reliance on a response acquisition response, problems of generalisation will probably remain. Many authors now stress the importance of additional procedures such as homework assignments in promoting generalisation. Findings vary concerning the additional benefits of incorporating cognitively based techniques such as problem solving or the use of self statements, although self statements form a major component of most work in the field of anger control. The issue of optimal combinations of methods remains inconclusive because few studies are really comparable.

Methods

The following account of techniques refers to group interventions unless otherwise stated, although most are applicable or can be adapted to working with single adolescents.

Orientation

It is helpful to begin the intervention strategy with an introduction to rationale and methods. This represents a continuation of the process of structuring expectations which will have commenced with preliminary assessment and negotiation of goals. Ground rules for the group concerning confidentiality, members' right to express their viewpoints and the non-use of violence also need to be established. Discussion can move at an early stage to the benefits of improvements in target areas. This need only be a brief recapitulation, with the opportunity for some additional discussion, if techniques such as the ABC approach were used in the initial assessment. Points made can be listed and referred back to throughout the group. For example, the benefits of conversation, friendship, romantic relationships or of controlling temper can be examined briefly.

Discussion can be extended to acknowledge possible disadvantages, and the overall balance of positive and negative aspects of such training. Handout sheets summarising main points and giving background information on problems such as shyness and loneliness are valuable. Here, relevant issues such as literacy and the feasibility of retention of documents should be considered. Experience suggests that handouts are much appreciated in groups: the credibility of the group can be enhanced at an early stage by accurate representation of personally relevant problems and feelings.

Modelling

Before modelling is attempted, the rationale behind use of specific examples should be explained. This is part of the process of teaching adolescents to analyse social behaviour and to think in terms of skills and their relevance; it also aids identification with the situation. Stylistic aspects of modelled behaviour should be mentioned in advance. A permanent display of lists of verbal and non-verbal behaviour, after these facets have been introduced, is helpful. Models should be as similar as possible to adolescents on attributes such as age and background; this is particularly important with adolescent clients and adult therapists. Modelled episodes should be kept under five minutes, lest it be difficult to keep track of what is being demonstrated. After the model has performed, detailed questions focusing on aspects of verbal and non-verbal behaviour, strategies and performance improvements can be asked.

Modelling is also an established way of modifying self statements. The model can move from voicing self statements out loud during performance of a task to whispered, and then non-verbally indicated covert self statements, with the client trying out the modelled routine following each stage. The procedure can be used to demonstrate self statements which maintain a focus on the task in hand, and it is a small step to extend this to the modelling of problem solving.

Rehearsal and feedback

Rehearsing real life situations demands making scenes as realistic and personally relevant to participants as possible. This principle should guide the selection of participants. In the interests of promoting generalisation, however, each group member should be exposed to variations in models and situational demands. A clear description of the scene should be agreed, with clear instructions as to what is being looked for.

Goals, roles and rules or norms should be explained by the group and the main actor, with due regard for personal dimensions (e.g. 'a situation where you are the centre of attention') as appropriate; it is often in terms of 'idiographic stimulus and response equivalences' (Mischel 1968) that generalisation takes place. Scenes can be repeated, with coaching and increasing difficulty (e.g. the partner in the interaction adopting the role of an uncooperative acquaintance). Feedback should be solicited from the group with an emphasis on what was done well, on specific details, and on what might be improved. This contributes to the development of greater awareness, vicarious learning, and for participants, direct experience of enacting different styles. The protagonists should also be asked to comment, not missing opportunities for reinforcement and watching out for boredom thresholds. Repetition of successful performance increases chances of generalisation of gains. Video feedback can be helpful but can also distract.

Questions can be asked concerning likely thoughts and feelings of the adolescents if the situation had occurred in real life, along with problem-solving aspects such as alternative courses of action and their likely consequences. These give the opportunity to check and enhance use of cognitive skills. Group sessions can benefit from the use of games which reduce inhibitions and encourage an attitude of experimentation. Several collections of these games are available (e.g. Brandes and Phillips 1979). Excessive use can trivialise the activity, but as a rule humour is a significant aid to learning and performance. An extension is the use of Fixed Role Therapy (Kelly 1955) in which a new persona or role is fashioned from existing self descriptions for the purpose of short experiments in rehearsal. This procedure might be seen as drawing upon principles of changing perspectives through cognitive enactment.

The present author has outlined a similar idea termed the 'WOMBAT' (Needs 1988b). This stands for 'Way Of Me Behaving And Thinking'. Most clients warm to this. It is a way of communicating the idea of a *style of behaving* which carries with it characteristic ways of thinking (such as views of self, others, beliefs and self statements). Such a conceptual unit draws upon elements of Fixed Role Therapy and covert modelling: the latter facilitates change and prompts performance by the adolescent holding a mental image of successful performance. WOMBATs concerning roles such as being friendly, assertive and calm can be constructed in terms of detailed personal prototypes. This encourages development of new 'blueprints' for both thought and action that can help assimilation and integration of aspects of functioning which have received attention in the group. The main points of blueprints can be recorded on individualised WOMBAT cards. An important objective can then become what has been referred to in the context of anger control work as 'application training' – the elaboration, consolidation and validation of WOMBATs.

Homework assignments

Homework assignments can be regarded as experiments con- ducted outside group settings. This orientation (with its echoes of the Kellyian metaphor of 'man the scientist') is one which can be made explicit with some individuals or groups. A scientist carries out experiments in order to find out about the world and develop new and better ways of doing things. A scientist accepts complexity, uses his or her mind and is prepared to take a long hard look at what happened and try again in a modified way if events do not turn out as planned. This can encourage a focus away from merely short term concerns, or over-generalisation of failure, to resourcefulness and due affirmation of the importance of the problem-solving procedures of definition, generation and evaluation of alterna- tives, selection and trying out. It also engages the meaning system in encouraging reconstruction based on detailed reflection on the aspects that 'work'. This can be strengthened by repetition of the process and an emphasis on positive behaviours which are likely to be reinforced in natural settings.

The 'scientist' orientation allows an integrated approach to the development of WOMBATs, with homework assignments becoming experiments in their use and refinement. Experiments should be agreed with, and where possible suggested by, the adolescent. Aims should be specified, and details such as relevant skills, settings and target individuals formulated on the 'drawing board'. Attempt should be made to anticipate obstacles and ways of overcoming them. Trial runs can be held in the group with role plays being designed and examined in the usual manner. Assignments themselves can be specified and described on cards. Assignments should be challenging but attainable. Sometimes an area of experimentation should be broken down into smaller cumulative experiments. In true experimenter fashion, results and experiences can be recorded in a log or on record forms (Liberman et al. 1989). Results can be analysed subsequently in the group, leading to additional role plays, coaching, feedback and questioning as appropriate.

Limitations on homework assignments can of course occur in institutional settings where the range of types of interaction and interactants can be limited and where potentially a wider deviant culture can dominate. This is not a problem if institutional behaviour is the target. In addition, there are usually some skills (e.g. acquaintanceship, assertiveness or keeping calm) which can be exercised here, in preparation for outside the institutional setting.

Overcoming resistance

Likelihood of overt or passive lack of co-operation can be reduced by careful assessment, negotiation of goals, structuring expectations, establishing rapport and working with rather than ignoring the meaning system of the client. Resistance may still be apparent from time to time, and there are good reasons for this. These can include ambivalence regarding other people, social interaction and change. Anxiety can be debilitating in some adolescents. Some individuals who can be construed as personality disordered can be expected to test the credibility or good will of the therapist.

Power struggles should be avoided. Counselling techniques which communicate empathic understanding of the individual's concerns can be helpful in encouraging openness and keeping the focus constructive (e.g. paraphrasing, reflecting feelings). Additional tactics are possible. For example, the therapist can double for the reluctant group member in role play and ask the client for criticism. This can take pressure off the client, making him feel less trapped while at the same time keeping him involved and providing opportunities for vicarious learning. Observing the involvement and progress of other members can itself encourage participation. Ultimately, however, normal expectations should be maintained otherwise the structure of the entire group can dissolve. Sometimes an individual is not ready for a group and further one-to-one work is necessary.

Application

Social skills

Interventions which target basic communication skills usually include introduction to verbal and non-verbal elements of communication. This sets the scene for coverage of recognising and expressing emotions and the initiation and maintenance of conversational sequences, involving such aspects as open and closed questions and attentive listening. Some programmes go further into the realms of friendship, addressing shared activities, the role of pacing and reciprocity in self disclosure, giving and receiving compliments, joint decision making and compromise. Additional inputs can include problem solving, moderation of social anxiety and basic assertiveness such as refusing unreasonable requests or resisting peer pressure. Specific problems relevant to adolescents (e.g. job interviews, leisure activities, requesting instructions or clarification) may be incorporated, depending on the targets, length and degree of structure of the programme.

Dating and relationships

'Dating' or 'heterosocial skills' can form a module within a general course or separate group. Prior mastery of conversational skills (and, for some, grooming and hygiene) is necessary, where relevant norms and behaviour have been identified.

Areas for heterosexual skills training programmes include: initiating and eliciting conversation (e.g. by finding common ground, use of questions and listening skills, handling silences); self disclosure at different levels of relationship including talking about interests, experiences and feelings; empathy and reciprocity; making adjustments, resolving difficulties and assertiveness; intimacy and handling close relationships. Prominence has been given in some programmes to choosing/ recognising approachable partners for a date; planning, identifying resources and activities; the process of asking itself, and using problem-solving techniques to anticipate or negotiate obstacles.

There can be great advantages in having at least one woman therapist involved in work on 'dating' and it is desirable to examine assumptions and expectations concerning dating (and relationships in general) so that erroneous and self-serving beliefs can be identified and challenged. This might be linked to a programme of empathy training. Social skills without empathy can be a recipe for manipulation, and empathy and reciprocity are necessary for establishing true intimacy. Seeing other points of view can also help reduce anger and perhaps help attenuate a preoccupation with markedly idiosyncratic concerns and ideas.

It is possible to go beyond 'dating' to the conduct of deeper relationships. Otherwise notions of close relationships may remain governed to a large extent by models from an unsatisfactory past. From eliciting and acknowledging the benefits of close relationships, exploration can proceed to difficulties. If the focus of the group is not to shift dramatically, addressing the origins of such concerns is best undertaken outside the group (or in a different group). Yet some acknowledgement of the ways in which pressing personal issues can override other considerations helps provide a space in which alternatives can be recognised.

Anger control and assertiveness

Several intervention programmes aimed at modifying anger in adolescents have been reported in some detail (e.g. Feinder and Ecton 1986, Glick and Goldstein 1987, McDougall et al. 1987). This area of practice has gone beyond a 'response acquisition' approach more often than other areas of psychosocial treatment. This owes a great deal to the formulation by Novaco (1975). Not all reported interventions have covered the range of possible target components and techniques to an equal degree. Benefits have been reported from training in use of self instruction or self statements (Snyder and White 1979); problem solving (Guerra and Slaby 1990); assertiveness training (Rimm et al. 1974); and training in prosocial values (Arbuthnot and Gordon 1986). These focus on different facets or stages of the sequence of aggressive behaviour (Goldstein and Keller 1987). Individuals can be impaired in one or more of these areas which, as the earlier discussion of psychological factors should suggest, are likely to be interdependent to a large degree.

Adherence to positive aspects of aggression is much more likely to be dislodged if examples are drawn from episodes where group members have regretted losing control of their temper. Without such an emphasis group members can try to justify their own behaviour or attempt to impress and cultivate support amongst their peers.

Anger-provoking self statements can be identified from role plays, diaries or discussion exercises involving pairs of group members. Some workers use standard role play because any prolonged focus on the problems and circumstances of one individual tends to strain the patience of other group members. Others circumvent this problem by dividing into pairs to discuss personal episodes of anger. Each member then in turn recounts the episode and relevant self talk described by his partner.

Positive counters to negative and hostile self statements can be generated on the basis of role plays and discussion and their use can be modelled and rehearsed. Novaco (1975) describes four phases of self talk: *preparing for provocation* (e.g. 'You don't have to prove yourself'); *coping with arousal* (e.g. 'Time to take a deep breath'); *reflecting afterwards* (e.g. 'I'm doing better all the time'). Other responses are possible but the Novaco sequence is fairly easily understood by most adolescents. A large part of an anger control group should be concerned with 'application training' in the use of self statements in role-play sessions, anticipated situations and homework assignments. Some workers have recommended use of a structured diary or 'hassle log' to record experiences for discussion or further role plays. These techniques can help identify and neutralise thoughts which trigger or sustain anger, prompt the exercise of a task-orientated approach and aid the discriminatory capacity of individuals who are habitually impulsive or who have difficulty in differentiating emotional reactions.

Many chronically anger-prone individuals are also anxious while Novaco's model outlines that angry behaviour and cognition are influenced by physiological arousal, and vice versa. Some anger control programmes have included relaxation procedures with varying degrees of success. McDougall et al. (1987) reported that group relaxation techniques tended not to be taken seriously by participants who also on the whole did not adhere to practice using tapes outside group sessions. To be effective, procedures such as deep muscular relaxation with breathing exercises and guided visualisation need to be practised regularly. To do this, it helps to decide in advance details of time and setting, whether to sit or lie down, the use of imagery before commitment to a fixed sequence and to use self-reinforcement. In addition, procedures which do not divide the body into an exhaustive number of muscle groups and which then use enhancement procedures involving visualisation of deepening relaxation seem most convincing with anxious or impatient youngsters. A heightened awareness of what relaxation feels like might then influence effectiveness of cognitive techniques such as thought-stopping (e.g. counting backwards from ten then breathing slowly) in situations where heightened arousal or negative thoughts threaten to take over.

Orientation to typical anger sequences and alternatives to them can be necessary steps in dislodging an angry response. Strip cartoons can be used to great effect with adolescents to demonstrate self-fulfilling prophecies of expectation, behaviour and outcome in interactional sequences, as can selective video feedback on samples of behaviour in role plays or role reversal.

Several anger control programmes also make specific use of assertive strategies such as the 'broken record' and 'fogging'. The former involves keeping calm while repeating intentions and wishes in simple terms; the latter is similar, but a calm restatement of one's own position is prefixed by reflecting back an understanding of the other person. This is particularly relevant with the majority of abusive adolescents who are verbally inarticulate and have difficulty in sustaining a verbal interchange based on empathy and sensitivity.

Overview and implications

There are grounds for some optimism that major impediments to successful psychosocial treatments might be overcome with adoption of an approach which goes beyond a narrow emphasis on skill acquisition and employs a more comprehensive awareness of the processes involved in personal change. From this might come a more differentiated conceptualisation of the possible role of psychosocial factors in sexually abusive behaviour by adolescents.

Most obviously, impaired social functioning might restrict access to consenting age-appropriate sexual partners, with concomitant effects on a deviant self image and lack of re-inforcement of non-deviant arousal (e.g. Hayes et al. 1983), even though evidence on the previous and current sexual experience of adolescent sexual offenders is equivocal (e.g. Becker et al. 1986). Areas such as impaired empathy or a propensity to misread affective cues may impair social functioning and contribute to offending. In addition, themes derived from social experience (e.g. hostility) are likely to colour sexual encounters. Social isolation can lead to feelings of boredom which can act as a precursor to illegitimate searches for excitement and offending. It can also increase, for example, the time available for would-be child molesters to babysit. Unsatisfactory social and sexual relationships may undermine self esteem and increase susceptibility to culturally available sexual 'scripts' which emphasise forcefulness and adversarial views of sexual relations; isolation may compound idiosyncratic developments and reliance on fantasy. A lack of supportive and intimate social relationships may increase vulnerability to stress, and sexual sensations can provide an 'oasis' of distraction and freedom in the face of uncertainty and anxiety.

Unassertiveness can contribute to frustration and anger, which may be displaced on to a target different to the primary source. Feelings and memories from earlier trauma may be reactivated or resonate with current preoccupations and beliefs. Loneliness can foster attributions of blame against people perceived as its cause and lonely youngsters can act aggressively when they believe they have been rejected or are unappealing to girls. Sexual assault can be a vehicle for the expression of anger, and anger can exert a disinhibiting influence.

Concern with issues of control, power and dominance in sexual offending may be related to attempts at validation of self as competent and effective. To regard some adolescent sexual offending as containing elements of experimentation is not, from this perspective, to minimise or dismiss it as a passing phase. Initial, perhaps tentative explorations by an adolescent can be the first steps in elaboration and extension of the self into a dangerous and entirely self-serving form of social encounter. Psychosocial treatment, which to be effective must engage the self in a more constructive fashion, has the potential to make a significant contribution to steering development in a different direction.

6

Educational Approaches to Treatment

John L. Taylor

It is not surprising that the principles and practice of teaching and promoting learning are prominent in work with sexually abusive adolescents. Poor academic performance and educational difficulties are associated with delinquency in general and abusive adolescents in particular (Epps 1991). Development and maintenance of sexual offending in adolescents has been linked with poor social learning and exposure to inappropriate role models, as indicated in the last chapter. Treatment programmes for juvenile abusers aim to change behaviour, encouraging development of positive attitudes in part by providing information and increasing relevant knowledge. Educational processes commonly aim at the following objectives: (a) preparation for treatment; (b) modification of attitudes and values which contribute to abusive behaviour; and (c) structured social learning to facilitate re-socialisation.

In their review of 30 juvenile sex offender treatment programmes, Sapp and Vaughn (1990) found that psychological therapies and behaviour modification techniques were used extensively compared with other approaches. Group therapy programmes for juvenile sexual abusers tend to share a number of elements in which instruction and training play a significant part. These include development of insight into their offence cycle, cognitive approaches to understanding behaviour, victim awareness, knowledge of deviant arousal patterns, opportunities for social learning and rehearsing of newly acquired skills (Steen and Monnettee 1989, Zimpfer 1992).

Adequate motivation is necessary for initiating and carrying out any tasks. Abusive adolescents are generally poorly motivated to undertake 'treatment'. A major obstacle to adequate motivation is denial. Denial of the nature or extent of offending behaviour is often linked to cognitive distortions which allow abusers to abrogate responsibility for their actions. This process may be supported by the belief that the disclosure of offending will have a number of negative consequences, including prolonged incarceration or other restrictions.

Re-education and re-socialisation are important in helping adolescent sex offenders accept responsibility for their behaviour (Perry and Orchard 1992). O'Donohue and Letourneau (1993) showed that a treatment programme including elements of education about the nature of sex offender therapy and sex education had a positive effect in reducing long-held denials, which was maintained at the end of therapy. Perpetrators suggested that information about treatment demystified the procedures involved, reduced fears and helped them overcome their denial. Several educational devices for motivating abusers are available, including providing information concerning the limits of confidentiality, the purpose of assessments, treatments available and the role of the therapist (Garland and Dougher 1991).

It is also commonly agreed that therapists should communicate to perpetrators their understanding of abusers' reasons for denying their acts (Garland and Dougher 1991). Apart from giving information about the likely consequences of persistent denial, such as relapse and its consequences, such discussion also undermines confidence in the value of denial. Staff observations can increase perpetrators' doubts about the wisdom of continuing to deny or minimise their acts. Challenging abusers with inconsistencies between information in official records and from assessments and self-reports may also motivate perpetrators to consider treatment. Telling abusers that keeping a daily log or diary may provide a safeguard against future allegations of abuse, may be a useful method of directing them towards a therapeutic relationship. Learning that disclosure does not result in punishment is important, developing trust in the safety of reporting thoughts, feelings and actions.

Development of sexuality and acquisition of sexual knowledge

The onset of rapid sexual development in adolescence is normally associated with profound biochemical and physical changes. The increase in sexual arousal, interest and drive that reflects the biological changes of puberty does not account fully for complexities of adolescent sexual behaviour. A range of other influences is also involved in promoting change in the cognitive, emotional and social aspects of adolescent sexuality. Given wide cultural variations, sexual behaviour of adolescents cannot be understood separately from its social context. Adolescents are generally less concerned with reproduction than with pleasure. However some tension between the two remains. This is in the context of all societies' attempts to control sexuality in order to regulate fertility. Thus, society's attempts to influence adolescent sexuality tend to focus on reproductive and biological aspects. The consequence is that the emotional and social aspects of sexuality are often ignored or underplayed, resulting in uncertainty about how to deal with them. This may lead to activities which are harmful, both to individuals and society, including unsafe sex, premature sexual experience and sexual aggression.

Williams (1991) describes a developmental model which attempts to integrate three key aspects of human sexuality. She considers sexuality as comprising 'three coats which individuals wear' during their lives:

1. a biological stimulus–response coat that represents physical feelings and reactions.
2. a reproductive coat that individuals put on at puberty and wear until the end of their reproductive lives;
3. a coat that represents sexual attitudes, values and identity. Others see this as reflected in the person's behaviour. This coat is worn from birth and gradually develops and becomes visible as external influences are applied to it.

Generally the three are indistinguishable, but on occasions they stand out clearly. They cannot be separated easily and damage to one coat will have marked effects on the other two. This approach is easy to understand and explain when discussing sexuality with adolescents. It also suggests why attempts at influencing or manipulating the 'reproductive coat' only are unlikely to have major effects on feelings, attitudes or values which determine behaviour.

We would expect adolescents to develop sexual behaviour through the same learning mechanisms that are involved in the development of any other type of behaviour. These include association with and imitation of models in the environment; direct experiences resulting in rewarding or punishing consequences; appraisals and expectations arising from socio-sexual encounters. Such learning can be inhibited by:

- a lack of appropriate models (particularly relevant with regard to intimate sexual behaviour), such as a young person never witnessing his parents expressing affection or being physically close in an appropriate way; frequently viewing pornography on videotape recordings;
- unpleasant experiences resulting from behaviours which might be considered competent in other situations (or re-inforcement of inappropriate behaviours), such as an adolescent who is responsible and honest in discussing the possibility of sexually transmitted disease being denied intercourse and stigmatised;
- cognitive limitations which interfere with the ability to appraise situations accurately and possibly result in nega-tive emotional states including anxiety and fear – for example, the adolescent who is concerned about his sexual performance being anxious about his partner's feelings for him.

Another important factor influencing development of sexuality is access to information. Sources of sexual information available to adolescents are many and varied, the most frequent being friends/peers, followed by schools, books and magazines and parents, in descending order of frequency (e.g. Rice 1987). However, the impact and access to information varies greatly among different groups. The media and popular culture are considered by some workers and parents to have a dispropor-tionate and negative impact on adolescents' sexual education (e.g. Klein and Gordon 1992), even though adolescents, when asked, do not concur with this view.

Sex education for adolescent abusers

Adolescent abusers, like other young people, are likely to benefit from education which helps them better understand their sexuality, clarify their personal values and make more appropriate decisions about their sexual behaviour (Klein and

Gordon 1992). However, for a number of reasons, sexual abusers are more in need of education in these areas as part of a comprehensive treatment programme:

- For some adolescents, difficulties in relating to peers, and consequent social isolation, result in limited access to the most readily available source of sexual information and reduced opportunities to develop appropriate sexual behaviours (Hacker 1986).
- For many others, knowledge and attitudes regarding sexuality are based on direct and indirect experiences of sexual abuse and tend to be, therefore, either distorted or deviant in nature (Finkelhor and Brown 1985).
- Adolescent abusers who have been victims of male perpetrators sometimes develop intense homophobic attitudes as a defence against anxiety about any homosexual feelings they may have, or feelings of guilt concerning pleasure they may have experienced during the abuse (Scavo and Buchanan 1989).
- Reoffending by adolescent abusers is associated with limited sexual knowledge and poor understanding of sexual values.
- Psychosexual educational approaches have been shown to be successful in increasing adolescent abusers' sexual knowledge, improving their attitudes and modifying their values (e.g. Kaplan et al. 1991, Zimpfer 1992).
- Improved sexual knowledge, attitudes and values enhance the probability of success of other offence-specific treatments.
- As their sexual values and beliefs are less ingrained and distorted, re-education can be successful in disrupting younger abusers' offence cycles and reducing the probability that these will become habitual and repetitive.
- Psychosexual education, as part of the treatment programme, should be given to abusers as early as possible, as it is known that the careers of many adult offenders began during adolescence and the seriousness of offending behaviour escalated as they moved from adolescence into adulthood (e.g. Murphy et al. 1992, Perry and Orchard 1992).
- Psychosexual education can help counteract negative attitudes and values promoted by inappropriate exposure to pornography in childhood, which many abusers experience in the context of abusive situations (e.g. Carter et al. 1987).

- As some abusers use pornography during both antecedent and maintenance phases of their abusive acts, educational approaches can sensitise abusers to its influence on their behaviour (Fisher and Barak 1989).

At the beginning of treatment adolescent abusers are often anxious about and, therefore, resistant to the prospect of having to discuss their behaviour. Providing sex education at this stage can be a relatively non-threatening introduction to treatment issues. This may help challenge the taboo of disclosure acquired by those offenders who have themselves been victims of abuse. It will provide the foundations for later work on abusive behaviour and facilitate the formation of working relationships with therapists. Also, despite being sexually active, abusers are often ignorant of key areas of sexual knowledge. Introducing sexual education early in the treatment programme will provide abusers with the information and vocabulary they need for later work on abuse-specific issues. Adolescent offenders frequently have a history of educational difficulties and low attainment. Beginning treatment with a high quality education programme may establish a learning pattern that will prepare and motivate abusers to engage in later treatment with a strong educational component.

Assessment of sexual knowledge and attitudes

The primary aim of assessing adolescent sex offenders' sexual knowledge and attitudes is to gain information concerning those areas requiring intervention, and provide a baseline against which progress can be evaluated. Given the sensitive nature of this area of assessment, it is unlikely that an abuser will provide the information required until a trusting relationship has been established. Consequently a thorough assessment is time consuming, requiring a number of sessions. Also, if the offender's anxiety about discussing sexuality is matched by the clinician's discomfort in dealing with it, the assessment is likely to drift and lose direction. Because of these problems, this area of assessment is often ignored or dealt with superficially. In order to facilitate development of a working relationship, and deal with the problem of drift, it is important that assessment sessions are structured and carefully planned to maximise the likelihood of engaging the abuser and gaining the information required for a comprehensive assessment.

Another difficulty concerns the reliability and validity of measures used to assess sexual knowledge and attitudes. Quantitative measures of sexual knowledge rely on questions based on accepted scientific facts. However, the reliability of these 'facts' is sometimes uncertain, particularly in such areas as HIV infection. Assessments of attitudes are frequently referenced to the sexual behaviour and preferences of the general population. Unfortunately, there is insufficient good research to be sure of actual sexual behaviour and the preferences of adolescents as a whole. Further, quantitative assessments of attitudes often do not reflect the real depth and complexity of adolescents' sexual values and beliefs (Morris 1991). Finally, the applicability of standard tests of sexual knowledge and attitudes to adolescent sex offender populations has not been adequately investigated.

Despite these difficulties, there appears to be general agreement among workers regarding the areas that need to be included in assessment of sexual knowledge and attitudes. Table 6.1 summarises these.

Since different methods of assessment have not been comparatively evaluated, many clinicians continue to believe that the most useful approach to this type of assessment is through clinical interview. Assessment of sexual knowledge and attitudes can form part of a comprehensive sexual history comprising the abuser's sexual development, experiences, identity and orientation (e.g. Murphy et al. 1992). The use of guidelines for clinical interviews may help structure and facilitate completion of a comprehensive sexual history with adolescent abusers.

In addition to clinical interviews, other approaches to assessment of adolescent sexual abusers' sexual knowledge and attitudes are often used. Commonly these include questionnaires, pencil-and-paper tests, and inventories. Although there may be broad agreement on what should be assessed, there appears to be no consensus about which specific instruments are most useful.

Table 6.2 selectively describes a number of measures which may be helpful in assessing sexual knowledge and attitudes.

Table 6.1   *Areas for assessment of sexual knowledge and attitudes*

1. Biology of reproduction
   - Vocabulary for body parts, reproductive process, and terminology for behaviours associated with sexual intercourse and reproduction
   - Knowledge of mechanics of reproduction – including sexual arousal, foreplay and sexual intercourse

2. Puberty
   - Understanding of changes associated with male and female sexual development during adolescence – including reproductive changes, development of secondary sexual characteristics, and cognitive/ emotional maturational processes

3. Sexual health
   - Knowledge of, and attitudes towards contraception, use of contraceptive devices, and safe sex
   - Awareness of sexually transmitted diseases (including AIDS), how they are transmitted, and appropriate responses following contraction

4. Masturbation
   - Attitudes and beliefs concerning auto and mutual masturbation, and the role of sexual fantasy during masturbation

5. Comprehensive sexuality
   - Understanding of the different aspects of sexuality – including physical, emotional and behavioural components
   - Attitudes towards different sexual orientations, knowledge of factors affecting sexual drive and dysfunction, and sexuality as a function of age.

6. Development of relationships
   - Understanding of how relationships develop – including concepts of communication, trust, mutuality and responsibility
   - Knowledge of, and attitudes towards 'dating' as a particular form of relationship development

7. Sexual intimacy
   - Understanding of, and attitudes towards power, consent, and choice in relationships which become sexual
   - Knowledge of signals which communicate a partner's approval/arousal or discomfort in response to sexual intimacy

8. Sex roles
   - Attitude and beliefs about sex roles associated with gender; sexual stereotyping and sexism

9. Sexuality and the law
   - Understanding illegality of certain sexual acts including rape, sexual contact with children and incest
   - Appreciation of distinction between unusual sexual preferences, illegal expression of sexuality, and socially inappropriate sexual behaviour.

Table 6.2   *Measures for assessing socio-sexual knowledge and attitudes*

Title	Author(s)	Description
Adolescent Problems Inventory (API)	Freedman et al. (1978)	Describes 44 scenarios involving social problem situations. Inventory gives a measure of respondents' abilities in solving social and interpersonal problems.
Attitudes Towards Women Scale (ATW)	Spence and Helmreich (1972)	A 15-item scale that measures attitudes to a number of aspects of women's roles including vocational, educational and interpersonal relationships. Provides information regarding offenders' degrees of sex role stereotyping.
Inventory of Attitudes to Sex	Whalley and McGuire (1978)	Comprises 91 true–false items, and additional multiple choice questions, which produce scores on nine attitude scales including heterosexual nervousness, sexual curiosity, sexual hostility, promiscuity and prurience.
The Math Tech Sex Education Test	Kirby (1984)	This test is in two parts. First part is a sexual knowledge test comprising 34 multiple choice items; second part is made up of 70 items using scale responses relating to 14 sexual attitude and value categories.
The Psychological Inventory	Kirby et al. (1979)	A 140-question inventory using Likert scale responses. Provides scores for 25 scales measuring attitudes to a range of sexuality issues. Examples of scales are sex roles, use of birth control, heterosexual interaction and sexual pressure.
The Sexuality Development Index (SDI)	Johnson (1981)	Developed to assess gender identity, socio-sexual behaviours and sexual knowledge of adults with developmental delays. Videotaped vignettes are used so that respondents can indicate who they identify with in terms of gender and sexuality, can respond to questions about socio-sexual scenarios relating to issues such as privacy, coercion and masturbation. Questions relating to basic sexual knowledge also included.

Table 6.2   *cont.*

Title	Author(s)	Description
The Socio-Sexual Knowledge & Attitude Test (SSKAT)	Wish et al. (1980)	240-item test developed to assess individuals, with learning disabilities level of socio-sexual knowledge, and attitudes towards socio-sexual practices. The SSKAT is administered as a semi-structured interview and responses are scored on a range of knowledge and attitude sub-tests including intimacy, intercourse, birth control, masturbation and homosexuality.

Even though several of the measures described above were not developed explicitly for assessment of *adolescent* abusers' knowledge and attitudes, they can be adapted and modified to make a valuable contribution to this area of assessment. For example, despite the SSKAT having a number of difficulties, including too many 'yes/no' responses limiting the quality of information received, some outdated stimulus materials and the failure to deal with some important areas of socio-sexual functioning, its basic format and approach provides a useful model. The present author and several colleagues are currently developing the Sexual Information, Reasoning and Attitudes Test (SIRAT). This test is based on SSKAT format, but in addition to assessing basic sexual knowledge, it utilises updated stimulus materials, covers contemporary socio-sexual issues, and uses a broader semi-structured interview approach to explore the reasoning on which respondents' attitudes and values are based (Taylor et al. 1997).

Similarly the content of the SDI described by Johnson (1981) may not be particularly relevant to adolescent offenders. However, the creative and innovative approach to assessment used in the SDI could be adapted by clinicians working with adolescent abusers in order to develop an interesting and relevant addition to the more traditional forms of assessment. In general, the use of inventories and questionnaires should augment clinical interviews which form the backbone of assessment of adolescent abusers' sexual knowledge and attitudes.

Psychosexual education programmes

Context

Group work with abusive adolescents is the most frequently utilised treatment method. If managed correctly by trained therapists, groups can provide abusers with the safe environment in which to explore their sexuality, have their attitudes and values challenged, and contemplate behavioural change. The main dynamics at work in successful groups are mutual support, modelling of positive attitudes and empathic behaviour (Kirby 1985). These can be powerful allies to therapists leading psychosexual education groups, both in their own right and to augment individually tailored work (George and Behrendt 1985).

There seems to be some consensus that groups should not involve more than seven members and two co-therapists, preferably one male and one female. When planning a group, which is intended to become cohesive over time, the developmental stage of the abusers, their age and nature of their sexual offending should be considered. Ideally group sessions should take place once a week for approximately one and a half hours each. The room in which the group meets should be large enough to allow easy movement and not make the abusers feel hemmed in, but not so large that the participants feel distant from one another. It should be in private, without large glass windows or doors that may inhibit offenders' participation.

A few basic ground rules for group meetings should be established at the outset. It is particularly important that offenders agree to listen to each other and guarantee one another confidentiality regarding the content of sessions. If practicable, simple refreshments should be shared at the end of each session as reinforcement for a successful session, to promote group cohesiveness and to provide an opportunity for socialising.

As for other young people, psychosexual education programmes for sexually abusive adolescents should be guided by a number of key principles. They should:

- attempt to provide accurate information;
- help abusers clarify attitudes regarding their own and others' sexuality;

- impart decision-making skills that allow them to use the information provided to guide their own behaviour;
- be relevant to interests and concerns of participants and realistic about their sexual interests;
- provide concrete messages that have immediate impact;
- present varied educational materials to engage adolescents and hold their attention;
- make use of film, videotape, TV soap opera vignettes, role play, psycho-drama, group discussion, and appropriate games to develop learning points.

The major difference in psychosexual education programmes for adolescent abusers is that the information provided and skills taught *must* be linked to their abuse cycle. When discussing, for example, masturbation in group work, the relevance of altering masturbatory attitudes or behaviour to disrupting the offence cycle should be emphasised. Obviously the delivery of such a multi-modal programme requires a good deal of careful planning and preparation by therapists. A number of sources for teaching materials and techniques to help with this task are listed later in this chapter. Some ideas for linking educational material to abusive behaviour are provided below.

Content

The content of a psychosexual education programme follows from those areas included in the assessment of knowledge and attitudes described in Table 6.1. To establish a curriculum, and how it may be linked to abusive behaviour, the content is divided into three parts related to the main aims of sexual education: sexual information, psychosexual attitudes and values, and responsibility and decision making associated with sexual behaviour (Hains et al. 1986) (see Table 6.3).

Although offence-related teaching points potentially overlap with several of the educational areas, therapists are able to judge when, and if, to link the two areas depending on the individuals involved in the programme, the nature of their abusive behaviour, and the atmosphere and cohesiveness of the group.

Table 6.3 *Psychosexual education programme – an outline*

Content of programme	Examples of how content might be linked to offending behaviour

Section 1: sexual information
• Biology of reproduction and anatomic terms
• Changes during puberty:
  – physical, emotional and cognitive
• Sexual health:
  – contraception, sexually transmitted diseases and safe sex
	– Understanding pre- and post-pubescent developmental differences to challenge offenders' beliefs regarding children's ability to respond in a positive way to sexual contact.
	– an improved understanding of physiological arousal to help those offenders who are themselves abuse victims to cope more effectively with any pleasure, and consequent guilt, they have experienced.

Section 2: psychosexual attitudes and values
• Masturbation:
  – including sexual fantasies
• Comprehensive sexuality:
  – physical, emotional and behavioural aspects
• Sex roles:
  – stereotypes and sexism
• Sexual intimacy:
  – power, consent and choice
	– the role masturbatory fantasy plays in the lead up to, and maintenance of offending behaviour.
	– interaction of the different components of sexuality to illustrate impact of abuse on offenders' own sexuality, and that of their victims, and thus improve empathy and reduce denial.
	– discussion of abusers' own experiences of powerlessness and lack of choice to help them appreciate their victims' feelings.

Section 3: responsibility and decision making • Responsibility in relationships • Communication skills • Problem-solving skills • Sex and the law	– discussion of personal responsibility in relation to choice to help challenge offenders who attempt to avoid responsibility. – improving communication and problem-solving skills to help abusers reduce the risk of reoffending if interpersonal conflict is involved in the abuse. – a clear appreciation of laws, and society's perspective on offending behaviour to modify distorted thoughts about the seriousness and consequences of their behaviour.

Appendix: teaching materials for psychosexual education programme

The following are sources of materials and ideas that are relevant to the development of a psychosexual education programme for sexually abusive adolescents.

Academy Television. Healthwatch Video Catalogue. 104 Kirkstall Road, Leeds, LS3 1JS, England.

> This catalogue contains a number of videos relating to sexual abuse, adolescent sex education, developmental problems in adolescence and interpersonal skills which can be used to inform and generate discussion in groups.

Mazur and Michael (1992)

> This paper outlines a 'human sexuality interaction education' programme and refers to five videos used to facilitate adolescent offenders' education in the biological and reproductive aspects of human sexuality.

Steen and Monnettee (1989)

> A wide range of helpful and practical ideas for running adolescent therapy groups are provided in this book. In particular, games and techniques for encouraging adolescent sex offenders to confront a number of key issues relating to sexuality are described.

Sex and the 3Rs: Rights, Responsibilities and Risks (McCarthy and Thompson 1992)
Living Your Life (Craft 1991)

> These packages are designed to help people with learning disabilities understand, explore and appropriately express their sexuality. Both contain teaching materials, resources, and ideas for dealing with a broad range of sexuality issues. The materials can be adapted and modified to work with adolescent offenders regarding their sexuality.

7

Cognitive-Based Practice with Sexually Abusive Adolescents

Graeme Richardson, Surya Bhate and
Finlay Graham

The term 'cognitive' refers to the mental processes that enable
us to know and evaluate our external world. More specifically,
it incorporates ways in which knowledge of environment is
attained, retained and utilised, associated with higher-order
mental functions. These include attention, memory, perception,
language, thinking, problem solving, reasoning and concept
formation.

In psychotherapeutic practice, 'cognitive' has assumed a
more limited definition and focus. It refers primarily to person-
accessible thoughts and their content, as judged by the person's
self statements or self talk. This is a form of internal dialogue
which is equivalent to a running commentary on actual or
planned reactions to events and interactions with other people.

Studies of cognitive factors in sexually abusive behaviour
have tended to focus on the products of cognitive processes
rather than their structure or operations. 'Cognitive products'
are the thoughts, images and evaluations which can be
abstracted from the abuser's internal dialogue, i.e. self statements, attributions, perceptions and inferences (Segal and
Stermac 1990).

Basic cognitive theory and practice

A basic tenet of cognitive psychology is that people *actively*
participate in perceiving and shaping their environment.
Hence, perceptual processes are influenced by a person's thinking and emotional state at the time. A central tenet of cognitive

psychology is that some human beings respond not to some 'objective' reality but to a subjectively 'perceived' environment.

Cognitive therapy is the clinical practice based on cognitive psychology (Ellis and Grieger 1977, Beck 1976). In maladaptive reactions which demand help, cognitive processes are seen as irrational, erroneous or distorted. Specifically, irrational self statements are believed to be associated with emotional distress and impaired social functioning. The process is conceptualised thus: an event in the environment (A) triggers erroneous and self-defeating beliefs (B). These 'cause' dysfunctional emotional and behavioural consequences (C). The major impetus was given by Beck's work (1976) on clinical depression which showed how depressed patients exhibit a negative bias in their thinking which results in a distorted and pessimistic interpretation of themselves, their relationships and their future. Therapeutic intervention seeks to identify, challenge and correct these debilitating cognitive processes (Murphy 1990).

The clinical practice of cognitive-behavioural therapy (CBT) emerged from an amalgamation of behaviour therapy and cognitive psychology. Three responses to external events are identified: (1) overt behaviour, (2) thinking and (3) physiological activity in the body. Problem behaviours are regarded as involving all three elements. Cognitions are seen as critically influencing emotions and behaviour. For example, hostile thoughts lead to angry feelings which increase the probability of a violent assault. The importance of antecedents (A) and consequences (C) of behaviour (B) and thinking is stressed.

Self control therapies (Kanfer 1970), self instruction training (Meichenbaum and Goodman 1971) and problem solving techniques (Shure and Spivack 1978) are all variations of cognitive-behavioural therapy. This approach has *self management* of the clinical problem as its therapeutic goal. Accordingly, learning and practising cognitive skills of self monitoring, self evaluation and self reinforcement are critical practice elements to facilitate self management. Dysfunctional or problem behaviour, including related thoughts and feelings, is seen as *learned*. Cognitive *and* behavioural skills training are used to reduce the frequency and severity of these behaviours to manageable levels.

Cognitive-behavioural interventions are structured, time limited, instructional and skills based. The adolescent is provided with a clear rationale for the proposed interventions and motivated to believe he can modify or control his behaviour. He learns and practises skills to help him reduce the problem behaviour and more effectively cope with daily life events. He is encouraged and given exercises in using these skills in real life situations and attributing effective self management and improvement in problem behaviour to his increased skills and self control, thus increasing self confidence (Kahn 1990).

Cognitive interventions with conduct disordered children and adolescents

In our own research (Richardson et al. 1995a) and practice we have found that the majority of sexually abusive adolescents meet the diagnostic criteria for conduct disorder (*DSM III-R*: American Psychiatric Association 1987) and behaviour problems shared with other conduct disordered adolescents. Research shows that aggressive and conduct disordered behaviour is associated with cognitive factors (Hughes 1988). Thus, cognitive interventions used in the treatment of conduct disorder are considered relevant to the treatment of *some* sexually abusive adolescents.

More specifically, evidence shows conduct disordered and aggressive adolescents to present *social cognition deficits*. These include:

- *social perspective-taking*: impaired ability to take another person's point of view and tune into others' perceptions, thoughts and feelings;
- *social problem-solving ability*: difficulty in generating pro-social non-aggressive and effective solutions to social problems;
- *positive outcome expectancies for aggressive behaviour*: expecting aggression to pay and get them what they want
- *attributional biases*: over-attribution of hostile intent to other people in ambiguous and social situations; and
- *inattention to social cues and impulsivity*: not reading all the available social cues in a social encounter, making rapid decisions about the situation and reacting quickly to them.

Cognitive behavioural treatment with these adolescents includes self-instructional training and social-cognitive skill training, outlined below.

Self-instructional training

Self-instructional training (Meichenbaum and Goodman 1971) is a procedure to help reduce impulsivity and increase self control in critical areas such as aggressive behaviour. The adolescent is taught to 'stop and think' before acting. This represents verbal mediation of overt behaviour, to slow down reactions and encourage thinking through problems. Typically, (1) practitioner describes technique; (2) models technique in practice; (3) adolescent practises technique; (4) is given corrective feedback by practitioner; and (5) is rewarded for successful application of technique. This is repeated and *over-learned* until established. In best practice, parents or others may be taught to go through debriefing sessions at irregular intervals with the youngster in order to reinforce the technique.

Social-cognitive skills training

An example of this approach is interpersonal problem-solving training (Spivack and Shure 1974). This procedure is taught through the use of verbal instruction, modelling, discussion of hypothetical problem situations, role play, corrective feedback and social reinforcement. The aim is to improve social adjustment by helping the adolescent solve interpersonal problems. The procedure consists of teaching six specific skills:

1. *Generating alternative solutions*: getting into the habit of thinking there are alternative solutions to a problem;
2. *Considering consequences of social acts*: development of ability to consider consequences of social behaviour on oneself and others and ability to generate a range of probable consequences for a specific social action;
3. *Developing means–end thinking*: skill in generating the step-by-step actions or means in order to resolve an interpersonal problem;
4. *Developing 'causal' thinking*: ability to recognise that one's own actions and feelings are related to actions and feelings of others and that each affects the other in some way;
5. *Sensitivity to problems*: ability to remain alert and aware of the range of difficulties that may arise in social interactions;

6. *Dynamic orientation*: ability to recognise that behaviour may reflect motives or antecedents that are not always apparent.

Cognitive theory and criminal behaviour

In daily work (Richardson et al. 1995a) we find that the majority of our sexually abusive adolescents exhibit anti-social tendencies, including non-sexual criminal behaviour. They seem to share common cognitive-based problems with other young offenders. These include lack of consequential thinking, exclusively focusing on the positive aspects of offending, lack of concern about rule breaking and lack of victim empathy (see also Hollin 1990).

Cognitive explanations of general criminal behaviour maintain that particular thinking styles and cognitive skills deficits are also associated with individuals who commit criminal acts. Offenders generally experience difficulties of self control which lead to impulsive behaviour which are themselves criminal or precipitate criminal acts. Associated with poor self control and behavioural impulsiveness are deficits in cognitive processing, which ordinarily mediate between an impulse or urge to act in a particular way and the action itself (Ross and Fabiano 1985). This cognitive mediation is one factor in moderating human behaviour, exerting a critical role in the development and maintenance of self control and internal modification of behaviour to external circumstances. Overall, offenders are regarded as lacking the specific cognitive skills required for mediating appropriate social behaviour (Chandler 1973, Higgins and Thies 1981). For example offenders have not learnt to think before they act or develop effective thinking skills to generate alternative responses to situations and interactions. Consequently their thinking tends to be both impulsive and concrete.

Although there has been no similar work on adolescents, Yochelson and Samenow's (1977) work on the thinking errors of heterogeneous adult criminals seems applicable to adolescents. They identified a number of cognitive tendencies said to be pervasive in the life of the criminal and the correction of these was considered crucial to the treatment of offenders. They include concrete thinking; fragmented thinking; failure to empathise with others; lack of perspective of time; irresponsible decision making and perceiving self as victim.

Examples of thinking which support generalised criminal behaviour include:

- *minimising*: when adolescent makes behaviour sound acceptable or less serious, such as 'We were only pretending to kiss'; 'I only hit him a few times'; 'I only put my hand on her chest';
- *not accepting personal responsibility*: when the abuser denies personal obligations or holds someone else responsible – 'I didn't know it would get me into trouble'; 'I was just doing what my mates do'; 'She made me do it'; 'It wasn't my fault';
- *beliefs about ownership*: when the abuser thinks he is entitled to others' possessions – 'I haven't got anything'; 'They can afford it'; 'I was only borrowing it'; 'I can take what I want';
- *beliefs about self control*: when the adolescent says he cannot stop doing what he does or does not want to stop – 'I just can't help myself'; 'why should I stop?';
- *ignoring others' rights and injury to them*: when adolescent only considers himself, feels no obligation and has no regard for welfare of others – 'I don't care'; 'I can do what I want';
- *victim stance*: when abuser sees himself as unfairly treated and wronged – 'I didn't moan when it happened to me'; 'She started it'; 'It's not my fault. It just sort of got out of hand'; 'I was bored. We have nothing else to do'; 'They've only picked on me because I've been in trouble before'.

Current explanatory models do not consider these thinking styles and distortions to be causative in the aetiology of sexual abusiveness but they are viewed as critical in its maintenance through minimising, justifying and distorting (Abel et al. 1984, Rouleau et al. 1986, Wolf 1984).

A different aspect of the cognitive processes involved in abuse focuses on social and cultural attitudes which support sexual aggression against females. These have been identified as 'rape myth acceptance', adversarial sexual beliefs, acceptance of interpersonal violence against women and sex-role stereotyping. These beliefs and attitudes are considered to be a direct cause of sexually abusive behaviour (Burt 1980, Koss and Dinero 1987, Malamuth 1986, Murphy et al. 1986).

Adolescent cognitions

Cognitive work with sexual abusers

Both research evidence and clinical experience suggest that six target areas should be considered when drawing up an individual treatment plan following completion of the assessment. Not all abusive adolescents will require intervention in all these areas.

Education and motivation   The preliminary phases of cognitive intervention with sexual offenders are educational and motivational. This phase involves giving information about and explaining the role of cognitive distortions in sexually abusive behaviour. It indicates to the abuser that engaging in sexual abuse involves aspects of his thinking which are distorted and inappropriate. Information drawn from initial assessment, which should include assessment of abuse and victim-related cognition, would be utilised to create awareness of these patterns.

The motivational phase involves utilising this explanation and information to convince the abuser of the need to change those aspects of thinking which are associated with abusive behaviour. Specifically, their role as a significant risk factor involved in 'relapse' should be emphasised. This possibility is linked to a description of the probable negative consequences of relapse elaborated in Chapter 9.

Cognitive distortions   Studies have shown that adults who sexually abuse children differ from other groups of men, in terms of perceiving (a) less adult responsibility for initiation of sexual contact, (b) child's complicity in the acts, (c) child benefiting from sexual contact and (d) sense of injustice about being punished (e.g. Segal and Stermac 1990). Cognitive restructuring techniques are used to modify the abuser's thinking.

Knowledge   It is questionable whether an abuser's cognitive distortions are influenced by the victim's reactions to abusive behaviour. As seen in Chapter 1, sexual abusers go on to offend time after time and against numerous victims. There is evidence that when a child victim's reaction is ambiguous (for instance staring at the offender, saying nothing or not moving), then adult child molesters interpret this response as suggesting acceptance of sexual contact (Segal and Stermac 1990). We have no reason to believe the same is not true of adolescents. Thus, a standard component of treatment involves providing information about how victims typically react to abuse and assault and about the harmful effects on victims. This knowledge seeks to offset the abusers' tendency to concentrate exclusively on self-gratifying aspects of their abusive behaviour immediately prior to approaching a victim.

Attitudes   It is evident that adverse beliefs and attitudes disinhibit individuals and increase likelihood of sexual violence in certain situations. There is evidence that rapists are deficient in the ability to process women's signals in heterosexual interactions, especially negative ones (Lipton et al. 1987).

Thinking styles   Earlier in the chapter we briefly described cognitive distortions associated with both conduct disordered adolescents and young offenders. It is necessary to remedy these. The adolescent is unlikely to be able to benefit from this treatment if he does not possess the cognitive skills necessary for constructive participation. This approach critically addresses thinking *processes* as well as thinking content, contrary to what seems to be the common practice.

Modifying cognitions

A number of clinical approaches and techniques have been developed for changing the content and style of an individual's thinking (Beck 1976, Ellis and Grieger 1977, Meichenbaum 1977). These procedures have been employed in the treatment of sexual offenders (Abel et al. 1984, Lange 1986). Modifying cognitions is usually called 'cognitive restructuring'. Like any clinical intervention there are both processes and specific techniques involved in cognitive restructuring. The process involves (a) providing the abuser with a rationale for the role of cognitions in the development and maintenance of sexually abusive behaviours; (b) persuading the abuser of the need to modify aspects of his thinking; (c) assisting him in identifying specific cognitive distortions; and (d) providing him with alternative interpretations and corrective information in order logically to challenge and dispute his distortions.

This 'challenging process' is often referred to in literature as a 'confrontational' approach. 'Confrontation' suggests an approach that may be aggressive or humiliating and would undoubtedly result in fear and resentment and may, in fact, lead to resistance by the abuser. We believe the analytical process described above should be used consistently and firmly to 'confront' the abuser but not to have a confrontation.

Disputing cognitive distortions

Identifying and confronting an offender's cognitive distortions may be carried out in individual or group sessions. Consensus in the literature suggests that this practice is best conducted in groups. Other group members, who are also sexual abusers, together with the group leader, challenge the accuracy of the abuser's account of his behaviour, associated beliefs and cognitions. The group leader, therefore, needs a good working knowledge of (a) the range and content of cognitive distortions typically expressed by abusers; (b) attitudes and beliefs which are associated with sexual aggression against victims; and (c) details of the negative impact of sexual abuse and assault on victims.

Explaining cognitive treatment to the adolescent – the main points

- Adolescent sexual abusers share some common problems.
- They may know their sexually abusive behaviour is wrong.
- They may know the harm they cause their victims.
- After abusing someone they may feel guilty and ashamed.
- These feelings are unpleasant and the adolescent will want to avoid them.
- They develop ways of avoiding or reducing these unpleasant feelings.
- One of the ways is to convince themselves that what they did was not bad.

- They tell themselves that the victim agreed to sexual contact.
- They tell themselves that the victim was not harmed by the sexual contact.
- They eventually say these things almost without thinking and believe them to be true.

- An aim of treatment is to help you recognise that things you tell yourself are untrue.
- These things excuse and justify your behaviour, which is actually wrong and harmful.
- These excuses and justifications are called 'cognitive distortions'.
- Part of the treatment is to help you stop and think about your behaviour. This includes thinking about the harm you have caused your victims and not making excuses for your behaviour.
- This may make you feel uncomfortable but it is necessary to help you avoid getting into more serious trouble. If you continue to tell yourself these sorts of things you are likely to abuse someone else in the future.

Analysis of cognitive distortions

A cognitive distortion is expressed in the form of a 'self statement'. The tasks are as follows: (1) identify adolescent's abuse-related self statements; (2) understand offence-related *belief* which underpins the self statement; (3) make explicit the belief statement and explain how it supports abusive behaviour; (4) challenge this belief through expressing alternative statements which undermine abusive behaviour.

Discursive dialogue between the practitioner and the abuser may follow, during which the practitioner seeks to persuade the abuser of the wrongness of his belief and the correctness of the alternative. In some cases, there is no such discursive dialogue and opportunity for genuine persuasion does not arise. In these cases, the adolescent tends not to challenge alternative statements, but appears simply to comply with the practitioner's position. It is not clear whether such adolescents are simply being compliant and unchallenging, or are pretending to accept the practitioner's position whilst passively rejecting it.

Example of the disputing process

Self statement	– 'If she had said no I wouldn't have done it.'
Cognitive distortions	– A child is able to consent to sexual contact.
	– It is the child's responsibility to stop the abuse.
	– If a child does not say no she has agreed.
	– If a child says nothing she has agreed.
Alternative statements	– A child is too young to negotiate an agreement to engage in sexual contact with an older person.
	– A child does not have sufficient knowledge to make an informed choice about participating in sexual behaviour.
	– A child does not have sufficient knowledge to understand the consequences of sexual contact.
	– Children find it difficult to say no to older people.
	– Children find it difficult to say no to things they do not understand.

Evaluation of treatment outcomes   The overall treatment programme is most often evaluated in terms of recidivism rates following successful completion of treatment. A cognitive component would be evaluated in terms of the achievement of specific changes within the abuser. The adolescent's account of his abusive behaviour, including his thoughts, mental pictures and feelings, can be analysed at different times during treatment. Treatment effectiveness may be judged by the reduction in identifiable cognitive distortions regarding (1) justifying his abusive behaviour, (2) blaming the victim, and (3) misperceiving consequences for the victim. Discrepancies between the victim's account and the abuser's account of the abuse also indicate the continued presence of misperceptions and cognitive distortions.

Questionnaires that specifically state cognitive distortions and ask for the abuser's response may be administered before and after cognitive interventions. Effectiveness would be judged, however, by a reduction in the number of cognitive distortions endorsed. It should be noted that these questionnaires are not subtle: adolescents are generally able to detect what the questionnaire is about and fake socially desirable responses. The ability of the adolescent to engage in 'Socratic' questioning and correct biased thinking and beliefs would seem to be a more robust measure of treatment effectiveness. This requires a more active input by the adolescent and a degree of improvisation and generalisation based on what was learned in therapy sessions. This may be tested out in role reversal situations during sessions. Similarly, the adolescent's ability to generate various scripts that indicate consequential thinking may be used to evaluate any improvements in this area.

Cognitive control of sexually abusive behaviour

In our own practice we find it necessary to develop a standardised approach based on and driven by assessment of individual abusers. The critical difference between this and other suggested plans is our emphasis on the *thinking style* of the adolescent, which derives from our experience of the paucity of their thought processes and skills. The following material provides an instance of how comprehensive cognitive modification may be pursued, within the specific content to be decided by an individual adolescent's profile.

The aim of this procedure is to: (1) remedy offence-related cognitive distortions and provide the adolescent with training in offence-related thinking. In the development of this procedure we have utilised the information-processing model of social behaviour (e.g. Dodge and Murphy 1984, Hughes and Hall 1987) with adolescents who have attentional difficulties, impulsive behaviour and conduct problems (Douglas 1976, Kendall and Braswell 1985).

We structure this process around seven sessions whose contents are : (1) the role of offence-related self statements; (2) flow of self talk to facilitate self control; (3) practice of cognitive self control techniques, such as 'thought stopping' and self instruction; (4) thinking ahead; (5) self control self statements; (6) issues of inappropriate sex; (7) appropriate thoughts and beliefs. This appendix provides some examples of material to be used in these sessions, although individual workers will tailor their material to particular clients.

Generally, cognitive factors appear to be important targets for intervention and modification, as they seem to play some role in mediating the expression of sexually abusive behaviour and may contribute to the risk of reoffending. It is not clear if cognitive factors are of equal significance in the abusive behaviour of all adolescents, nor how these factors interact with others also shown to be implicated in abusive behaviour. Currently, cognitive factors are often tackled in comprehensive treatment programmes, even if their role in causation of the behaviour and its recurrence are not solidly established.

Appendix

Themes of offence-related thinking

Thinking about children as sexual partners; children's sexual parts; children participating in sexual acts; persuading children into sexual acts; places and times when you can get children on their own; teaching children about sex.

Offence-related self statements about younger girls

'There's a girl on her own, it won't hurt to go and talk to her'; 'The girls I have touched in the past enjoyed what I did to them . . . this girl will too'; 'If I'm gentle and kind to that girl she will keep a secret . . . she will not tell'; 'I like the look of that young girl . . . I wonder what it would be like to have sex with her'; 'Adults taught me about sex when I was a child . . . so it will be OK for me to teach that young girl'.

Self control self talk script

Offence-related thought:

> *'There's a young girl on her own . . . it won't hurt to talk to her.'*

Self control statements:

> Don't fool yourself! It will hurt to go and talk to her; It will hurt me and her; I've done this in the past – say I'll talk to her, but it never stops there; I see her as an easy target; I see her as someone I can do sexual things to; In the past I thought I would not get found out; I'm not really interested in

talking to her . . . I want to touch her; It will hurt her . . . she will be frightened; She will be frightened of being on her own; If I abuse her she will tell someone; I will get caught; I will be arrested; I'll have to go to court; I'll be put in prison or be taken into care; People will hate me; People will call me a pervert; I don't have to do it; I can control myself; I can go away and masturbate on my own; I can get a girlfriend; I must get out of this risky situation; I am in control . . . I am going now . . . I'm walking away now . . .

Thought stopping and self instruction script

Offence-related thought:

> '*I like the look of that young girl, I wonder what it would be like to have sex with her.*'

Thought stopping:

> 'STOP! that thought is unhealthy . . . It is going to get me into trouble . . . I have to stop thinking of that girl right now!'

Self instruction:

> 'I must think of something that will stop me getting into trouble. I must have thoughts that help me control myself. I have practised these before. I know what to do. I can do it. I must say these things to myself right now!'

Self control self talk:

> I'll feel terrible if I do anything to that young girl; I'll worry in case she tells her parents and they tell the police; I'll be waiting for the police to come knocking on my door; I'll worry about being locked up; I can't go through with it . . . I'll feel bad afterwards . . . I'll regret it; I can't afford to be caught again; Next time I'll be locked up in prison; I've got to stop myself; this situation is dangerous; If I stay here I'll do something I shouldn't; I must turn away from this young girl; I must stop looking at her; I must begin to walk away now!; I must get amongst other people; I must go to a place where there are lots of people; I must occupy myself . . . I must go and do something else now!; There . . . I'm walking away from this dangerous situation.

Self control script

Offence-related thought:

> '*Adults taught me about sex when I was a child . . . so it's OK for me to teach her.*'

Self control statements:

> Get it right; Don't con yourself; They did not teach you about sex; They sexually abused you!; They used you . . . they did not ask your permission; That's not the same . . . it's very different; What they did was for themselves; They did not care about you or the hurt they were causing you; They did not care how you felt about it; They just did it; They frightened you; They hurt you; You didn't like it; It wasn't your fault they abused you; They did wrong . . . it was their fault; They should have been punished; It wasn't OK for them to 'teach' you about sex like that; It's not OK for you to 'teach' that girl about sex; You don't teach children about sex by touching them; That's sexual abuse!; You are conning her; You are conning yourself; You just want to touch her; You are doing it for yourself; You are not concerned about what she wants; She will not want you to do it; She will not like it; She will be hurt by it; She will tell someone; You will be caught; You will be punished; Stop! It's wrong to sexually abuse children; Walk away now!; Keep yourself safe; Keep yourself out of trouble.

Alternative appropriate thinking: thinking about
children as children doing childlike things

Imagine yourself in a situation where children are playing together. They are playing children's games. They are laughing, shouting, running around. They are children and look like children. They are not physically developed and do not look like you or adults. You know they do not think like people your age or like adults. They think like children, they do not know about adult things, they are concerned with childish things like playing on swings. You know they do not think about sex, they have no sexual thoughts and no sexual urges. You know they are too young to think about sex and too young to know about sex. You know if you talk about sex with them, you are doing wrong. They should not be told about sex at their age and should not have sexual things done to them.

You know that children are not physically developed. They do not have the bodies to do sexual things or enjoy sex. Children cannot enjoy sex because they are not physically built to do sexual things. You know that children do not become sexually aroused. They do not think sexual thoughts. They do not see people as sexually attractive. They do not feel sexually aroused because their bodies are not properly developed. You know they are children. You know it is illegal to talk to them about sex, see them as sexual, to touch them in sexual ways, to have them touch you in sexual ways. You know it is wrong. So don't do it!

Appropriate sexual thinking

Any scenario that allows the youngster to visualise legally permitted sex with a female above 16 years, or an alternative means of achieving sexual release.

8

Behavioural Treatment Techniques

Dawn Fisher and Gail McGregor

Like all complex human action, sexually abusive behaviour results from a range of external and internal antecedent factors. Many sex offenders report having engaged in thoughts about their sexually deviant behaviour prior to offending and appear to maintain and develop their deviant interests by masturbating to such thoughts (or fantasies). It should be noted that, in this context, the term 'deviant' is used to refer to behaviours which would be considered abusive if acted out and the term 'non-deviant' to legal, consenting and non-abusive sexual behaviour with an age-appropriate partner. In clinical settings, the continued experience of such fantasies by abusers is seen as an indication of increased likelihood of further abusive acts.

As a result, the modification of sexual fantasies has become a key element in many treatment programmes for abusers and, more specifically, persistent sexual offenders. These techniques have, therefore, become the subject of numerous evaluative studies (Laws and Marshall 1991, Marshall et al. 1991b) and much professional and ethical debate. The general findings suggest that these techniques are effective in modifying deviant arousal and fantasy patterns for a number of abusers (Quinsey and Marshall 1983, Quinsey and Earls 1990). Their efficacy is greatly enhanced, and maintained in the longer term, when they are used in the context of an overall treatment programme dealing with patterns of distorted thinking which support offending, high risk behaviours and lifestyles which facilitate abusive behaviour (Maletzky 1991, Barbaree and Cortoni 1993).

However, the use of behavioural methods with adolescent abusers raises a number of unique practical and ethical issues in addition to those pertinent to their use with adult sex offenders. This is the reason for the relative paucity of behaviour therapy reports on adolescent abusers. We will briefly outline the theoretical origins of behavioural methods, review the various techniques in use primarily with adult abusers and discuss the issues relevant to their use with adolescent sex offenders.

The importance of fantasy in sexual offending

A number of research studies have lent support to the clinical opinion of professionals working with sexual offenders – that offences occur, at least in part, as a result of the individual having developed a deviant interest prior to the commission of the offence (Finkelhor 1984, Lane and Zamora 1984, Lanyon 1991). One of the most influential theoretical models of sexual offending currently in use, Finkelhor's Four Preconditions Model (Finkelhor 1984), suggests that the first step towards becoming an offender involves the individual becoming sexually aroused by the thought of the deviant activity (Marshall and Eccles 1993).

This suggestion is supported by earlier theoretical work on the development of sexual behaviour and interests, such as McGuire's model of masturbatory conditioning (McGuire et al. 1965) and by conditioning and learning theory explanations of the principles by which individuals acquire and maintain both sexual and non-sexual behavioural responses (Laws 1989, Laws and Marshall 1991, Orford 1985). Simple, or classical conditioning models imply that certain behavioural responses are provoked by the presence of specific stimuli (Abel et al. 1983, Marshall and Eccles 1993). In the case of non-deviant sexual behaviour, this refers to the ability of sexual stimuli (e.g. the presence of an appropriate sexual partner and setting) to evoke feelings of sexual arousal.

Further refinements of this model have resulted in operant conditioning models. The key element here is that behaviour is gradually learned and maintained by its consequences for the individual (Orford 1985). If a behaviour produces negative or punishing consequences, such as social rejection or failure, then this will reduce the likelihood of the behaviour occurring again. Similarly positive or rewarding consequences, such as social acceptance or success, are likely to strengthen the behavioural response and lead to its repetition. Repeated associations between certain behaviours and positive consequences are likely to lead to strongly established behaviour patterns which are resistant to change.

When applied to sexual behaviour, it is evident that these rules normally lead to the acquisition of sexual interests and behaviours which are expressed in non-deviant ways – since these are condoned by society and are more likely to be rewarded. However, these behavioural rules also allow us to explain the development of deviant sexual behaviour (Howells 1981, Lanyon 1991, Orford 1985). In the case of sexual abusers, those behaviours and situations which have positive consequences for the majority of people may have had the opposite consequences for the offender. For example, adolescent attempts at exploratory sexual relationships may have been met with rejection and perceived humiliation. Similarly, engaging in deviant sexual behaviour has acquired strong positive consequences for the offender in contrast to the general population. The reasons for this reversal of the usual learning processes in some sexual offenders are likely to vary among individuals according to their learning history and this may be elicited during assessment (Longo and Groth 1983, Marshall et al. 1991a). Abusive behaviour may have provided the only available outlet for sexual behaviour: this is particularly important in considering sibling incest. To that extent, abusive behaviour is 'rational and adaptive' from the abuser's point of view. O'Brien (1991) highlights the view, borne out repeatedly in the previous chapters, that in adolescent abusers sexual acting out represents only one aspect of the general psychosocial difficulties experienced.

If the sexual arousal patterns of offenders are further examined in this context, it is clear that if an individual becomes aroused to deviant thoughts, this arousal may be strengthened and maintained due to the positive experience of subsequent masturbation and orgasm (McGuire et al. 1965). If non-deviant fantasies are less arousing to the individual, then these are likely to be used during masturbation less often and, therefore, will not be associated as strongly with the reinforcement of orgasm. Over a period of time, the offender's sexual arousal pattern is likely to be increasingly skewed towards deviant sexuality via masturbation (Bownes 1993, Laws and Marshall 1990). In the case of both adolescent and adult abusers, this is also true of *contact* with sexual partners. If appropriate sexual encounters are either rare, perhaps as a result of social difficulties (O'Brien 1991), or non-rewarding, due to sexual dysfunction, feelings of inadequacy or humiliation, then these will become less attractive and the individual may become increasingly reliant on deviant sexual behaviour and interests (Bownes 1993, Finkelhor 1984, Marshall et al. 1991a, Ryan and Lane 1991a).

The early work focusing on the concept of an 'offence cycle' with adolescent sexual offenders by Lane and Zamora (1984) is a practical adaptation of the conditioning models described above, and is incorporated into a large number of current treatment programmes. This approach emphasises the repetitious or cyclical nature of 'pre-abusive' behaviour (such as the rehearsal of abusive acts during masturbation) prior to the eventual engagement in deviant acts and the active use of memories of these acts as fantasy material for future masturbation. The majority of adult abusers who acknowledge their difficulties report that deviant fantasy played an important role in the development and maintenance of their sexual offending (Abel et al. 1987). However, a number of authors (Becker and Kaplan 1993, Marshall and Eccles 1993, Morrison and Print 1995) have cautioned against the application of theories of adult offending to child and adolescent abusers without further theoretical examination of the processes at work in each group. Specifically, the importance of deviant fantasy as a rehearsal for abusive behaviour may be reduced or different in an adolescent as opposed to adult context.

A number of studies have examined the role of fantasy in maintaining arousal patterns in abusers (Abel et al. 1983, Becker and Kaplan 1993, Laws and Marshall 1991, Quinsey and Earls 1990) and there has been considerable debate regarding the implications of deviant fantasy and arousal mechanisms for future risk. The acquisition of deviant sexual interest during the adolescent development of adult offenders has also been recorded (Abel et al. 1987, Faller 1991, Longo and Groth 1983, Weinrott and Saylor 1991). It is acknowledged that there are likely to be many people who have deviant fantasies which they find sexually arousing but never act out. However, given that sexual abusers have obviously acted out their fantasies in reality, it is possible that continued experience of deviant fantasies will encourage repetition of such behaviour (Fisher and Thornton 1993, Laws and Marshall 1991, Quinsey and Earls 1990).

Behavioural treatments, as one set of tools within the overall treatment package, are aimed at promoting sexual interest in, and arousal to, appropriate non-deviant sexual fantasies and decreasing the attractiveness of deviant fantasy so that it is no longer arousing for the individual. Treatment outcome studies indicate that simply stopping the deviant fantasies is less effective in the long term than methods in which offenders are taught techniques to enable them to substitute the deviant fantasy with non-deviant imagery (Marshall et al. 1991b). The theoretical models previously outlined provide a means of explaining the reasons for this in terms of allowing the abuser to learn how to achieve positive outcomes from appropriate non-deviant imagery and behaviour. These findings have important clinical implications for using a variety of behavioural techniques with abusers. They suggest that effectiveness of techniques may be improved by using them in conjunction, rather than separately. The combination of specific techniques and the structure of a complete behavioural programme will obviously be determined on an individual basis to meet particular abuser profiles. They are, therefore, best utilised in individual rather than group settings (Morrison and Print 1995).

Fantasy modification techniques

Techniques for increasing an individual's control over deviant fantasy and redirecting sexual interest are based on the effect of positive and negative outcomes on behaviour. Additional refinements of conditioning models have incorporated notions that cognitive processes, such as thoughts and fantasies, can be considered in the same way as overt behaviours and are governed by the same learning processes. This reflects more recent developments of conditioning theory to emphasise the importance of cognitive and emotional mediation of behaviour. Behavioural treatments have been aimed at modifying both actual behaviours (overt techniques) and the cognitive/affective processes (covert techniques).

These behavioural techniques fall broadly into two main categories:

1. Those which *decrease* the attractiveness of the *deviant* fantasy – by linking it to negative or aversive consequences;

2. Those which *increase* the attractiveness of *non-deviant* fantasies – by linking them to rewarding consequences.

Within each category, both 'overt' and 'covert' techniques are utilised. Overt techniques involve modification of actual behaviour by direct action (such as masturbatory reconditioning). Covert techniques involve cognitive or imaginal processes (such as thought stopping and covert sensitisation). Complete treatment packages, however, are likely to involve aspects of both methods. Treatment programmes must take account of the developmental level of individual clients. In the case of adolescents, modification techniques must be limited to those behaviours they have already experienced.

Although various methods will be separately described below, their concurrent use in clinical practice has made evaluation of individual techniques difficult. This is exacerbated by the lack of research studies dealing with individual treatment components and the low numbers of subjects used in some of the research studies. An added complication, from an evaluative standpoint, is the lack of standard procedures for use of behavioural techniques. In consequence, clinicians tend to adapt both the techniques and the explanations given to abusers on how to implement them, rightly to suit individual circumstances, but rendering sensible evaluative commentary difficult.

The techniques within the behavioural treatment field described below have been developed within an adult offender framework and their use with younger abusers should be considered carefully before the treatment package is drawn up (Becker and Abel 1985, Becker and Kaplan 1993).

Decreasing arousal to deviant fantasy

Overt methods – aversive techniques These techniques involve the pairing of a highly unpleasant outcome with the occurrence of deviant behaviour. The use of electric shock administered after description of deviant fantasy was one of the earliest aversive techniques described in the literature. Although widely used in the 1960s, it is generally no longer considered acceptable on humanitarian grounds as a method of treatment (Maletzky 1991, Quinsey and Earls 1990). However, other less invasive forms of aversive techniques have been utilised.

Olfactory aversion   (the pairing of unpleasant smell with the deviant behaviour). This has acquired wide currency as an alternative to the use of electric shock. Some researchers have suggested that the powerful effect of this method results from the direct and rapid impact of the stimuli on the sensory areas of the brain and the relative controllability of the stimulus presentation (Maletzky 1991). Consequently, any attempts by the abuser to dismiss, ignore or otherwise minimise the effects are rendered less effective.

The general procedure involves pairing an unpleasant odour (usually ammonia) with the deviant fantasy so that the abuser begins to associate the fantasy with a nasty but not harmful experience, rather than with the pleasures of sexual arousal. As treatment progresses, the individual can be encouraged to carry a foul-smelling, but containable substance, such as smelling salts, and to sniff this whenever a deviant thought occurs. Initially, however, the therapist delivers the aversive odour to the individual at the same time as deviant imagery is presented.

Typically, the deviant image or fantasy would be presented as a visual image or as an audiotaped description and the abuser would simultaneously be brought into context with the unpleasant smell. Introduction of the odour would occur at random intervals over the course of repeated presentations of the deviant fantasy. This random pairing is based on the conditioning theory principle that some of the most powerful influences on behaviour are consequences which are intermittently but predictably associated with that behaviour (Maletzky 1991). Olfactory aversion is frequently coupled with a covert aversive technique, known as covert sensitisation, described later.

Shame aversion therapy   A variation on this olfactory method which has been reported in the literature on adult exhibitionism is that of 'shame aversion therapy'. Originally developed in the 1970s, the method involves the abuser simulating the deviant act in front of an audience, who may be instructed to ridicule the individual. The embarrassment and anxiety experienced as an additional consequence then become associated with the offending behaviour, replacing the previously pleasurable associations. A variant of this procedure has been used in some treatment programmes in North America (Maletzky 1991). This involves the abuser being videotaped performing the act with a life-sized doll. The abuser then watches the video with the therapist and perhaps a co-worker or parent. In practice, this is a highly aversive technique which aims to set up negative associations with the deviant act. Maletzky comments on the use of the technique with offender groups other than exhibitionists, often with rapid results. He considers the technique and its variants as particularly useful with individuals who are making slow or little progress with other techniques. However, the very mechanism which is likely to produce these effects, the experience of shame or humiliation, may render it of lesser value with adolescent groups in view of the fragility of self esteem and interpersonal relationships within this group (Morrison and Print 1995).

Masturbatory satiation or orgasmic conditioning   This is based on the conditioning theory premise that behaviour which is not reinforced eventually becomes 'extinguished', i.e. ceases altogether. In this method, the abuser is required to masturbate to the deviant fantasy for up to an hour *post-ejaculation* (Marshall 1979). As each subsequent ejaculation becomes more difficult, the act of masturbating becomes more painful, boring and less rewarding. If this experience is accompanied by active fantasy, then the latter is likely to become associated with unpleasant experiences and therefore will gradually become less frequent (Abel et al. 1983, Marshall 1979). Verbalising the fantasy aloud on to an audiotape during each masturbatory episode (Abel et al. 1983, Maletzky 1991) allows random checking by the therapist to ensure the adolescent is carrying out the procedure regularly and correctly.

Studies using masturbatory satiation (Becker and Kaplan 1993, Maletzky 1991) indicate that while successful reductions in the deviant fantasy frequency may be obtained relatively quickly for both adults and adolescents, the problem of increasing arousal to appropriate fantasies remains. If there is no substitution of appropriate for deviant imagery, the net effect may be an overall loss of fantasy experience. Clinical experience casts doubt on the long term efficacy of the technique, which underscores the importance of including it at best as one technique within a battery.

In addition to the difficulties such as ensuring compliance and adequate monitoring in implementing the techniques described above with the adult population, with whom they were developed, there are additional problems with child or adolescent abusers. There may be some adolescents with vivid and extensive use of deviant fantasy life. If so, then the technique may be useful, if genuine compliance can be gained. However, in those for whom fantasy is not obviously relevant to abusive behaviour, where the content is not sophisticated or where detailed fantasy is not well established, the use of the techniques raises both practical and ethical issues. In such cases a flexible and adaptive approach which produces an individualised programme is likely to be more beneficial. The role of the therapist in assessing and facilitating compliance is of particular relevance.

Vicarious sensitisation   Weinrott (1994) has recently developed a procedure of 'vicarious sensitisation' for juvenile abusers within his treatment programme. This involves the video presentation of extremely aversive and individualised scenarios detailing the consequences of sexual abuse. For each adolescent, a brief audiotaped description of his offence is immediately followed by a segment of the video showing the terrible consequences of offending (Weinrott has devised 15 aversive vignettes which cover topics such as the juvenile abuser being caught by his mother, his arrest being broadcast on television news, court process and resulting social difficulties). The audio and videotape segments are alternated during each session and the treatment package consisted of twice-weekly sessions for a period of 12 weeks. The individual is required to state the positive reasons for therapy and for not offending at the end of each session.

A preliminary evaluation of efficacy showed promising results in those undergoing this procedure as compared to a waiting list control group. This represents a positive step in the development of treatment techniques specifically designed for an adolescent population.

Covert methods
Thought stopping   This cognitive technique enables people to inhibit unwanted thoughts and to interrupt excessive rumination on deviant or otherwise disturbing thoughts. It has already

been described in the context of cognitive interaction but is essentially a behavioural technique. It typically involves the abuser implementing a strategy to interrupt an unwanted thought as soon as it is identified. For example, the abuser would initially be instructed to shout the word 'no' aloud the moment a deviant thought occurs, and immediately to switch to an appropriate or distracting thought, previously identified and agreed with the therapist. This might include focusing on a non-deviant sexual topic or completing a non-sexual distraction task, such as naming objects in the immediate surroundings or counting backwards. Over time, the abuser would begin to think the word 'no' rather than say it aloud. Although this technique has been successfully used in relation to a wide range of clinical problems and there is clinical evidence of its efficacy with sexually abusive behaviour, Maletzky (1991) notes that there have been no large scale evaluative studies of its efficacy.

Thought stopping may be used in conjunction with an overt aversive technique in order to enhance the distraction or interruption effect. This might, for example, involve an elastic band fitted loosely round the wrist which the adolescent plucks in order to cause an unpleasant physical sensation. The interruption effect is thereby achieved using both cognitive and physical sensations. This then acts as a cue to begin the thought stopping procedure. This aversive strategy also has the advantage of being immediately available to the individual within a 'real life', as opposed to 'therapy session' setting. Many clients report that this aids greatly in helping them to stop ruminating on the deviant thought. However, the method requires a degree of insight and self awareness in addition to cognitive flexibility, which may limit its applicability in any given individual or population.

Covert sensitisation   This technique involves the abuser imagining and producing a written record of an emotionally unpleasant event associated with the deviant fantasy and at the point at which the deviant act would be imagined, to switch to an extremely detailed description of the unpleasant event or *aversive scene* (Abel et al. 1983). A list of such seriously unpleasant thoughts would have been previously elicited by the therapist and given or used as cue cards by the adolescent. It is important that the aversive scene has a strong emotional impact on the individual, arousing feelings of fear, repulsion or disgust. This is again so that the abuser experiences a strongly negative emotion associated with the fantasy rather than a positive one. By regularly pairing the deviant fantasy with imaginal aversive events, it is hoped that the deviant fantasy will lose its ability to be sexually arousing and pleasurable and will be avoided as a result of new, negative associations.

The full covert sensitisation procedure also incorporates *covert positive reinforcement* in the form of relief produced by a realistic 'escape scene'. This scene is incorporated into the fantasy at the point at which the deviant act is about to occur. The adolescent imagines leaving the fantasy scene without abusing and then reviews or incorporates the positive consequences of doing so into the fantasy. So there are three stages to the treatment:

- increased sexual arousal associated with the deviant act in the fantasy;
- a negative consequence associated with the deviant act;
- relief or escape from the negative consequences because of successful avoidance of the act in the fantasy.

Abusers may be given the scenes on audiotape or in written form in order that they can practise regularly between therapy sessions.

The effectiveness of this technique has been found to be greatly enhanced when combined with other behavioural methods, such as olfactory aversion. This is known as 'assisted covert sensitisation' (Maletzky 1991).

This technique appears to be ethically acceptable in that considerable time is spent collaborating with the therapist in the development of aversive and reinforcing imagery and the abusers themselves are in control of the aversive process. Unpleasant, punitive procedures are not inflicted upon them by 'authority' figures. The effectiveness of such techniques with both adult and adolescent offenders appears to be dependent on their co-operation, their understanding of the rationale and procedures and their ability to derive imagery which is both vivid and personally relevant.

Verbal or cognitive satiation   A cognitive variation on the overt technique of masturbatory satiation has been reported as successful in the treatment of adolescent abusers (Becker and Kaplan 1993) as well as adults (Salter 1988). This procedure involves the abuser verbalising the deviant fantasy repeatedly for between 30 minutes and one hour in order that the fantasy may become boring and lose its ability to arouse the individual. Variants include the adolescent repeatedly verbalising an offence-related phrase while viewing a visual stimulus depicting an individual with similar characteristics to his own victim. The therapist may provide direction as to appropriate phrases arising from activities known to have occurred during the offence or deviant fantasy. Separate phrases and sessions are used for each fantasy. Becker and Kaplan (1993) note that this procedure is effective in reducing deviant arousal within 8 to 16 sessions for adolescents in their treatment programme.

The conditioning principle used is identical to that of masturbatory satiation but the technique avoids the need for adolescents to be instructed to engage in masturbatory activity, of which they may have had little or no prior experience.

Increasing arousal to non-deviant fantasy

As with the previous category, techniques aimed at enhancing appropriate arousal include both overt and covert methods and, commonly, a combination of the two. They are often considered together under the grouping of *masturbatory reconditioning techniques* (Laws and O'Neil 1981).

Overt methods

Directed masturbation This involves the individual masturbating exclusively to non-deviant fantasies and being instructed to completely avoid masturbating to deviant fantasies. In order to help the abuser focus on appropriate imagery, visual stimuli may be suggested or provided by the therapist and may include photographs depicting consenting adult sexual activities or adult nudes. It is thought that the act of touching the genitals in the presence of a particular stimulus will increase arousal to that stimulus even where the individual has previously had no arousal to this. Studies using this approach report successful results and it is generally regarded as a technique which merits further empirical scrutiny (Maletzky 1991), particularly regarding its use with adolescents (Becker and Kaplan 1993).

Perhaps more than the previously described techniques, directed masturbation requires careful consideration of the level of functioning and developmental characteristics of the adolescent. The use of sexually explicit materials in this and other methods is fraught with ethical pitfalls even with adults. The exposure of immature adolescents to such material must, therefore, be based on strong evidence of clear therapeutic merit. The use of visual imagery depicting children and adolescents raises serious ethical and professional issues. Further guidelines on the use of sexually salient and pornographic materials with both adults and adolescents are provided in the publication of the Policy and Ethics Sub-Committee of the National Association for the Development of Work with Sex Offenders (NOTA 1994).

Covert methods

Thematic shift This technique involves pairing the pleasurable experience of orgasm with the appropriate fantasy. The abuser is initially instructed to masturbate to the deviant fantasy to ensure arousal. At the point of 'ejaculatory inevitability' a mental switch to an appropriate fantasy image is made. Gradually, this switch from the deviant to the non-deviant fantasy is brought forward in the masturbatory sequence, so that eventually the abuser can become aroused and masturbate to orgasm, using the non-deviant fantasy. This method is used to increase non-deviant arousal and it is particularly for those individuals whose previous sexual fantasy preferences have been almost exclusively deviant.

Studies of the effectiveness of this method appear to show mixed results. Those studies in which an improvement was indicated, in terms of the abuser's ability to use non-deviant imagery, also indicated that the level of deviant interest itself remained unchanged (Quinsey and Earls 1990). Further therapeutic improvements were gained only when the thematic shift method was used in combination with aversive techniques whose aim was to reduce the level of deviant interest.

A technique used in conjunction with thematic shift to promote arousal to non-deviant imagery is 'fading and shaping'. This involves the abuser initially being shown an image of the deviant stimulus (to promote initial arousal) which is gradually faded out and replaced by a non-deviant image. If the abuser then shows a decreased level of arousal the deviant image may be reinstated. Eventually, the individual is able to become aroused by the non-deviant stimulus alone. As with other behavioural techniques, good short term treatment outcomes have been reported using this technique (Barlow and Agras 1973, Laws and O'Neil 1981 cited in Quinsey and Earls 1990).

Fantasy alternation This requires the abuser to verbalise his fantasy aloud while masturbating to orgasm (Laws 1985). The individual is required to alternate his use of deviant and non-deviant fantasies, either on a weekly basis or every other session in order to ensure that a degree of arousal is maintained. The aim of the method is to lessen the exclusive association between arousal and deviant imagery but, since the young person is masturbating to the deviant fantasy as often as to the non-deviant fantasy, it is likely that the deviant imagery will continue to be arousing for the client. Not surprisingly, the limited amount of literature relating to this technique has indicated generally poor results, and in some instances an increase in deviant arousal has been noted (Laws and Marshall 1991).

Limitations of fantasy modification procedures

Despite the widespread belief amongst practitioners in the role of fantasy in sexually abusive behaviour, rigorous empirical evidence, particularly in relation to adolescents, is in short supply (Becker and Kaplan 1993, Laws and Marshall 1991, Morrison and Print 1995). There are a number of issues implicated in the use of these techniques:

While the procedures are based on conditioning theory, there is conflicting evidence from the available research studies on whether sexual behaviour is conditioned in a similar way to other voluntary behaviours (McGuire et al. 1965, Marshall and Eccles 1993). Similarly, for ethical reasons there is no empirical evidence to suggest that sexual offending is exclusively the result of behavioural conditioning. Further investigation of the extent to which sexually abusive behaviour may be understood within a conditioning framework is required.

The use of the techniques described requires a high level of co-operation from the abuser. Given that the procedures are highly intrusive and that most individuals, particularly young people, find them embarrassing, only highly motivated clients are likely to agree to them or carry them out as instructed (Becker and Kaplan 1993). In our clinical experience we have found that it is generally very difficult to engage young people in using these procedures effectively in the early stages of their treatment. In the case of abusers living in the community, it can prove especially difficult to persuade individuals to use such techniques in the face of their anxieties about being overheard or having someone discover their written work. In the case of adolescents living with other youngsters, the issue of privacy is an even greater limitation. Where young abusers feel so uncomfortable with what is required of them, their continuing attendance for therapy may be jeopardised.

Where the procedures require the use of images, the nature of the images being used must be considered carefully and many professionals have serious concerns about such sexual material. It is generally agreed that stimulus materials should be non-sexist and non-abusive, creating grave difficulties for the availability of such materials depicting young children. Similar concerns are raised about the continued demand for the production of such materials for future use. A more detailed review of such issues and guidelines for the ethical use of such materials is provided by NOTA (1994).

The use of aversive techniques, based as it is on infliction of imaginary unpleasantness, is not acceptable to some professionals. The intrusive, unpleasant nature of the techniques, the variable ability of abusers to give informed consent, to understand the rationale of treatment and implications of their withdrawal from treatment create difficulties for ethical practice and their use must be carefully considered.

There are difficulties in assessing the efficacy of these procedures. The abuser's self-report is unlikely to be completely reliable, but the alternatives are highly intrusive. In those North American programmes which make regular use of fantasy modification procedures, abusers are often required to verbalise their fantasies during the procedures and to tape these for evaluation by the therapist. Adolescents may be particularly resistant to doing so due to embarrassment and anxieties over privacy. Additionally, not all therapists may feel comfortable about having to check the tapes, especially where the client may be aroused by this involvement or where the therapist may be a focus of the fantasies. Indeed, this process may in some instances become an even more convoluted route to rewarding fantasies. The need for the techniques to be used primarily in individual settings, in which a high level of trust has been achieved, is also apparent.

To be effectively used, fantasy modification techniques require a thorough understanding of the psychological principles and theories from which they derive. Many practitioners in the UK do not feel that they have the clinical expertise or level of training required to undertake such work. Consultation with and supervision by a psychologist experienced in the application of such theories and techniques to the field of sexual offending is not always available.

Since much treatment in this country is conducted in a group setting and detailed fantasy modification work requires individual sessions, there are also resource limitations on its widespread use.

Special considerations with adolescent sex offenders

When considering the use of fantasy modification techniques with adolescent sex offenders, there are a number of additional issues to be taken into account. Many young people who act in a sexually abusive manner may be completely lacking in specific 'rehearsal' fantasy due to the genuinely opportunistic nature of their behaviour. For this group, fantasy modification is not appropriate.

The issue of what constitutes an 'appropriate' fantasy is particularly pertinent for adolescents. As with adults, there is little empirical research into the nature and content of fantasy within both general and offender populations. Some young offenders may have had no appropriate sexual experiences and may have to be taught to develop an appropriate fantasy. Appropriate fantasies include the following features:

- *full consent* in that both the parties are *able* to give consent (they are developmentally advanced enough to know what they are doing). Therapists should be guided by legal definitions of the age of consent;

- *equal power relationship* – they exert or are capable of exerting equal influence over the sexual activity by virtue of their similar age, intellectual level and position or status;
- *mutual agreement* on the activity;
- *positive emotions* in terms of attachment and affection;
- *no coercion*, particularly physical, either active or threatened;
- the *focus of fantasy* should not be someone with whom the adolescent is angry or dislikes.

Identifying a person who may become focus of 'appropriate' fantasy can present difficulties for the adolescent and the therapist. Using a person who is known to them personally (such as neighbours or school friends) may be inadvisable as it may encourage inappropriate sexual behaviour. Individuals such as media personalities, who are usually 'unobtainable', may present a better choice.

The content of the fantasy raises the problem of what constitutes appropriate fantasy material for an individual who is younger than the legal age of consent for homosexual or heterosexual intercourse. Should the techniques 'allow' or 'encourage' the use of images of activities which the adolescent is too young legally to engage in? Perhaps the majority of practitioners working with abusive adolescents take the view that provided the fantasy fulfils the requirements for appropriateness defined earlier and that the individual is already sexually experienced to a degree, then this issue need not be too problematic. This might suggest that, as a general guide, adolescents should not be encouraged to develop fantasies about activities *beyond* those they have already experienced. This point illustrates the professional uncertainty and moral ambiguity of so much work with adolescents in such a sensitive area as sexual abuse, and the potential legal pitfalls, even when an adolescent is already experienced, should a challenge be made.

Regarding the procedures used with adolescents, the American National Task Force on Juvenile Sexual Offending (National Adolescent Perpetrator Network 1988) have produced guidelines following lengthy consultation with practitioners across North America. They suggest that where a procedure involves masturbation, only those adolescents who have already engaged in masturbation should be required to carry out such a procedure. As a result, verbal satiation is far more widely used with adolescents than masturbatory satiation. They also recommend that the least intrusive methods should always be used. In particular, aversive techniques (primarily olfactory based) should be used only when other methods have proved ineffective and with the informed and voluntary consent of the individual and their parents.

The National Task Force also recommended that adolescents should never be exposed to stimuli beyond the range of behaviours that are reported or exhibited by the individual. With regard to the use of Penile Plethysmography (PPG) assessments, they recommend that this procedure is useful for those individuals who strongly indicate deviant arousal patterns but should be conducted with the consent of both adolescent and his parents and should only be used where less intrusive methods are unlikely to succeed. In the UK, the National Children's Home Report on Juvenile Sex Offenders (1992) did not recommend the use of PPG assessments in any circumstances. Further British consideration of the issues is provided in Morrison and Print (1995) and NOTA (1993).

In view of the role that fantasy is believed to play in the development and maintenance of sexually abusive behaviour, fantasy modification procedures would appear to be an important part of a treatment approach. However, the research literature reveals that efficacy of individual techniques is not known, treatment outcome measures for some of the procedures are lacking and mixed results have been reported in others. The clinical application of the procedures is fraught with difficulty due to their highly personal and intrusive nature and the interaction of these with the adolescent's developmental level, intensity of motivation and social circumstances.

Despite these reservations, the use of fantasy modification techniques with individuals who have an obvious problem with deviant fantasies can contribute significantly to an overall package of treatment in which practitioner training, resource and ethical issues have been addressed. The procedures of verbal satiation and vicarious sensitisation appear to be among the most appropriate for use with adolescents provided the skilled resource issues can be satisfactorily resolved.

9

Relapse Prevention

Graeme Richardson and Finlay Graham

'Relapse prevention' as a treatment model was developed in work with substance abusers where it was recognised that 'cure' was unrealistic. The goal of treatment is instead teaching behavioural and cognitive skills which may (a) prevent relapse from occurring or (b) minimise the extent of a relapse (Marlatt and Gordon 1985). It is a 'maintenance' model aimed at sustaining changes made during treatment. The model was adapted for work with sex offenders (Pithers et al. 1983, 1988; Pithers 1990). Sexually abusive behaviour is seen as 'addictive' in nature, following a relapse course just like other cravings, such as smoking or drinking. In both, relapse is characterised by a process or chain of behaviours which occur sequentially over time (Hildebran and Pithers 1992).

It should, however, be noted that this approach was developed with adult sexual offenders rather than abusive adolescents. Ward and colleagues have shown that the modification of the model during its application to sexually abusive behaviour creates theoretical difficulties (Ward et al. 1995). Nevertheless, we consider the model to be useful for practice.

Relapse process

This refers to the transition from a high risk situation to a lapse and then a relapse. The desire for immediate indulgence in pleasure is the starting point. This desire and subsequent deviant decision increase chances of a lapse, referred to as the 'problem of immediate gratification' (PIG). When a person lapses, physiological and psychological effects then reinforce desire for further gratification and the probability of a relapse.

In Marlatt and Gordon's (1985) model, 'abstinence violation effect' (AVE) is hypothesised as a mediator between a lapse and a relapse. This is a cognitive (thinking) and affective (feeling) reaction to an initial violation of an 'abstinence rule' which prohibits a particular behaviour, which varies in intensity, and is more intense when a relapse occurs. The intensity of the AVE depends on the extent to which a person is able to justify the lapse to himself; is associated with the motivation to remain abstinent, with social support from other significant others to help him abstain, the personal cost of abstinence in terms of perceived effort and self-denial, and the period of successful abstinence preceding the relapse.

The AVE is believed to be predictive of a person's ability successfully to follow the abstinence rule and regain control over behaviour. If the lapse is attributed to external, unstable and specific factors, the AVE is of lower intensity, thereby reducing the risk of a relapse. If, on the other hand, the lapse is due to internal, dispositional factors then the person experiences a negative emotional reaction and loss of control. This lowers expectations about coping with future risk and loss of confidence about managing lapses. Behaviour recurs, becoming worse with each violation until a new cycle is set in motion.

Unlike addiction, lapses in abusive behaviour constitute a criminal offence against a victim. It is the first indicator of losing self control, such as buying pornography or a deviant sexual fantasy. A relapse is defined as the occurrence of *any* abusive episode, even if it is a lesser offence when compared with previous ones.

Pithers (1990) described the critical role of 'seemingly unimportant decisions' (SUDs) in placing the abuser in high risk situations, in which his sense of control over abusive behaviour is threatened. A seemingly unimportant decision for a child molester might be to go to the local swimming baths which is used by schoolchildren.

Relapse prevention in practice

The book *Relapse Prevention with Sex Offenders* (Laws 1989) and the treatment manual *A Structured Approach to Preventing Relapse: A Guide for Sex Offenders* (Freeman-Longo and Pithers 1992) provide the practitioner with two useful resources. This approach may inform all phases of clinical intervention including assessment, treatments, external supervision of the adolescent and management of the risk he poses.

Basic principles

The key assumptions underpinning relapse prevention practice are:

- Sexual aggression is not an impulsive act.
- A series of abuse precursors precedes and leads to an act of sexual aggression.
- These abuse precursors (or precipitants) can be identified.
- The abuser can learn to identify his particular pattern or sequence of precursors (the relapse process).
- The abuser is never 'cured' but has the potential to relapse (reoffend).
- The abuser can learn to intervene in and control this relapse process and avoid further acts of sexual aggression.

Introducing abusers into the model

In the early stages of treatment, abusers are introduced to the concepts of the model. To establish a working relationship, practitioner and abuser must use the same map of intervention and the abuser must accept it is relevant and beneficial to him. The abuser is instructed into the model and begins to apply it to his own abuse characteristics, life history and circumstances.

Elements of the model and relationships between them are then explained and their implications for the abuser's self control explicitly stated. The elements described and discussed with the abusers are:

Abstinence This is defined as a lifestyle free of sexually abusive behaviour. It includes an absence of 'lapses' such as abusive sexual fantasies, misuse of pornography, use of drugs and alcohol, if these were associated with abusive behaviour.

Offence precursors These refer to situational, intrapersonal and interpersonal antecedents of sexually abusive behaviour. Abuse precursors include seemingly unimportant decisions (SUDs), high risk factors (HRFs), maladaptive coping responses (MCRs), lapses and the abstinence violation effect (AVE)

Pithers and colleagues (1983) have identified a range of factors commonly found in adult child molesters and adult rapists.

Early precursors

- chronically dysfunctional family and upbringing
- maternal absence/neglect
- paternal absence/neglect
- parental marital discord
- physical abuse as a child
- sexual abuse as a child
- precocious sexual behaviour (before age of 12 years)
- late sexual experience
- intellectual impairment (IQ under 80)

Precipitating precursors

- anger at time of offence
- stable and generalised anger
- social anxiety
- depression
- emotional inhibition and over-control
- inability to cope with life stressors
- boredom
- social isolation
- divorce/break-up of a close relationship
- sexual dysfunction
- abusive sexual fantasy
- deviant sexual arousal

Precipitating precursors (cont.)

- absence of victim empathy
- low self esteem
- poor social skills
- lack of assertiveness
- lack of sexual knowledge
- alcohol/substance misuse
- viewing of pornography
- opportunity to abuse a victim
- planning to abuse a victim

Perpetuating precursors

- anger
- denial of sexual problems
- abusive sexual fantasies
- alcohol/substance misuse
- relationship problems
- isolation
- social competency deficits
- visits to places which allow access to potential victims

Seemingly unimportant decisions These are apparently inconsequential and irrelevant decisions which increase exposure to high risk situations and in which the abuser chooses whether or not to reoffend. Ignoring or covering up lapses, even minor ones, increases the risk of relapse.

High risk factors   Probability of relapse is increased when the abuser encounters a 'high risk situation' (e.g. a child abuser is asked to babysit) because it tests and jeopardises his self control. Specific thoughts and feelings which increase the chance of a lapse or relapse are regarded as high risk factors and abusers are taught to cope better with them (Marques and Nelson 1989).

Relapse process   Pithers et al. (1983) have identified a common sequence of precursors that constitute the relapse process:

(a)   Change in mood
(b)   Sexual fantasies
(c)   Distorted thinking
(d)   Planning
(e)   Disinhibition
(f)   Abusive act

For most adult sexual offenders the first identifiable lapse is the return of deviant sexual fantasies. The working assumption is that most sexual abusers set the stage for lapses by placing themselves in high risk situations. This occurs as a result of their distorted decision making.

Lapses   Lapses are the presence of 'offence precursors' or 'risk factors'. They include thoughts, fantasies, feelings and behaviours. They represent a step along the path towards a relapse, though in themselves they are not abusive or illegal. Examples of 'lapses' include: talking to a potential victim; being alone with a potential victim; viewing pornography; alcohol/substance misuse; thinking about abusive sex with an actual or potential victim; abusive sexual fantasy; sexual arousal by children; feeling angry; feeling lonely; feelings of not coping with life.

Maladaptive coping responses (MCRs)   These represent the abuser's responses following a lapse. They are maladaptive because they do not halt the relapse process, but actually precipitate further steps. For example, an abuser has an abusive fantasy about a child; he then masturbates to it; consumes alcohol and then walks down to the local park where he knows children are playing.

Abstinence violation effect (AVE) A high risk situation generates tension between self control and its lapse. The abuser may become self critical and pessimistic about his self control (self deprecation), leading to self doubts about the effectiveness of treatment and his own failure (failure expectation).

Problem of immediate gratification (PIG) This arises when the abuser focuses on the positive pay-off and ignores negative consequences of potential relapse, thus increasing its probability.

Level of perceived self control If an abuser believes he is 'cured' he may react adversely to any opportunistic or transitory lapse, seeing it as an irreversible loss of self control. He should be advised to expect the possibility of lapses and use it as an opportunity to exercise and improve on self management skills.

Adaptive coping response (ACR) This represents the abuser's response following a lapse. It is adaptive if it halts the relapse process by preventing further lapses. A range of adaptive responses is required as part of the treatment, and these target the abuser's risk factors, such as how to deal with an abusive sexual urge or fantasy.

Relapse This is any sexually abusive act or offence.

Sexual abuse cycle

The abuser is also introduced to the abuse cycle model. The abuser is taught to make the links between events which trigger particular thoughts, activate feelings and behavioural responses as a means of controlling his sexual behaviour, and break one of the links in the chain to prevent a relapse. Ordering of these chains is variable, since feelings can precede thoughts and vice versa.

The abuse cycle is used by Freeman-Longo and Pithers in their Relapse Prevention treatment manual (1992).

This cycle consists of four distinct phases. The 'build up' phase, the 'acting-out' phase, the 'justification' phase and the 'pretend normal' phase. The *build up* phase may include feeling lonely, having abusive fantasies and thoughts, watching pornography, planning an abusive act, and giving oneself permission to go ahead with the planned act. The *acting-out* phase represents the abusive sexual act. In the *justification* phase the abuser feels anxious about being found out, but rationalises his behaviour by minimising or excusing it, telling himself he will not do it again. In the *pretend normal* phase the abuser returns to his daily routine and unresolved difficulties.

This approach makes use of a sexual abuse cycle in treatment. Offence precursors are identified as a sequential process of thoughts, feelings and behaviour which link together and precipitate the abusive behaviour. Treatment focuses on providing the abuser with the skills necessary to interrupt this sequence and avoid a relapse.

In our experience this approach can be a useful technique but there is a danger that the process may become unduly prescriptive. We should remember that models of the sexual abuse/assault cycle are theoretically driven and not empirically validated. It is good practice to guard against making the individual fit the model rather than the other way round.

Treatment in relapse prevention

Treatment follows comprehensive, individual assessment. Relapse prevention utilises the same range of techniques as in other treatments, but is more clearly integrated. It focuses on (1) internal self management and (2) the external/supervisory dimension. The internal self management dimension involves helping the abuser avoid lapses and preventing a lapse becoming a relapse. Self management alone may be insufficient in some cases. The external supervisory dimension is designed to help overcome this difficulty through improved monitoring and communication of 'offence precursors' by a range of other people.

Internal self management

Avoiding lapses The following procedures are utilised to help the abuser learn skills to avoid lapses.

Identification of offence precursors   This is an educational stage. The abuser is encouraged to understand the elements and dynamic of his relapse process. Situations, thoughts, feelings and behaviours that precipitate lapses can be anticipated and circumvented by:

- teaching the abuser to recognise the offence precursors involved in his relapse process;
- assisting him to identify high risk factors and any seemingly unimportant decisions that precede them;
- identifying *his* complete relapse sequence;
- identifying the precursors which precipitate the first lapse – typically an emotional state, a distorted thought, or a particular behaviour.

Stimulus control procedures   Certain external stimuli may be the initial trigger to abusive chains and cycles. Self control may be enhanced if such stimuli as viewing pornography or watching children are avoided.

Avoidance strategies   The abuser identifies and seeks to avoid situations which are known to elicit lapses such as swimming baths, children's play areas or babysitting.

Programmed coping responses   The abuser learns a standardised problem solving response to anticipated high risk situations. He rehearses this through repeated practice in role-play scenarios. Such programming and rehearsal helps responses to become 'automatic' and thereby more likely to be utilised in an actual high risk situation.

Escape strategies   Abusers are likely to encounter situations that could precipitate a lapse. They must, therefore, learn and frequently practise rapid escape strategies from unexpected high risk situations.

Coping with urges   The urge to act abusively is conceptualised in terms of positive pleasure whilst the negative consequences (arrest, social disapproval, guilt) are ignored. The abuser is encouraged to think of giving in to an urge as an active decision which he makes and for which he is responsible. The adaptive response is to focus thinking on its negative

consequences, rather than its gratifying aspects. Self statements about negative consequences are rehearsed, as are
aversive images depicting negative consequences.

Skills training   If skills deficit features in the overall
formulation as being significant in abusive behaviour then it
warrants treatment as set out in Chapter 5.

Preventing lapses becoming relapses   It is to be taken for
granted that lapses will occur, so each abuser needs to practise
how to prevent them becoming relapses. The following
procedures assist the abuser in dealing effectively with lapses.

Cognitive restructuring   The abuser is encouraged to view
lapses as mistakes from which he has to learn about his relapse
process and further enhance his coping skills. Reminder cards
are produced which include the definition of a lapse; a description of abstinence violation effect and negative self attributions; reassurance that he does not need to give in to deviant
urges and that these will weaken with time; instructions to
analyse precursors to the lapse in order to learn from the lapse,
and finally a list of adaptive coping responses to maintain self
control.

Contracting   In contracting the abuser formally agrees to limit
his exposure to high risk situations and a 'lapse limit' is
specified. This represents the extent to which lapses will be
tolerated, and requires the abuser to report any lapses to the
therapist. The lapse limit should be established with care so as
not to create a point of no return for the individual.

Maintenance manuals   These are developed by the abuser
himself to help remind him of the adaptive coping responses he
has learned and in what situations these may be required in the
future. The manual might include: reminder cards; a rationale
for avoidance and escape strategies; emergency telephone
numbers; a list of seemingly unimportant decisions, high risk
situations and offence precursors; self statements; and self-
monitoring forms.

The self management of sexually abusive behaviour may falter
for several reasons: abusers may not apply acquired skills in a

high risk situation; abusers may fail to report lapses to the therapist and return to a stance of denial/rationalisation/ minimisation; the abuser's motivation may be low. Attention should be given to external supervision and other aids to prevent relapse.

External supervisory dimension As there is no 'cure' for abusive behaviour, lifestyle management must be planned, self control techniques learned and applied on a lifelong basis. If the abuser manages this effectively he reduces the risk of further abuse. The external supervisory dimension has three functions: (1) external monitoring of abuse precursors; (2) establishment of an informal network of contacts which assists professionals to monitor the abuser's behaviour; (3) establishment of a collaborative relationship amongst professionals involved in the treatment of abusers.

The objectives of this approach to risk management are: effective supervision of the abuser's behaviour in the community; monitoring of ongoing risk of reoffending; taking action when risk is increasing; development of a support network to assist the abuser to maintain treatment gains and cope effectively with high risk situations.

The external supervisory dimension tries to involve relevant professionals and significant people in the abuser's life to assist him in maintaining lifestyle changes and self control. They may include the abuser's immediate family members or care-givers, social worker, probation officer, general practitioner and/or the abuser's employer.

Both the abuser and other identified people need to monitor his lifestyle, his current level of personal and social functioning, and his commitment to reporting and coping with lapses. The main point is that risk management should not rely on the abuser's self report. The following areas should be monitored by other people: lifestyle routines, activities and habits; emotional state; current level of coping; sexual urges and fantasies; re-emergence of any of the antecedents previously identified as precipitants of sexually abusive behaviour (lapses).

Differences between adult and adolescent abusers

Our work with sexually abusive adolescents leads us to conclude that the basic framework of a relapse prevention approach, despite its origins in adult work, has much to offer. There are, however, significant differences between adult sexual offenders and abusive adolescents which need to be considered. Sexual knowledge is poorer in adolescents; behaviours are much less fixed; cognitive distortions are less fully developed; adolescents live in a social world with different values, beliefs and expectations; they tend to be more emotionally labile; the role of family is more critical with adolescents; there are fewer incidents of abusive behaviour in adolescents; personality is still developing; perpetration/ grooming strategies are less consistent and sophisticated; the abuse process is still developing, thereby limiting detailed offence cycles or relapse processes that might be targeted; situational and opportunity factors appear to feature more as precursors and internal cognitive factors less frequently; many abusive adolescents (like their adult counterparts) have themselves been sexually abused but the adolescents are temporally closer to these abusive experiences; learning about sex is developing more markedly; the role of fantasy as a precursor of abuse is less clearly understood in adolescents and appears to be less significant; younger adolescents experience and expect significant degrees of external control of their behaviour by parents or carers; motivating and engaging with adolescents requires a different approach and different skills and is generally more difficult than with adults; there are significantly different ethical and legal contexts for adolescents and adults.

The living contexts in which adolescents are located are usually different from adults'. They are often still at home or being cared for in homes. In our experience, relapses in care are very common. The following guidelines seem useful in working with abusive adolescents:

- The adolescent's family should be involved in relapse prevention. In practice this is most effective when a parallel programme for the parents is run and occasional joint meetings with parents and adolescents held.
- If the adolescent has been removed from home as a result of sexually abusive behaviour, then it is critical to adopt a similar strategy with carers.
- Relapse prevention should be more behaviourally orientated than with adult offenders.

- In relation to Pithers' 'internal' and 'external' dimensions, more focus should be placed on the 'external' dimension when working with adolescents.
- Monitoring sources tend to be more numerous and arguably more reliable with adolescents than with adults (e.g. parents, carers, school, social worker).
- Diversion from high risk situations is more feasible with adolescents (e.g. increased use of structured time, greater parental supervision, respite babysitter, outreach work by Youth Care Team, etc.).

The development of an effective risk management plan through external supervision and support might include working with the abuser and his family; educating others involved in treating, caring, supporting and supervising the abuser in the basic principles of relapse prevention; regular meetings of professionals involved in the case to review progress; visiting the abuser at home and checking discreetly for obvious precursors, e.g. children hanging around, pornography, reduced level of functioning.

Clinical practice

In practice, we do not explicitly state the 'no cure' principle when working with adolescents. Establishing motivation to address their behaviour and providing them with optimism about gaining mastery over their problem are crucial both to them and to their parents/care-givers.

Equally, we find the full relapse prevention model too complex for many young abusers. We use simpler analogies and examples to help explain the basic principles of relapse and related treatment. We talk about the process of 'losing control of sexual behaviour', in terms of feelings, thoughts, images in their mind's eye, reactions to situations and people, places, opportunities, decisions and behaviours. We describe prevention plans in terms of knowing when and how to stop walking towards the potential victim, turning around and walking away. Identifying the abuse precursors and relapse process before the adolescent enters a relapse prevention treatment group means that group time is not wasted on preliminaries and takes account of alternative models of abuse cycles (e.g. Bera 1994, Marshall and Eccles 1993, Ryan et al. 1987).

We recognise limitations of the abuse cycle approach. The developmental histories and sequence of precipitants of many adolescents do not neatly fit it. Many of the assumptions are of questionable validity, such as those concerning previous incidents and the likelihood of others unless the individual is treated. Dangers of labelling are evident and risk tends to be overestimated. We must recognise the possibility of spontaneous desistance.

We have identified the following precursors in our clinical work with adolescents.

Adolescent specific offence precursors

Early or predisposing precursors

- Socio-economic deprivation
- Absent father
- Criminal parents and peer group
- Physical abuse by at least one parent
- Lack of parental supervision
- General conduct disorder
- Peer relationship difficulties
- Low intelligence, particularly verbal intelligence
- Sexual abuse by a known male perpetrator, more often than not a relative, and abuse penetrative
- Premature exposure to sexually explicit materials
- Mother having series of co-habitees
- Divorce of parents
- Witnessing parental violence
- Conflict with stepfather
- Weak attachment bonds to parents
- Truancy
- Physical aggressiveness
- Generalised offending
- History of care as a result of family difficulties
- Weak boundaries within the home, e.g. privacy, sharing bedrooms and baths
- Sexually deviant parent
- Pre-pubertal sexual experiences

Immediate or precipitating precursors

- Babysitting
- Access to pornography
- Arguments within family
- Rejection by peer group
- Negative self image
- High proportion of unsupervised time with younger children
- Opportunity
- Anger

- Low social competency
- Cognitive distortions about victims
- Abusive fantasy
- Fun fighting
- Expression of increased comfort with younger children
- Joint involvement with peers
- Rehearsed interaction and game playing with younger children
- Calculated decision to abuse
- Retaliatory thoughts (getting back)
- Homosexual thoughts/urges
- Absence of peer sexual outlets
- Victim of bullying
- Loneliness/alienation
- Sexual anxiety re same-age girls
- Developmental sexual urges and curiosity
- Sexual arousal to children
- Planning
- Frequenting places where children play
- Poor coping skills in responding to life's difficulties
- Befriending and grooming of targeted children
- Non-sexual physical touching of younger children

Maintaining or perpetuating precursors

- Continuing life changes in terms of placement and carers
- Continuing rejection by peers
- Unresolved angry feelings
- Unresolved victimisation issues
- Unresolved family issues
- Continued contact with a previous victim
- Continuing thoughts of retaliation and revenge
- Abusive sexual fantasies
- Cognitive distortions about victims
- Continued lack of opportunities for normal sexual experiences
- Denial of homosexual thoughts and urges
- Continued difficulties relating to peers
- Poor supervision by adult carers
- Inappropriate care placement
- Continuing opportunities to be alone with potential victims

'Relapse prevention' provides a practical model with a good deal of face validity and has been shown to be effective in reducing recidivism in sex offenders (e.g. Marshall et al. 1992a,

Pithers 1990). It needs careful, individually tailored application particularly with younger adolescents, sexually reactive children or youngsters with learning difficulties. Workers should be prepared to innovate in the interest of their clients, rather than pursuing an approach which is still organically developing.

10
Working in Context

Julie Hird

The preceding chapters have discussed different aspects of assessment and treatment of sexually abusive adolescents. This chapter considers some of the important features of the context in which this work occurs. Sexually abusive behaviour is a complex issue, because its occurrence has implications for many different agencies. It is not possible to categorise it as primarily a medical, psychological, social or criminal disorder. No single profession can provide a totally adequate response to this problem, in terms of either assessment, treatment or risk management. In addition to a variety of agency contexts, this kind of treatment work has a characteristic 'therapeutic context' which is in many ways different from other traditional psychological therapies.

Agency context

Up till the mid-1980s there was no offence-specific treatment available for adult offenders and abusers in Britain. Most went to prison, although some were referred to health settings and received treatment for various difficulties, including depression, poor self image or family problems. In the case of adolescents who committed abusive acts, the statutory authorities, such as police and social services, were often not informed and the behaviour was either viewed as experimental, requiring no intervention, or as a symptom of underlying psychological difficulties and the young person was referred to a child guidance clinic and probably diagnosed as having 'adolescent adjustment problems'. Shoor et al. (1966) for example wrote about the 'syndrome' of the sexually abusive adolescent in a psychodynamic framework, but provided little insight about treatment, unlike Striar and Ensor's (1986) helpful overview.

In the United States, during the 1980s, interest in the cognitive-behavioural treatment of sexually abusive behaviour, which focused directly upon the offending behaviour, began to develop and publications about this approach began to accumulate. Several authors noted that sexually abusive behaviour in adults often had its origins in adolescence (Longo and Groth 1983) and suggested that if treatment were aimed at the younger age group, there would be a greater chance of preventing continued offending into adulthood. Knopp (1985) proposed that such treatment optimism was justified due to the recency of the problem in adolescence and the supposed malleability of sexual identity during this developmental stage. As a consequence treatment centres for sexually abusive adolescents flourished in the United States and in 1986 the National Adolescent Perpetrator Network, comprising more than 800 individuals involved in such interventions, was established.

The development of treatment services for sexual abusers in Britain followed a similar sequence. Isolated treatment programmes sprang up in the late 1980s and were largely the result of enthusiastic professionals getting together, reading the American literature and searching out and organising relevant training and conferences.

Such initiatives were planned and carried out by workers themselves, since there were no mandates within the various organisations to provide such services. Those who chose to work with sex offenders often suffered from the curiosity and even alienation from other colleagues who searched for hidden motives to explain their attraction to this particular client group. Morrison (1992) described how workers sometimes felt as if they were viewed as 'quasi-perpetrators' and were not really trusted.

The newness of the cognitive-behavioural approach often meant that managers were totally unskilled in this area, so that they had difficulty in supervising their staff. Another consequence of the lack of organisational structure and support was that services could abruptly disappear, due to 'burnout' or when particular individuals moved on to other jobs.

It was against this general background that a North-West organisation, ROTA (Regional Offenders Treatment Association) was formed by a group of multi-disciplinary practitioners. They aimed to offer consultation and support to themselves and others in their work with sex offenders. The general drive was towards the development of more widespread treatment services for sex offenders.

In September 1991 ROTA began operating as a national organisation and became NOTA (The National Association for the Development of Work with Sex Offenders). The interest group in the North-West remained and other areas of the UK formed regional groups. The Association offers advice and consultancy on all aspects of working with sex offenders, organises conferences and training events and produces publications on various pertinent issues. For example, NOTA recognises the complex contextual aspects of this kind of work and offers its own guidelines for good practice (NOTA 1993).

In 1990, National Children's Home (NCH) surveyed treatment facilities available for sexually abusive adolescents. It discovered that under half of local authorities in England and Wales had any such facilities; there were no management structures; no consensus on the preferred style of intervention or on treatment goals. Consequently, NCH set up a committee of enquiry to examine the whole issue of children and young people who sexually abuse other children and they reported their findings in 1992. The report recommended that the Child Protection System should become responsible for co-ordinating the response to this problem, but also acknowledged that other agencies had important roles to play in enabling assessment and treatment to take place. The report also stressed the need for a 'continuum of care', which would involve a wide range of services based in a variety of settings, varying from community-based agencies to residential and secure facilities. Thus a young person could receive the kind of supervision and treatment required, depending upon his particular needs and the level of risk he posed to others.

At the present time treatment facilities for sexually abusive adolescents are available in a number of different settings, including social services and Youth Justice teams, voluntary agencies, such as Barnardo's, the probation service, the National Health Service, education, the prison service and other institutions such as centres for young people. Some of these are community based and others have an institutional setting, which may include conditions of security.

Social services

Within social services community work with abusive adolescents used to fall within the remit of the Youth Justice teams, who work with all kinds of adolescent offenders. However, it has become increasingly acknowledged that young abusers are different in some important ways from other young offenders and that the work with them should be based on different considerations. Juvenile justice philosophy promotes minimal intervention with young offenders, believing that many of them will grow out of criminal behaviour (NACRO 1991). This is, unfortunately, probably not the case for the majority of adolescent abusers, many of whom have already established a cycle of offending, which has become repetitive. Contrary to what many people want to believe, few young abusers are motivated by experimentation, peer group pressure or curiosity.

It used to be advocated within Social Services that their limited resources should be concentrated on working with the victims of sexual abuse rather than with the perpetrators. However since the *Strategic Statement on Working with Abusers* (Department of Health 1992) and the publication of the 1992 NCH report it has been increasingly recognised and accepted that abusive adolescents often have more in common with children in need and at risk, than with other types of adolescent offenders. As recommended in the NCH report, many area child protection committees have started to take on the role of co-ordinating the response to this client group to bring it into the child protection arena. In some areas separate conferences are held for the victim and the abuser, so that a strategic response can be formulated to address the needs of both groups. Masson (1995) comments that although this development has been slow, there is now evidence that procedures have been implemented in many areas. Several different models of practice are emerging, in terms of the relationship between child protection services and youth justice, particularly in relation to which agency takes the lead role.

Children who are taken into the care of social services are generally placed in foster homes, residential homes and secure units. The placement of adolescents who exhibit sexually abusive behaviour is especially difficult, since other children who may be living with them are at risk of becoming victims. In most cases a foster family with no younger children is the ideal environment for young sexual abusers, but demand for these places exceeds supply and there is often little alternative but to place them in residential settings with other children (Marsh et al. 1988).

When this occurs, it is imperative that managers of such facilities alert all staff to the risks that the abuser might pose to other children, in order to minimise the possibility of further victimisation. This will encourage closer supervision and arrangement of the environment to increase protection of the more vulnerable residents. Staff training is crucial for such work. Sexually abusive adolescents often present as victims, rather than perpetrators, so that some staff may underestimate their potential for reoffending. Without specific education about how sex abusers operate, sexually inappropriate behaviours in residential establishments may be misinterpreted or even overlooked.

Voluntary organisations

Several voluntary organisations, principally Barnardo's, have, in recent years, set up projects which employ specialist staff and undertake treatment work with young abusers. There are presently 12 such initiatives in the United Kingdom, which are generally linked to social services, but sometimes to other agencies. For example the 5A Scheme in Liverpool is funded equally between Barnardo's and social services and employs a co-ordinator, a senior practitioner and a practitioner, all of whom spend their time working with young abusers. Another example is the joint venture between Barnardo's and adolescent health services in Belfast.

The probation service

The probation service principally works with adult offenders, but the Criminal Justice Act (1991) stated that adolescents can be placed on a probation order from the age of 16, so many adolescent sex offenders will be found on probation.

Concern used to be expressed amongst probation staff about concentrating too many resources on sex offenders, since they represent a small percentage of all their clients. However, in recent years, following the Probation Inspectorate Report in 1991 (HM Inspectorate 1991), the probation service has recognised the importance of working with sex offenders and has approved of specialisation for some of its workers to address the difficulties of this client group. The emphasis to date has been on group treatment for adults, in almost all probation departments, but the Home Office is currently considering the issue of the 16–18-year-old sex offenders who are placed on probation (Morrison 1992).

Typically the probation officer is an advocate for the offender and this could give rise to a clash of interests when working with abusive clients, since the protection of victims must always be the primary concern of the worker.

The health service

Within the National Health Service, outpatient treatment facilities for adolescent sex offenders tend to be located in adolescent or forensic services and in some in-patient departments that specialise in adolescent mental health. The extent to which any treatment work is carried out in any particular setting tends to depend on the skills and interests of individual staff members, since work is viewed as highly specialised. Hence, there is a huge variation in availability of services across different areas. Health authorities regard themselves as having no clear statutory role to provide treatment to this client group, since the group is in the grey area between justice, health and social services. Nevertheless, there seems to be a growing recognition that, given the specialist psychological and psychiatric resources required for such work, the service is best provided by health authorities.

Education

Within the education system there is no general strategy for working with sexually abusive adolescents, although, as in other establishments, some teachers and educational psychologists are addressing this issue, especially in residential schools which cater for learning disabled or behaviourally disturbed pupils.

The prison service

The recognition of the need for specialist treatment of sex offenders has also been made by the prison service. At present core group treatment programmes are being run in six prisons in England and Wales, for those sex offenders who are serving a sentence of at least four years and are, therefore, judged to be most at risk of serious reoffending. In young offender institutions there is no national initiative and treatments for sexual abusers will depend on availability of interested and skilled staff. A 1993 report from the British Psychological Society noted that six of these institutions now have their own psychology staff.

Secure establishments

Secure residential facilities are available for those adolescents whose specialist needs cannot be met elsewhere and who pose a danger to themselves or others. A large number of these young people will have been sentenced under Section 53 of the Children and Young Persons' Act 1933 and will, therefore, be the responsibility of the Home Office. In addition to a limited number of secure places available within local authority community homes with education, there are two national facilities – the Glenthorne Youth Treatment Centre in Birmingham and Aycliffe Young People's Centre in County Durham. Both these national centres aim to provide offence-focused work. The Aycliffe Centre has a specialised residential unit for sexually abusive adolescents, which enables intensive treatment in an environment in which they do not have to conceal the nature of their difficulties from the other residents.

A few adolescent sexual abusers are also found in special hospitals, which are being incorporated into the National Health Service. These patients have been deemed to be suffering from a mental disorder within the meaning of the 1983 Mental Health Act. Some of them will have a mental illness, others will have brain damage and yet others have psychopathic disorders (see also Perkins 1991).

Secure residential facilities encounter serious obstacles to successful intervention. Local authority secure units often have little access to specialised services and many offenders will spend their time without receiving any offence-focused treatment. Epps (1994a) describes treatment interventions for sexual abusers in a Youth Treatment Centre and warns about the problem of generalising behaviour from the institution to the community. He also highlights the demoralising situation of releasing clients from security who are still judged as posing a serious risk, or detaining those who no longer do so, simply on the basis of the lifespan of a detention order. Briggs (1994), working with sexually abusive adults in a special hospital setting, stresses the need for continued offence-focused treatment when the client returns to the community. Both writers emphasise the need for staff training, which is often lacking. They also recognise the challenge of maintaining staff motivation when working with seriously damaged clients over a long period of time, often with little evidence of therapeutic change.

Multi-agency programmes

The 1992 NCH report recommended multi-disciplinary collaboration between agencies in the provision of community based treatment services for adolescent sexual abusers. Although there have been several such initiatives in recent years, some have floundered at the planning stage and others have had to close due to staffing changes and the lack of appropriate management support. The Greater Manchester Adolescent Programme (G-MAP) is probably the best example of a long running multi-agency project. It was set up in 1988 between social services, probation, the NSPCC and the health service and provides assessment and both group and individual treatment. A fuller description can be found in O'Callaghan and Print (1994) and the issue is widely discussed in a number of publications (e.g. Marshall and Eccles 1991).

Therapeutic context

Relationship between practitioner and client

Before embarking on any assessment or treatment work with sexually abusive adolescents the practitioner must appreciate the specialised nature of the therapeutic relationship with the client. The extent to which this relationship is different from those with non-abusive clients will depend on the agency in which the worker is located.

Psychological problems have traditionally been addressed through psychotherapy and counselling and this form of interaction with the client requires belief in what the client describes and the ability to maintain a non-judgemental stance. These are viewed as essential in order to promote emotional and behavioural change (e.g. Rogers 1959). Indeed, there is some evidence for the view that simply experiencing this kind of interaction with a therapist, or having a 'therapeutic alliance', is the most important factor for change and that the type of therapy is irrelevant (Luborsky et al. 1985).

There are two main reasons why this traditional kind of 'therapeutic alliance' is not suited to treatment work with sex offenders: it does not serve the needs of potential future victims and it rarely promotes behavioural change.

Staff sometimes feel they must apologise if they 'like' their abusive clients, so strong is the view that a 'person is his behaviour'. However, as in all kinds of psychological and counselling therapies, feeling positive regard for the client is essential, since a therapeutic alliance must still be formed. If staff feel unable to respect clients who have abused others – that is, they are unable to separate the abuse from the individual – they are probably not suited to this kind of work.

Motivation in the client

One of the preconditions for inclusion in most treatment programmes addressing other kinds of psychological problems is strong motivation to change. The view that unmotivated individuals can be helped will not be accepted easily by traditional therapists. But in reality, few sexually abusive adolescents are sufficiently uncomfortable with their behaviour to seek out treatment. Their denial of the problem helps them to preserve a reasonable level of self esteem. So the starting point for treatment cannot depend on an abundance of self motivation.

Mandated attendance for treatment is, in many ways, preferable to voluntary participation. Many abusers only present for treatment because there is a short term gain, such as a community disposal following a court appearance. Moreover, there is a high risk of early dropout or withdrawal when sessions become emotionally demanding.

Attendance can be mandated in a number of ways, either by legal requirement, or linked to other statutory agency involvement. A supervision order with specific requirements, a probation order with a condition of treatment, statutory supervision on release from custody or a deferred sentence are examples of the former; case conference recommendations relating to concerns about the safety of other children in the household are an example of the latter.

Once the adolescent has joined a treatment programme he has to be encouraged to take responsibility for his difficulties, because although attendance can be mandated, actual behaviour change can only occur from within the client. The techniques of motivational interviewing (Miller and Rollnick 1991) can be useful in this regard. Using non-confrontational techniques the therapist aims to increase the discrepancy between the client's view of his present problems and his possible future behaviour. Another way of increasing client motivation in group settings is to employ the support and encouragement of fellow group members who are highly motivated.

Working in the criminal justice system

Therapists who offer psychological treatment in more traditional settings rarely become involved in making decisions about people's lives and indeed would resist any opportunity to do so. However, in the case of sexual abusers, it is often necessary to inform the court and other agencies about the assessment and treatment process and, in some cases, be a party to decision making which will have a major impact on the life of a young person. For example, risk assessment might indicate that an abuser needs to be placed in a secure setting, or failure to respond to treatment may prevent the implementation of a previous plan for family reunification. The issue of public safety has always to be uppermost, which means that therapists who work with this client group have to exert considerable control over clients' lives.

Another consequence of the imperative to protect others is the need for open communication between all professionals involved in a case, so that there is limited confidentiality. In an important sense, society is the primary client since, although the adolescent abuser may be receiving treatment, the overarching aim of the intervention is to protect other potential victims; any general psychological improvement in the abuser is a bonus. Naturally the two goals are often closely linked.

Open communication also means access by all professionals to all the documentation about the abuser. Statements made by abuse victims are indispensable in an assessment of the likely truth of an abuser's account, although it also has to be borne in mind that sexual abuse victims tend to play down, rather than exaggerate, the facts. The typical abuser minimises aspects of his abusive behaviour, most typically the seriousness of the assaults, the frequency of their occurrence and the use of threats or force in carrying them out or ensuring secrecy. It is unfortunate that the adversarial nature of our criminal justice system encourages minimisation, due to the defence solicitor's role, which is one of representing his client's interests above all others. The nature of evidence and the burden of proof also result in extensive plea bargaining practices.

The limited nature of confidentiality in treatment work with abusers must be communicated to them at the start of contact, particularly in relation to disclosure of previously unreported abusive behaviour. It is generally the case that if there is an identifiable victim, the relevant agencies will be informed.

Treatment philosophy

All those in a treatment programme should be informed about the basis of intervention. Issues such as what constitutes sexually abusive behaviour and an explanation of the rationale behind intervention are particularly important, since these are often misunderstood. Points of emphasis should include the fact that adolescent abuse of young children is rarely a one-off experiment and that the goal of treatment is control and not cure of sexual attraction to children.

Treatment outcome is not always successful and the worker has to be able to accept that some clients are unchanged after lengthy interventions. This may be due to the complexity of the problem, personality difficulties or other contextual factors such as family rejection.

Interaction with the therapist

The style of interaction between the therapist and client is quite distinct from traditional styles of counselling. The usefulness of insight-based therapies, which search for unconscious feelings, has yet to be demonstrated in the reduction of risk. Instead, work focuses on the adolescents' thoughts, feelings and behaviours within a cognitive-behavioural framework.

Most individuals hope that others will like them and approve of them. This is especially true of sexual abusers and is one of the reasons why they minimise their account. By playing down what they did they believe that the therapist will like them more. Indeed they will have presented their modified account to many listeners, some of whom will have willingly accepted it, thus reinforcing that particular version of events. The therapist should convey the idea that society's view of sex offenders is misguided and that such people are not 'evil' or 'perverted', but have behaved inappropriately and caused distress to others. This explanation then leads into why sexual abusers typically present for treatment in a state of denial and minimisation, unable to face up to the reality of what they have done and therefore unlikely to achieve behaviour change.

The therapeutic style is one of confronting, firmly housed within a framework of support and respect for the individual. This challenging style is often misunderstood by some professionals as being punitive or conveying dislike to the clients. It should never appear to be either of these, but as a way of respectfully challenging the abuser's story in order to help him become fully accountable for his actions.

Unreported abusive behaviour

Those who work in certain settings, particularly health, may be faced with the dilemma of a young person asking for help with his sexual abuse of a child, without the statutory agencies being aware of the incident. His parents may request that there is no reporting and investigation of the assault, but are nonetheless supportive of their son's need of treatment, to avoid its repetition in the future.

However, treatment without statutory involvement is considered to be bad practice. Firstly there is an identifiable victim, who may be in need of help and counselling. Secondly, the lack of a victim's statements renders the worker totally dependent on what the abuser says. Thirdly, if the abuser abruptly ceases to attend, there is no way of persuading him back, and fourthly, working in this manner would collude with the secrecy on which sexual abuse thrives. The best course of action is to explain the difficulties and encourage the young person and his parents to report the matter, so that the victim's interests can be taken into consideration.

Rights and responsibilities

Regardless of the variety of agencies dealing with the abuser, attempts must always be made to balance society's rights and those of the abuser. Professionals are often faced with the dilemma of deciding who is their primary 'client'. Is it the offender, the agency, their institution, or society at large? Further confusion abounds in deciding what they are trying to do. Is it treatment? Is it an 'intervention'? Is it a diversion from custody scheme, or a mixture of all three? Whichever label is chosen has implications for the way in which the agency manages abusers and will dictate the form and content of service delivery. Consideration of these issues is essential for all practitioners if they are to be able to make the correct ethical and legal choices for their clients (Bohmer 1983).

Whilst it is important to be able to mandate treatment for sexually abusive persons, as with all other treatments, the individual has the right to refuse it. It is pointless for a court to mandate that a young person attend a treatment programme if he does not want to go. Apart from being possibly unethical, it would probably be ineffective, since behaviour change requires commitment from within the individual. In situations of this kind, it might be more appropriate to further assess the abuser's motivation and address those aspects which may be causing resistance. Often there is denial in the family itself and the parents are unwilling to accept their child has a problem. The effect of the family members upon the level of motivation in the young abuser cannot be over-emphasised (Thomas 1991).

Such issues are also pertinent in the case of people who drop out of treatment programmes and decisions have to be made about what should be done with them. Ultimately, one has to accept that a young person may choose to face other legal consequences, such as a period of imprisonment, rather than become involved in, or remain committed to, a treatment programme.

All young people who have committed abusive acts should have the right to receive treatment and this should take account of their particular needs, including race, culture and disability. With the current limited availability of treatment facilities, it is likely that these aspects are often overlooked or unsatisfied.

In addition to the right to treatment, the intervention should also be the most effective and least intrusive available and set in the least restrictive environment, dependent upon the level of risk. All these considerations are likely to be controversial, since this area of work is in its infancy and research knowledge is slow to accumulate. There is a view, however, that offence-specific cognitive-behavioural work is more effective than insight-based therapies (Ryan 1987) and most treatment programmes are developing along these lines. The American literature also views group work as being the treatment of choice (Ross and Loss 1991), but such groups are still thin on the ground in this country. So, an exact fit between treatment needs and available facilities rarely exists. Moreover, on a practical level there is often ignorance of what treatment facilities are available in the locality, or a mistrust of other agencies and a consequent reluctance to refer a young person elsewhere.

Many young clients have other psychological or psychiatric problems. These must be considered in their own right and referrals should be made to the relevant services. Becker et al. (1991) found that 42% of their sample of juvenile sex offenders had appreciable depressive problems and that the symptomatology was more severe in those who had themselves been victims of sexual abuse. Moreover, the risk of suicide should always be considered in a young person.

Many professionals fall into the trap of feeling responsible for behaviour change in their clients. Whilst it is their responsibility to be aware of and address the factors that may impede progress, they have to accept that ultimately their client may not be able or ready to change his behaviour. At this point he may have to be excluded from a treatment programme, in order to maintain its credibility and to prevent the mistaken assumption that being in treatment is equivalent to behaviour change.

In practice, the most sensible approach to the issue of the client's rights is through the drawing up of a contract at the start of contact with the young person. This should spell out many of the aspects described above, including what the agency expects of him and what the client can expect from the agency.

Perhaps the most important right of the young person in treatment is to be regarded as an individual of equal worth to everyone else, so that aside from his sexually abusive behaviour, full consideration is always given to his feelings, his welfare and his future life plan.

Monitoring outcomes

Most of those who practise in the field of sex offending seem to have faith in the value of their treatment programmes, but this does not address society's concern regarding treatment efficacy and stopping future abusive behaviour. Ironically, the issue of treatment effectiveness is often the least concern of the busy professional and few treatment programmes appear to incorporate any attempt to measure outcome. Moreover, their expectation is not to prevent all future abuse, since treatment can only aim to control and contain, not cure, deviant sexual interests.

The ideal test of outcome would involve monitoring all those individuals who have been treated and untreated, recording further commission of sexual offences over the next 20 years and comparing the differences between the two groups. Unfortunately, there are obvious drawbacks in this research design.

It cannot be assumed that all sex offenders who do not receive treatment will go on to commit future offences. Indeed, West (1987) argued that the typical sex offender appears in court only once in his lifetime. Such claims are countered with recognition of the fact that only a small minority of all sexually abusive behaviour is reported and reaches the courts (Fisher and Thornton 1993).

So, the only pure test of treatment effectiveness is to record the recidivism rates of a treated group and compare them to the recidivism rates of a matched control group who have received no treatment. In most areas of practice, however, this would be an ethically unacceptable experimental design, since some sex offenders would have to be deprived of treatment. Even if this were achieved, the period of time over which recidivism rates should be recorded would have to be a number of years. Clearly, all treatment could not remain on hold until publication of results. There are already some early results concerning adult sex offenders that have overcome ethical difficulties, employ matched control groups (Marques et al. 1994) and indicate a tendency towards lower reoffending rates in the treated group.

Most treatment programmes depend upon estimates of recidivism rates for untreated and treated adult offenders. Such estimates vary widely, depending upon the type of offender studied, the length of treatment programme and the length of follow-up period. Marshall and Barbaree (1990) quote untreated recidivism rates of 12.5% after 1–2 years, 27.3% after 2–4 years and 60% after 4 years. They present treated recidivism rates of 5.5%, 7.1% and 25% after the same follow-up periods.

The relationship between adolescent and adult sexually abusive behaviour is still poorly understood. A small number of studies have attempted to follow up adolescents who have been in treatment programmes and record the rates of sexual reoffending. A full review can be found in Vizard et al. (1995), who report that most of the studies employed only small numbers of sexually abusive adolescents and that the follow-up periods were relatively short. Smith and Monastersky (1986) followed 112 adolescent offenders for an average of 29 months after treatment and found that 14 of them reoffended sexually and 35 reoffended non-sexually. Becker (1990) reported new sexual offences in five out of 205 adolescent abusers after a follow-up period of one year. Although such results seem impressive, Vizard et al. also report the early study of Doshay (1943) which recorded the recidivism rates for 106 untreated adolescent sex offenders over six years and found that just two of them reoffended sexually.

The present state of knowledge about sexually abusive behaviour does not yet elucidate which aspects of a treatment programme are clearly linked to risk reduction. Nonetheless, despite the lack of experimental treatment outcome data, there is fair agreement within the field about the desired goals, or outcomes of an intervention programme, which are believed to be linked to a reduction in future risk. These are usually a decrease in denial, accepting responsibility for offending behaviour, understanding the offence cycle and development of victim empathy. Other peripheral aspects, not directly offence focused, but probable mediators of abusive behaviour, are also seen as important, including self esteem, self efficacy, and social isolation. All of these aspects of an individual's behaviour can be 'measured' before treatment begins and after it finishes, to see if there are any differences. The outcome measures utilised by different programmes vary and some goals are more difficult to measure than others. Ideally, all treatment programmes should aim to use the same outcome measures, to enable comparisons and further empirical knowledge of the dynamics of adolescent abusive behaviour. One such project is already under way in Britain (Debelle et al. 1993) which is attempting a multi-centre treatment outcome study.

An outcome evaluation study of group treatment programmes for adult abusers of children has been recently published (Beckett et al. 1994). This utilised 11 different questionnaire measures, some of which were related to offence behaviour and others to more general aspects of personality and social functioning, administered pre- and post-treatment. The report identified changes in many of the measures following treatment and confirmed the value of cognitive-behavioural treatment for sex offenders. The future offence records of those men who participated in the study will be monitored for several years to see if there is any significant relationship between acquisition of treatment goals and the commission of future sexual offences.

There are a number of means at the disposal of practitioners who are concerned to incorporate an outcome evaluation aspect. The most common method is based on professional judgement of progress, linked to treatment goals earlier described. However, this approach is often criticised as subjective and therefore open to bias and distortion by the individual practitioner. Ratings by other practitioners involved with an individual help overcome some of these difficulties. Moreover, if treatment has taken place within a group setting, it is useful for the members to be involved in a peer rating of progress exercise, in which they rate their own and each other's progress against some identifiable standard, usually with outstanding similarity to professional ratings. One clear and useful measure for this group exercise is the six-step progress rating model devised by Smets and Cebula (1987).

There are several questionnaires available which can be administered before and after treatment to produce a more objective measure of change. In some cases they are restricted for use by particular professions, or require specific training before they can be reliably used. Few of these measures specifically address sexually abusive behaviours in adolescents, with the notable exception of the Multiphasic Sex Inventory (Nichols and Molinder 1984) which has a version for young people. It is a 300-item true/false questionnaire, for use with known abusers, which asks about all aspects of individuals' sexuality, including child abuse, rape and indecent exposure. It is intended as an assessment tool and can also be used as a measure of treatment outcome. It provides a profile of the different features of sexually abusive behaviour such as denial of deviant interests, sexual obsessions, social sexual desirability, cognitive distortions, justifications for sexual abuse and motivation for treatment. In its use with adolescents it is sometimes criticised for the sexually explicit and distasteful nature of some of the items, but this is probably unavoidable when working with clients who have sexually deviant interests.

Several questionnaires which have been developed for use with adult sex offenders could also be administered to adolescents. Other questionnaires can be used to assess the more peripheral issues and adolescent versions are usually available. For example, the Offer Self-Image Questionnaire (Offer et al. 1982) gives a profile of how an adolescent views himself in relation to his body, his family, his school, his work performance and other variables.

One of the most difficult areas in which to measure change is victim empathy. The fear is often expressed that abusers simply learn what to say about the experiences of their victims and can therefore tick the correct answers on questionnaires, but that their actual level of empathy with what their victims experienced remains unchanged. What abusers think and feel about their victims is a complex issue, with attitudes embedded at different levels of awareness. There is no valid, objective measure of victim empathy yet available.

In practice victim empathy is best assessed by careful observation of comments that abusers make about their situation. They often state that the abuse was all their own responsibility, but will reveal victim-blaming beliefs at other times, when they are off guard. In group treatment this often occurs when they are asking questions of other members in a 'hot seating' scenario, when they personally feel less under scrutiny.

The concern that abusers in treatment can learn what to say about their victims, but not really change, is a criticism often levelled at all aspects of cognitive-behavioural interventions. This is, of course, a possible outcome of participation and should always be borne in mind when assessing progress. Most importantly, it underlines the need for co-operation and good communication between agencies, so that information about behaviour both inside and outside treatment can be shared. Any occurrence of sexually abusive or sexually inappropriate behaviour, poor anger control, lack of assertion skills, social isolation or worsening school or work performance should be communicated with the treatment centre, since it provides one of the essential means of monitoring outcomes. Effective communication between professionals will highlight those individuals who can talk about their sexually abusive behaviour, but whose level of risk remains unchanged. But, as with every other aspect of work in this area, workers need to be cautious and modest about the extent of probable achievement.

11

Professional Reports on Abusive Adolescents

Surya Bhate and Masud Hoghughi

Many professionals are requested to provide reports regarding abusive adolescents to the court, solicitors or tribunals, yet few have received formal training in report writing. Such reports are different from those written for other professionals, such as GPs and social workers, since writers may be required to give verbal evidence as expert witnesses. Reports for the criminal court (youth court for most juveniles) may vary according to the writer's profession but are likely to have a similar structure and, in the case of abusive adolescents, to cover broadly the same areas.

Purpose of the report

Report for the judicial process may be requested by the defence, prosecution or the court. It may be requested at different stages in the prosecution process. Prosecution or defence may seek a report before the trial but the judge or magistrates may request a report after the defendant has pleaded guilty or has been found guilty but prior to sentence being passed.

The report, to be useful, will need to take account of the purpose for which it was requested. The content and focus may vary according to the source of the request. It is, therefore, important to ascertain the brief before writing the report. The request for the report should contain detailed instructions from the solicitor or the court regarding their areas of concern. Sometimes referral agents are not sure of what is of concern, in which case discussion should gradually identify their wishes. The writer may then address additional issues which increase understanding of the adolescent's behaviour, as he or she sees fit. The defence solicitor or local authority may be looking for explanations of the offending, further risk to the victim or the adolescent and others of the community, commentary on suggested dispositions and a specialist view of what the best outcome would be. Each statement needs to be evaluated against possible hostile examination.

Occasionally a defendant's fitness to plead and fitness to stand trial are raised by the defence solicitors. These issues are usually raised when the defendant is facing serious charges or there are circumstances which suggest that the adolescent may have been in an abnormal state of mind at the time of the offence.

The professional as expert witness

Expert witnesses are now called to provide opinions whenever the case is out of the ordinary. They are called when the issues at stake are sufficiently ambiguous for either party to be able to use them to advantage or for the court to feel that it needs an independent assessment of the critical issues. All these referrals are dependent on the expert witness who, by virtue of special knowledge, skill, training and experience, can bring 'added value' to the judge or jury (Freckleton 1987).

This presumes that not only is the individual expert sufficiently qualified in the subject to regarded as 'expert' but also that the subject matter is solid enough to be relied upon by the court in accounting for the areas of concern. In the UK, the qualifications of the 'expert' who may give evidence in regard to sexually abusive adolescents are not usually in doubt. In the US, expert witnesses are required to have had additional training and qualifications irrespective of their primary discipline, be it psychology, psychiatry or social work. Hostile cross-examination on this point seeks to ensure, more than in the British system, that the expert witness really knows what he or she is talking about.

Even the expert, however, cannot go beyond the limits of the discipline and here the solidity of the subject matter leaves much to be desired. As can be seen throughout this book, there are major uncertainties about the scientific status of work in this area. Despite some sterling work, there is not enough consistency in the interpretation of material or agreement on assessment and treatment methodologies; nor is there a generally accepted body of knowledge, and above all, what is known has not enough predictive value to allow us to regard this area of activity as 'scientific'. Judged by these criteria, there are major difficulties in establishing the scientific basis of much expert opinion in the area of adolescent sexual abuse, particularly when the reliability and validity of many measuring instruments (e.g. deviant fantasy) are seriously questionable.

Nevertheless, it has been cogently argued (Gudjonsson 1990) that psychologists in particular have clinical, experimental, actuarial and advisory roles which are invaluable to the court. These utilise potentially the full spectrum of scientific psychology, rather than opinion, and can provide either valuable information for the court on specific issues about the case or generic reports on the status of a subject, such as treatment outcomes for adolescent abusers.

Ethical issues

Theoretically at least, the expert witness is briefed to provide a report that represents the views of his or her discipline regarding the abusive adolescent. In reality, because the discipline is not yet scientific, the vagaries of the parent discipline (e.g. psychiatry or psychology) compound individual differences among practitioners and produce sometimes startlingly divergent assessments of the adolescent's condition and risk potential. It is important for the report writer to state the reliability and validity of the sources of information and the predictive solidity of the expert opinion. This seems important as a means of establishing the probity of the subject matter and opinions related to it.

A related difficulty arises from poor validity of risk estimation (see Chapter 3). There is little question that even in grave cases when a custodial sentence is certain, the court is interested in the likely level of continuing risk by the offender. The expert's dilemma is how far to state explicitly that risk estimation is an unreliable activity; how far to use subtle techniques of assessment to gain information not overtly understood to be incriminating the defendant; how far to try and protect the defendant against the worst court outcome or, alternatively, how far to try and protect the community.

It seems ethically reasonable to inform the defendant about the expert witness's role, base discipline, particular areas of interest to his or her inquiry, for whom the report is being written and the basis on which the expert will arrive at his or her conclusions. The current status of sex offenders in the UK and pressures of time, emphasised by legal aid constraints, make this form of exchange as rare as it is necessary. This is essential in relation to adolescents whose life is likely to be blighted by careless evaluation and disposal (see also Bluglass 1990, Chiswick 1985).

These difficulties interact with the expert witness's own attitude to sexual offending, especially against children. This might lead the clinician to over-value or underplay the different interpretations of the evidence, particularly when the report is for either prosecution or defence. Unless questions of criminal responsibility are involved, we believe it is best for the *court* (i.e. the judge or magistrate) to request the report rather then either party in the adversarial process. This may go some way towards mitigating the wholly understandable tendency to be economical with the truth for the defence and damning for the prosecution.

Admissibility and confidentiality

There are strict rules of evidence governing what may and may not be presented in court. Almost anything general regarding the case (e.g. intent of the abuser, how developmentally normal his behaviour may be) may fall into this category, leaving only specific issues to be presented to the court and jury. It is the judge's duty to admit certain forms of evidence. For example, the defendant may recount to the expert witness a history of abuse and subsequent conversations with his victim – both of which, as previous chapters have shown, are important in the defendant's assessment. However, they may not be recounted to the open court as they constitute hearsay.

Issues regarding disclosure of information will vary. Ordinarily, when a solicitor requests a report it is assumed that the adolescent has given consent for disclosure of information to the solicitor. Great care must be taken not to exploit clients, as the information they provide may be used not only to determine their management but also in relation to other overriding interests of public safety. Additional complications arise if a client gives a history of abusing children (other than the victim) or continuing to be a risk to children. Professionals have a duty to protect children and in the UK it is permissible, indeed required of professionals, to breach confidence in these circumstances. The best practice is not to promise the adolescent complete confidentiality. For example, an adolescent sex offender examined for indecent assault on a 5-year-old girl while babysitting, admitted to similar acts on several young children. The information was relevant to the assessment and included in report to the court. Apart from sexual offences, many adolescents admit to other delinquent behaviour and related difficulties. These may well be relevant to the assessment, treatment and disposal recommendations and should, therefore, be stated in the report. Whether the person who commissioned the report (typically the defence solicitor) will be prepared to convey them to the court is another matter and should not be the expert witness's concern.

Contents of the report

Magistrates often do not have more than 30 minutes to read the document pertaining to the case before the hearing. In Crown Court, judges may have somewhat longer but they need most of that time for evaluating the contending evidence, of which the expert's is only a small part. It is helpful to aim for conciseness, rigorous, solid though not abstruse arguments, written in plain unjargonistic language, and clear linkage between factual evidence and professional judgement. Clear structure, breaking up of text with subheadings and use of phrases and bullet points rather than full sentences to state 'facts' all help make the report more readable and useful. Rather than repeating readily available information from other reports, barest reference should be made to them.

Layout

It is essential that the layout of the report allows the reader to find relevant sections quickly and coherently. Subject headings with appropriate page numbers should be listed, commencing with client's (defendant's) relevant demographic details and concluding with recommendations and prognosis.

Basic information

This should include:

1. name, age, sex and current address of the defendant, dates, times and place of examinations for purpose of preparing report;
2. information about the report writer to include present post, experience and qualifications, with dates and special experience, if any;
3. details of the offence(s) and relevant sources of information, such as committal papers, including defendant's witness and victim statements.

Family background and personal history

Social inquiry reports usually provide relevant family background. However, whenever possible, the report writer should see both parents and, if relevant, extended family members as part of the assessment. Assessment should include views about parents, parental relationship and its vicissitudes, history of parental mental illness, intrafamilial abuse and criminality, if any. This information is important as studies consistently report a high prevalence of unstable and disturbed family backgrounds, including parental separations, violence and experience of physical abuse and neglect; only a minority of adolescents live with both natural parents.

The relevance of these areas will vary amongst offenders. However, it is probably safer to be over-inclusive rather than to skimp on certain areas. If the information elicited is not relevant or a significant amount or a whole category of information is not available this should be noted.

Educational and occupational history

This can be obtained from the defendant and parents and, where possible, should be corroborated by the school. Level of intellectual functioning, if relevant, can be easily ascertained from or by psychologists. A proportion of adolescent sexual offenders have educational, social and other handicaps. Teachers are a rich source of information. Areas of inquiry should include the client's educational achievement, potential, social skills, truancy and ability to get on with peers and staff in school. History of difficulties including violence, drug taking and suspension known to the school will be key factors in shaping assessment and recommendations. High incidence of disruptive behaviour, academic under-achievement, diagnosed learning disability and chronic truancy are often seen in abusive adolescents. Many find themselves in YTS programmes. Occupational history gives clues to the progress or otherwise of the young person in coping with the transition to work and the possibility of rehabilitation.

Personality and habits

Detailed assessment of the personality make-up using good instruments can be provided by psychologists. However, it is helpful to inquire about general sociability, impulsiveness, maturity, anger control, temperament, moral behaviour and the like through open-ended questions. Any significant abnormality can be subject to specialised assessment by a psychologist.

Many young people go through a phase of abusing substances. A detailed history of alcohol, tobacco intake and substance abuse is relevant in assessment of adolescent sexual offenders, as it has implications for treatment. Corroboration of this history is advisable though parents and others often do not know the full facts.

The examination

This is the crux of the report, reflecting the writer's own observations and citing reasons for reaching conclusions. This section may profitably commence with observations regarding the client's general presentation, demeanour and attitude. Presence of apparent mental abnormality, mannerisms, eye contact and level of co-operation will be noted. The interviewer aims always to create a relaxed atmosphere in which the adolescent can be helped to understand reasons for the assessment and limits of the confidentiality of the material. This needs careful explanation to both adolescent and family. Having dealt with the non-emotive aspect of the task, attempt should be made to inquire about his history of offending, tracing the development of abusive behaviour over time. This should be followed by discussion of the index offence, its antecedents and consequences for the offender.

The sexual offence may be (1) *non-contact* including exhibitionism, voyeurism and obscene phone calls; (2) *sexual molestation*, against the victim(s); (3) *sexual assault*, which is usually attempted rape or rape using physical force. Use of coercion as a means of overcoming victim resistance requires critical assessment. A small proportion of adolescent perpetrators may, indeed, use a much more sophisticated grooming process of befriending both the family and the victim. Information about location of the offence says much about the planned or opportunistic nature of the offence. Behaviour is more likely to be predatory and compulsive where the victim is attacked in a public place. Access to victim statements is important but not always possible. This will allow the adolescent's deliberate distortions, propensity to underplay or to present a plausible account to be tested.

In Chapter 4 the main areas of assessment were listed. That list or the worker's own should be followed rigorously, if necessary over a number of sessions, until 'adequate' information is available. As already noted, this has to be reconciled with exigencies of time and other commitments. A sensitive area is the perpetrator's own history of sexual abuse, still often denied by adolescent boys. This takes time and delicate questioning to produce accurate answers.

If there is evidence of mental abnormality at the time of the offence or examination, the adolescent may have to be referred for other expert opinion or specialised assessment carried out by the report writer.

Opinion

This section contains the formulation or primary hypothesis attempting to explain the adolescent's behaviour in the context of his development, life experiences, circumstances and the opportunities at the time the alleged offence was committed. Attempt should also be made to provide some risk assessment based on a detailed knowledge of the case. It should be made explicit that general risk assessment is context bound and imprecise.

Option appraisal

In this final section, attempt should be made to outline options available to the court, without overstepping its prerogative of deciding disposals. The report should comment on the presence or absence of abnormality, the client's commitment to change, likelihood of benefit from treatment and availability of treatment facilities. Often, treatment and supervision require joint working between agencies. Prior discussion and agreement between those agencies should be highlighted and confirmed, as in a supervision (or probation) order with condition of treatment. The writer should confirm that in the event of the court preferring this option, the named medical practitioner (usually consultant psychiatrist) and a social worker, are agreeable to this course of action. Where outpatient or other specialised work, such as drug rehabilitation, is available and acceptable, this should be stated.

Giving evidence in the court

Giving evidence in the court on a written report submitted is often a daunting and stressful experience, given the adversarial nature of British and American courts. There are no simple solutions. It is useful to have some idea of the layout of the court and outline of the case. The latter, termed 'skeleton', can normally be obtained from the instructing solicitor(s) and helps alert the writer to any sensitive issues that may be pursued under cross-examination. Report writers should familiarise themselves with details of the case the previous night and enter the court to hear relevant preceding evidence. Formal dress and presentation in court are normally expected. The witness will be asked to swear on oath (or affirm non-religiously) and asked to confirm name and qualifications. It is important to distinguish between qualifications and experience when establishing expertise. Witnesses are expected to focus on the judge, facing and addressing answers to him or her. Brevity will be appreciated, as will clarity and careful address, particularly since some questions may be repeated and witness will be caught out if inconsistent. It is generally inadvisable to score points off the cross-examining lawyer. They may not know as much about the expert's subject but they are expert at cross-

examination and entrapping the expert if the testimony is not
solid. Honesty, straightness and making defensible statements
are a secure way of proceeding, particularly since the expert is
not in the dock and judges watch over the probity of opposing
lawyers' cross-examinations.

Conclusion

There appears to be little specific training given to professionals to equip them adequately for the role of expert witness.
Most witnesses seem to learn by trial and error exposure, often
in lower courts, though this can be significantly improved by
training, which seems necessary, given the increasing involvement of expert witnesses in both civil and criminal cases.

The best current advice on writing expert witness reports and
giving evidence can be summarised as follows:

1. Interview the adolescent on several occasions to indicate
   thoroughness, to establish rapport and the reliability of
   comments.
2. Interview carers and relevant members of the family.
3. Keep detailed record of the interviews as you may need to
   refer to them in cross-examination.

If called to give evidence:

1. Dress conservatively and relatively formally.
2. Adopt a serious professional attitude, being neither humble
   nor hostile. Remember you are not on trial and the court
   wants and needs your expertise and assistance.
3. Restrict your testimony to areas of your expertise. You must
   also know when to say 'I don't know'. Do not be expansive or
   speculate. It may backfire.
4. When responding to cross-examination, listen to the
   question carefully and turn to the judge while replying.
   The few seconds gained will allow you to marshal your
   thoughts. If unclear, ask the lawyer to clarify the questions
   and do not let him bully you into giving yes/no answers
   when these are inappropriate.

12

Considering the Workers

Masud Hoghughi

As professional work with abusive adolescents has grown, so workers and researchers have paid more attention to the necessary and desirable characteristics of the workers and the impact of such work. The volume of specific research and writing on the topic is, nevertheless, quite small. This is in part because many of the issues are not dissimilar to those which arise in working with any other high profile or high risk adolescent groups. Because of this, detailed references will not be given in the text.

Many of the points arising from work with abusers is covered in the preceding chapters. Additionally, readers might find it helpful to refer to a number of sources, such as the following, where a focused view of the main issues is presented: Briggs (1994), British Psychological Society (1995), Erooga (1994), Hoghughi (1978, 1988, 1992), Ryan and Lane (1991a).

The abusive adolescent

We have so far identified the major and most common characteristics of adolescents and responses appropriate to their condition. As the authors have consistently pointed out, despite the common feature of their abusive acts, the adolescents themselves vary widely in terms of their profiles. These include physical; intellectual/educational; home and family; social skills; anti-social behaviour and psychological differences.

Their impact on the *worker* may be because of a specific feature (e.g. physical attractiveness or high level aggression) or the severity of their profile. In either case, as with all other social exchanges, the impact would be somewhat along the dimension 'good–bad' or 'attractive–repulsive', including the midpoint judgement of 'neutral'.

The elements of this judgement include perceptions of the physical and psychological risk to the integrity of the worker, amenability to treatment and, therefore, risk of failure and possible censure.

The physical risk arises from the tendency of some adolescents to react aggressively when under pressure of rigorous questioning in assessment or confronting in treatment. Given their frequently weak internal controls, they sometimes react to pressure by attacking the worker. This is more probable in solo as opposed to group sessions, with female workers and in physically isolated environments. It is essential to work out 'worst scenarios' with individual adolescents and groups and take preventive action, if necessary by refraining from or terminating the encounter. An unsafe worker is not the most effective and may inadvertently be provoking actions which will damage him/her and rebound on the adolescent.

Additionally, the abusive adolescent may transfer powerful or otherwise unresolved feelings about women to the female worker and become sufficiently aroused to attempt sexual assault. Such assaults are not unknown. The process of evaluating the adolescent should include a specific assessment of *risk to the workers*, and this should be regularly reviewed and discussed with a supervisor or co-worker to ensure that the risk is contained and minimised.

The development of feelings for the worker refers to the phenomenon of 'transference', much discussed in dynamic psychology literature, which can be positive or negative. We have little specific knowledge of the relationship between transference and treatment efficacy with abusive adolescents. Motivation for continued treatment, always a sensitive issue, is at least better sustained when the relationship is good. We can assume that the more positive the relationship the better the abuser's response, as long as professional distance is safeguarded. This is the more important because of the psychological impact of abusers on workers. The whole topic of analysing and attempting to shape intimate abusive behaviour provides immense potential for the adolescent to 'get at' the worker. This can be done by withholding information, giving vividly graphic accounts of his acts, using obscene language, asking personal and pointed questions and the like.

The impact of these factors varies between community and institutional settings but not in a regular and predictable way.

Abusers who are not thought to be serious risks continue to function in the community. They are likely to understand better the need for self control and maintaining proprieties. On the other hand, they are more free to move around, in environments where the workers may not be well protected. They can plan and perpetrate acts against the relatively unprotected worker's person and property, with greater impunity than is possible in an institutional setting.

In institutions the risk would be modified by the number and quality of other youngsters involved in assessment and treatment. The sheer numbers involved, especially in group treatments, significantly increase the pressure on workers. This is particularly the case when the attitude of the more dominant group members to the worker is negative. On the other hand, the presence of other staff and generally greater structure of institutional settings and availability of serious sanctions may provide a source of security that is lacking in community treatment of abusers.

An aspect of institutional care which gives cause for concern is the youngsters' sexual targeting of each other. Anyone who has dealt with such groups in social services, probation, prison or health settings knows that it happens, though the extent is not known. What is known is that not all the sex is consensual. Some of the sexual targeting is known to staff and is sometimes ignored as a means of keeping the peace, mollifying the bullies and controlling some of the other inmates/patients.

Therapeutic (as opposed to custodial) workers are aware of sexual victimisation but often feel powerless to do anything about it. A major reason given by adolescents for running away from institutions is that they are abused. Whilst the possibility of this cannot be eliminated, open communication, a confidential complaint system, a non-violent and therapeutic as opposed to power-oriented regime and a good working relationship with the young people would go some way towards containing this problem.

The core issue around which all these other concepts revolve is the 'treatability' of the adolescents. This will be the result of the adolescent's history interacting with his current condition and the impact of treatment. The relationship between these facets is organic and ever changing. Nor can we speak of a youngster's treatability other than in relation to those who are attempting to treat him.

The features identified above lead workers to make a judgement very early on about how treatable the adolescent is within the skill constraints of the workers and resources of the organisation. This judgement affects the kind and amount of effort expended in trying to treat the abuser. Because the abuser is almost invariably referred by another (usually public) agency, the issue of treatability is potentially a source of conflict and anxiety for the worker.

There are no simple or sure-fire answers to any of these issues. The only sensible approach for the worker is to be aware of possible difficulties, evolve appropriate processes, procedures and response patterns to the most common and share them publicly to ensure that they are adequately dealt with.

The workers

Even in pure sciences, the workers' attributes affect what they achieve. This is much more the case in 'helping' professions, where there is considerable ambiguity and ambivalence in the work undertaken and we recognise that 'but for the grace of God' we might have been where our clients are.

Like the adolescent, workers also have a history which may or may not have included experience of physical, emotional or sexual abuse. This history interacts with their temperaments and subsequent history to determine their personal thoughts, feelings and behaviour patterns towards abusive adolescents – along 'positive–negative' or 'resilient–vulnerable' dimensions.

The prevailing 'self concept' or views of 'self efficacy' of workers is the embodiment of their history of coping with stresses and opportunities in the course of growing up and in their current circumstances. Their sense of security, maturity, resilience and competence in the face of problems, and insight into their own problem-solving ability, will critically determine how they deal with the special pressures of working with abusive adolescents.

Many forms of serious psychopathology and anti-social behaviour, such as violence and depression, are sufficiently alien to workers to allow them to maintain 'proper' professional distance from their clients. Sexual abusers are different. As adults, workers are likely to engage in a wide range of sexual practices and fantasies. When young they may have been sexually abused or may have engaged in sex with younger children, or coercively with peers. The detailed history taking, analysis of deviant fantasies and abusive practices, as well as certain forms of treatment, may reawaken memories and create sexual and emotional tensions that must be resolved. These will affect the degree to which they can maintain professional distance and deal with their clients in a dispassionate way.

Just as the adolescent may develop feelings for the worker in the process of 'transference', so the opposite may happen in 'counter-transference' – again either positively or negatively. The workers' own sexual needs and level and means of coping with stimulation and frustration will affect the way they deal with their clients. The positive or negative reactions to the adolescent's behaviour may affect the way they deal with their own sexual lives. In the early days of dealing with child sexual abuse, it became known that many workers were put off sex and could not carry on their normal lives for some time after examining victims.

The feeling of some workers that they are sullied and 'dirtied' by the experience of working with abusive adolescents is an aspect of identification with the victim. In part this arises from some workers' guilty recognition that they may have, or might have liked to have, behaved in a similar way to the abusers. The degree to which workers have insight into these feelings and are able to articulate them without resorting to 'defence mechanisms', such as denial, suppression, reaction formation and the like, will be important factors in their overall adaptation.

A further difficulty concerns the motivation for working with abusers. Frankly, adolescent abusers are not the most attractive group of youngsters and what they describe is ghastly by any standards. It is reasonable to ask oneself (and to allow others to ask) what working with the group says about the individuals who do it. This question is much simpler to ask than it is to answer. We need not pursue the motivational question too rigorously for people, such as psychologists and social workers, who deal with it daily as part of a wider category of disordered and anti-social youngsters. However, for others who choose to specialise in abusers, the motivational question needs to be constantly and publicly asked to ensure that workers remain aware of its implications. The fact that the work is of considerable benefit to society and, after all, 'someone has to do it', takes us some of the way to answering the question satisfactorily.

Working with sexual abusers places the worker in a position of power and control over the abuser. In an institutional setting particularly, this superior position allows the worker to create opportunities for sexually exploiting the young people – as has been shown in a number of cases where youngsters were systematically victimised by their carers. This is tempting, as some adolescents recognise the sexual vulnerability of the workers and knowingly set about to compromise them by some form of personal indiscretion. The worker's gender is relevant here, as it is across a range of other issues in working with abusive adolescents, although these are only just beginning to be systematically explored. Male workers have been shown to be at greater risk of socially prohibited behaviour with children of either gender, although it is not clear why they should be thought of as inflicting more harm, unless the issue is penetrative sex.

These are all topics that have to be faced at the start of work with sexually abusive adolescents. Insightful calm and resilience in the face of pressure are two of the most critical personal qualities to be sought in workers. They are part of a much larger list of ideal attributes which include intelligence, maturity, stability, sensitivity and compassion. They augment professional skills in different approaches to assessment and treatment, based on knowledge and understanding of the issues and practices involved.

Organisational issues

The above outline briefly describes the complex pressures, conflicts and frustrations which beset workers with abusive adolescents. They are the collective source of the stress which workers face, some of which is unique to this population. It is, however, debatable whether workers in this area are, on the whole, subject to greater stress than those who work with a range of other disordered adolescents. In general, working with deviant adolescents requires the most rigorous staffing and resource management policies. A number of the issues involved have been intensively covered elsewhere in relation to disordered adolescents so will not be repeated here (e.g. Warner Report 1992).

The workers' motivation and the possibility of ulterior motives for working with abusers, particularly in an institutional setting, has already been aired. This demands the most careful recruitment, selection and supervision to exclude the undesirable and monitor the activities of all workers to ensure that risk to them and the youngsters is minimised. The need to do this rigorously and closely is significantly higher in institutions, where the level and quality of contact massively increases the risks to both parties.

Given these risks, it is imperative to create a safe environment, whether in the institution or the community. The organisation needs to ensure that it knows where the staff and the young people are, what they are doing at all times and that either party can raise the alarm *and* obtain assistance promptly. This may require that both workers and youngsters work in 'transparent' and externally visible environments, even though there will be occasions when the need to cut out distraction (e.g. in covert conditioning) or privacy (as in plethysmography) limits such transparency.

The organisational issue also extends to whether work is undertaken singly, in co-working or as part of a team approach. There is no simple or universally accepted 'best' way. In general, and other things being equal, co-working or a team approach seems best, particularly when there is a lead worker for every case and the work proceeds after explicit assessment according to a shared, integrative treatment plan. The adolescent gets a powerful mix of inputs from team members with diverse strengths and skills. This allows rigorous and open case discussions and the establishment of a system by which danger signals can be picked up and communicated. Other team members can then act as co-supervisors. The disadvantage is that therapeutic relationships are more difficult to establish and sustain.

Where such team or co-working arrangements cannot be established and work has to be done singly, it is necessary to set up a clear monitoring structure, where the impact of the agency's involvement can be *publicly* analysed and aired, in the presence of the adolescent, his family, social worker, probation officer and other significant people. As part of this, explicit questions should be asked of the adolescent and the workers about the impact of the intervention on them as individuals, especially if there is any hint of questionable practices.

Clearly *the way* this is done is as important (if not more so) as whether it is done or not. The *process* or style of operating is critical in any area such as sexual abuse where everyone has strongly held views. Thus, the procedures having been established, the service providers need to reflect on and cultivate a style of management of workers which gives them a sense of security.

This, in turn, devolves upon clear statement of legislative rights and responsibilities; articulation of the value bases of the organisation; clear definition of the tasks and the methods to be utilised; limits of the authority and responsibility of each worker in relation to designated tasks and clients, and the awareness of team support both for day-to-day work and in the event of difficulties.

In the end workers' impact on adolescent abusers reflects the assurance and rigour with which they use their knowledge, understanding and skills. These can only be exercised to the full if they feel good enough about themselves to be able to face the challenge of abusive adolescents openly and go on giving of their best. The best care for the adolescents approximates to the best care for the workers. We hope this book has given some idea of the complexity of the work involved with abusive adolescents and what may need to be done to achieve this best.

References

Abel, G.G. (1987) 'Surveillance groups'. Paper presented at the annual meeting of the Association for the Behavioural Treatment of Sexual Abusers. Newport, Oregon.

Abel, G., Becker, J., Murphy, W. and Flanagan, B. (1975) 'Identifying dangerous child molesters', in Stuart, R.B. (ed.) *Violent Behaviour: Social Learning Approaches*, New York, Brunner Mazel.

Abel, G.G., Becker, J.V. and Skinner, L. (1983) 'Behavioural approaches to treatment of the violent sex offender', in Roth, L. (ed.) *Clinical Treatment of the Violent Person*, Washington, DC, NIMH Monograph series.

Abel, G.G., Becker, J.V., Cunningham-Rathner, J., Rouleau, J.L., Kaplan, M. and Reich, J. (1984) *The Treatment of Child Molesters* (available from G.G. Abel, Behavior Medicine Institute, 5791 Kingston Cross, Stone Mountain, GA 30087, USA).

Abel, G.G., Mittelman, M.S. and Becker, J.V. (1985) 'Sex offenders: results of assessment and recommendations for treatment', in Ben-Aron, M.H., Hucker, S.J. and Webster, C.J. (eds) *Clinical Criminology: The Assessment and Treatment of Criminal Behavior*, Toronto, M.&M. Graphics.

Abel, G.G., Becker, J.V., Mittelman, M., Cunningham-Rathner, J., Rouleau, J.L. and Murphy, W.D. (1987) 'Self-reported sex crimes of non-incarcerated paraphiliacs', *Journal of Interpersonal Violence*, 2(6), 3–25.

Adams, G.L. (1984) *Normative Adaptive Behaviour Checklist*, London, The Psychological Corporation.

Adams-Webber, J. (1979) *Personal Construct Theory: Concepts and Applications*, London, Wiley.

American Psychiatric Association (1987) *Diagnostic and Statistical Manual of Mental Disorders*, 3rd revised edn, Washington, DC. American Psychiatric Association.

American Psychiatric Association (1994) *DSM-IV*. Washington DC, American Psychiatric Association.

Amir, M. (1971) *Patterns in Forcible Rape*, Chicago, University of Chicago Press.

Arbuthnot, J. and Gordon, D.A. (1983) 'Moral reasoning development in correctional intervention', *Journal of Correctional Education*, 34, 133–138.

Arbuthnot, J. and Gordon, D.A. (1986) 'Behavioral and cognitive effects of a moral reasoning development intervention for high risk behavior – disordered adolescents', *Journal of Consulting and Clinical Psychology*, 34, 208–216.

Awad, G.A. and Saunders, E.B. (1989) 'Adolescent child molesters: clinical observations', *Child Psychiatry and Human Development*, 19, 195–206.

Awad, G.A. and Saunders, E.B. (1991) 'Male adolescent sexual assaulters: clinical observations', *Journal of Interpersonal Violence*, 6, 446–460.

Awad, G.A., Saunders, E.B. and Levene, J.A. (1984) 'A clinical study of male adolescent sexual offenders', *International Journal of Offender Therapy and Comparative Criminology*, 28, 105–116.

Bagley, C. (1985) 'Child sexual abuse: a child welfare perspective', in Levitt, K. and Wharf, B. (eds) *The Challenge of Child Welfare*, Vancouver, University of British Columbia Press.

Bagley, C. (1992) 'Characteristics of 60 children and adolescents with a history of sexual assault against others: evidence from a comparative study', *Journal of Forensic Psychiatry*, 3(2), 299–309.

Bagley, R. (1984) *Sexual Offenses against Children: Report of the Committee on Sexual Offenses against Children and Youths*, Ottawa, Government of Canada.

Bancroft, J. (1989) *Human Sexuality and its Problems*, Edinburgh, Churchill Livingstone.

Bandura, A. (1977) *Social Learning Theory*, Englewood Cliffs, NJ, Prentice-Hall.

Barbaree, H.E. (1990) 'Stimulus control of sexual arousal: its role in sexual assault', in Marshall, W.L., Laws, D.R. and Barbaree, H.E. (eds) *Handbook of Sexual Assault: Issues, Theories and Treatment of the Offender*, New York, Plenum Press.

Barbaree, H.E. and Cortoni, F.A. (1993) 'Treatment of the juvenile sex offender within the criminal justice and mental health systems', in Barbaree, H.E., Marshall, W.L. and Hudson, S.M. (eds) *The Juvenile Sex Offender*, New York, Guilford Press.

Barbaree, H.E., Marshall, W.L. and Hudson, S.M. (eds) (1993) *The Juvenile Sex Offender*, New York, Guilford Press.

Barbaree, H.E., Hudson, S.M. and Seto, M.C. (1993) 'Sexual assault in society: the role of the juvenile offender', in Barbaree, H.E., Marshall, W.L. and Hudson, S.M. (eds) *The Juvenile Sex Offender*, New York, Guilford Press.

Barlow, D.H. and Agras, W.S. (1973) 'Fading to increase heterosexual responsiveness in homosexuals', *Journal of Applied Behaviour Analysis*, 6, 355–366.

Baron, L. and Strauss, M.A. (1991) *Four Theories of Rape in American Society*, New Haven, CT, Yale University Press.

Battle, J. (1992) *Culture-Free Self-Esteem Inventory*, Austin, TX, Pro-Ed.

Baum, J.C., Clarke, H.B., McCarthey, W., Sandler, J. and Carpenter, R. (1986) 'An analysis of the acquisition and generalization of social skills in troubled youths: combining social skills training, cognitive self-talk, and relaxation procedures', *Child and Family Behavior Therapy* 8, 1–27.

Beck, A.T. (1976) *Cognitive Therapy and the Emotional Disorders*, New York, International Universities Press.

Beck, A.T. (1978a) *Beck Depression Inventory*, New York, The Psychological Corporation, Harcourt Brace Jovanovich.

Beck, A.T. (1978b) *Beck Hopelessness Scale*, New York, The Psychological Corporation.

Beck, A.T. (1990) *Beck Anxiety Inventory*, New York, The Psychological Corporation.

Becker, J.V. (1988) 'The effects of child sexual abuse on adolescent sexual offenders', in Wyatt, G.E. and Powell, E.J. (eds) *Lasting Effects of Sexual Abuse*, Beverly Hills, CA, Sage.

Becker, J.V. (1990) 'Treating adolescent sexual offenders', *Professional Psychology: Research and Practice*, 21(5), 362–365.

Becker, J.V. (1993) 'Adolescent sexual interest cardsort', in Hall, G.C.N. (ed.) *Sexual Aggression*, Bristol, PA, Taylor and Francis.

Becker, J.V. and Abel, G.G. (1985) 'Methodological and ethical issues in evaluating and treating adolescent sexual offenders', in Otey, E.M. and Ryan, G.D. (eds) *Adolescent Sex Offenders: Issues in Research and Treatment*, Rockville, MD, US Department of Health and Human Services.

Becker, J.V., Abel, G.G., Blanchard, E.B., Murphy, W.D. and Coleman, E. (1978) 'Evaluating social skills of sexual aggressives', *Criminal Justice and Behavior* 5, 357–368.

Becker, J.V. and Kaplan, M.S. (1988) 'The assessment of adolescent sex offenders', in Prinz, R.J. (ed.) *Advances in Behavioural Assessment of Children and Families: A Research Annual*. (pp. 97–118). Greenwich, CT: JAI Press, Inc.

Becker, J.V. and Kaplan, M.S. (1993) 'Cognitive-behavioural treatment of the juvenile sex offender', in Barbaree, H.E., Marshall, W.L. and Hudson, S.M. (eds) *The Juvenile Sex Offender*, New York, Guilford Press.

Becker, J.V. and Stein, R.M. (1991) 'Is sexual erotica associated with sexual deviance in adolescent males?', *International Journal of Law and Psychiatry*, 14, 85–95.

Becker, J.V., Cunningham-Rathner, J. and Kaplan, M.S. (1986a) 'Adolescent sexual offenders: demographics, criminal and sexual histories, and recommendations for reducing future offenses', *Journal of Interpersonal Violence*, 1, 431–445.

Becker, J.V., Kaplan, M.S., Cunningham-Rathner, J. and Kavoussi, R. (1986b) 'Characteristics of adolescent incest sexual perpetrators: preliminary findings', *Journal of Family Violence*, 1, 85–97.

Becker, J.V., Kaplan, M.S. and Kavoussi, R. (1988) 'Measuring the effectiveness of treatment for the aggressive adolescent sexual offender'. Conference of the New York Academy of Sciences: Human sexual aggression: Current perspectives (1987, New York, New York). *Annals of the New York Academy of Sciences, 528*, 215–222.

Becker, J.V., Kaplan, M.S., Tenke, C.E. and Tartaglini, A. (1991) 'The incidence of depressive symptomatology in juvenile sex offenders with a history of abuse', *Child Abuse and Neglect*, 15, 531–536.

Becker, J.V., Harris, C.D. and Sales, B.D. (1993) 'Juveniles who commit sexual offenses: a critical review of research', in Nigayama-Hall, G.C., Hirschman, R., Graham, J.R. and Zaragoza, M.S. (eds) *Sexual Aggression: Issues in Etiology, Assessment and Treatment*, London, Taylor and Francis.

Beckett, R.C., Beech, A., Fisher, D. and Fordham, A.S. (1994) *Community-based Treatment for Sex Offenders: An Evaluation of Seven Treatment Programmes*, London, Home Office.

Bender, L. and Blau, A. (1937) 'The reaction of children to sexual relations with adults', *American Journal of Orthopsychiatry*, 7, 500–518.

Benoit, J.L. and Kennedy, W.A. (1992) 'The abuse history of male adolescent sex offenders', *Journal of Interpersonal Violence*, 7(4), 543–548.

Bentovim, A., Vizard, E. and Hollows, A. (1991) *Children and Young People as Abusers*, London, National Children's Bureau.

Bera, W.H. (1994) 'Clinical review of adolescent male sex offenders', in Gonsiorek, J.C., Bera, W.H. and LeTourneau, D. (eds) *Male Sexual Abuse: A Trilogy of Intervention Strategies*, London, Sage.

Bethea-Jackson, G. and Brisset-Chapman, S. (1989) 'The juvenile sexual offender: challenges to assessment for outpatient intervention', *Child and Adolescent Social Work Journal*, 6(2), 127–137.

Blackburn, R. (1993) *The Psychology of Criminal Conduct: Theory, Research and Practice*. Chichester, John Wiley.

Blaske, D.M., Bordun, C.M., Henggeler, S.W. and Mann, B.J. (1989) 'Individual, family, and peer characteristics of adolescent sex offenders and assaultive offenders', *Developmental Psychology*, 25(5), 846–855.

Bluglass, R. (1990) 'The psychiatrist as an expert witness', in Bluglass, R. and Bowden, P. (eds) *Principles and Practice of Forensic Psychiatry*, London, Churchill Livingstone.

Bohmer, C. (1983) 'Legal and ethical issues in mandatory treatment: the patient's rights versus society's rights', in Greer, J.G. and Stuart, I. (eds) *The Sexual Aggressor: Current Perspectives on Treatment*, New York, Van Nostrand Reinhold.

Bownes, l.T. (1993) 'Sexual and relationship dysfunction in sexual offenders', *Sexual and Marital Therapy*, 8(2) 157–165.

Brandes, D. and Phillips, H. (1979) *Gamesters' Handbook: 140 Games for Teachers and Group Leaders*, London, Hutchinson.

Breer, W. (1987) *The Adolescent Molester*, Springfield, IL, Charles C. Thomas.

Briere, J. and Runtz, M. (1989) 'University males' sexual interest in children: predicting potential indices of "paedophilia" in a nonforensic sample', *Child Abuse and Neglect*, 13, 65–75.

Briggs, D. (1994) 'The management of sex offenders in institutions', in Morrison, T., Erooga, M. and Beckett, R.C. (eds) *Sexual Offending against Children*, London, Routledge.

British Psychological Society (1993) *Sexual Offenders: Context, Assessment and Treatment*, Division of Criminological and Legal Psychology No. 19 BPsS.

British Psychological Society (1995) *Professional Practice Guidelines 1995*, Leicester, BPsS.

Brooks-Gunn, J. and Furstenberg, F. (1989) 'Adolescent sexual behaviour', *American Psychologist*, 44, 249–257.

Burt, M.R. (1980) 'Cultural myths and supports for rape', *Journal of Personality and Social Psychology*, 38, 217–230.

Campbell, T.A. and Campbell, D.E. (1990) 'Considering the adolescent's point of view: a marketing model for sex education', *Journal of Sex Education and Therapy*, 16(3), 185–193.

Carter, D.L., Prentky, R.A., Knight, R.A., Vanderveer, P.L. and Boucher, R.J. (1987) 'Use of pornography in the criminal and developmental histories of sexual offenders', *Journal of Interpersonal Violence*, 2(2), 196–211.

Chandler, M.R. (1973) 'Egocentrism and anti-social behaviour: the assessment and training of social perspective-taking skills', *Developmental Psychology*, 9, 326–332.

Chiswick, D. (1985) 'Use and abuse of psychiatric testimony', *British Medical Journal*, 290, 975–977.

Clarke, R.V.G. (1977) 'Psychology and crime', *Bulletin of the British Psychological Society*, 30, 280–283.

Coons, P.M. and Milstein, V. (1986) 'Psychosexual disturbances in multiple personality: characteristics, aetiology and treatment', *Journal of Clinical Psychiatry*, 47(3), 106–110.

Coyne, J.C. (1982) 'A critique of cognitions as causal entities with particular reference to depression', *Cognitive Therapy and Research*, 6, 3–13.

Craft, A. (1991) *Living Your Life*, Cambridge, LDA.

Criminal Statistics England and Wales (1991), *CM 2134*, London, HMSO.

Dale, P., Davies, M., Morrison, T. and Waters, J. (1986) *Dangerous Families*, London, Tavistock.

Davies, G.E. and Leitenberg, H. (1987) 'Adolescent sex offenders', *Psychological Bulletin*, 101, 417–427.

Davison, G.C. and Neale, J.M. (1990) *Abnormal Psychology*, 5th edn, New York, John Wiley.

Debelle, G.D., Ward, M.R., Burnham, J.B., Jamieson, R. and Ginty, M. (1993) 'Evaluation of intervention programmes for juvenile sex offenders: questions and dilemmas', *Child Abuse Review*, 2, 75–87.

Department of Health (1992) *A Strategic Statement on Working with Abusers*, London, Department of Health.

Dodge, KA. and Murphy, R.R. (1984) 'The assessment of social competence in adolescents', in Karoly, P. and Steffen, J.J. (eds) *Adolescent Behaviour and Contemporary Concerns*, Vol. 3, Lexington, MA, Lexington Books.

Doshay, L.J. (1943) *The Boy Sex Offender and his Later Career*, Montclair, NJ, Patterson Amith.

Douglas, V.I. (1976) 'Attention factors', in Knight, R.M. and Baker, D.J. (eds) *The Neuropsychology of Learning Disorders*, Baltimore, MD, University Park Press.

Dow, M.G. and Craighead, W.E. (1984) 'Cognition and social inadequacy: relevance in clinical populations', in Trower, P. (ed.) *Radical Approaches to Social Skills Training*, London, Croom Helm.

Elliott, M. (1992) *Protecting Children: Training Pack for Front-line Carers*, London, HMSO.

Ellis, A. and Grieger, R. (1977) *Handbook of Rational Emotive Therapy*, New York, Springer-Verlag.

Epps, K. (1991) 'The residential treatment of adolescent sex offenders', in McMurran, M. and McDougall, C. (eds) *Issues in Criminological and Legal Psychology*, No. 17 (Proceedings of the first DCLP annual conference). Leicester, British Psychological Society.

Epps, K.J. (1994a) 'Treating adolescent sex offenders in secure conditions: the experience at Glenthorne Centre', *Journal of Adolescence*, 17, 105–122.

Epps, K.J. (1994b) 'Managing sexually abusive adolescents in residential settings: a strategy for risk assessment', in Clark, N.K. and Stephenson, G.M. (eds) *Rights and Risks: The Application of Forensic Psychology* (Issues in Criminological and Legal Psychology, 21) Leicester, British Psychological Society.

Erooga, M. (1994) 'Where the professional meets the personal', in Morrison, T., Erooga, M. and Beckett, R.C. (eds) *Sexual Offending against Children*, London, Routledge.

Eysenck, H. and Eysenck, S.B.G. (1964) *Eysenck Personality Scale Inventory*, Windsor, Berks, NFER.

Fagan, J. and Wexler, S. (1988) 'Explanations of sexual assault among violent delinquents', *Journal of Adolescent Research*, 3, 363–385.

Faller, K.C. (1991) 'Polyincestuous families: an exploratory study', *Journal of Interpersonal Violence*, 6(3), 310–322.

Fehrenbach, P.A., Smith, W., Monastersky, C. and Deisher, R.W. (1986) 'Adolescent sexual offenders. Offender and offense characteristics', *American Journal of Orthopsychiatry*, 56, 225–233.

Feinder, E.L. and Ecton, R.B. (1986) *Adolescent Anger Control*, New York, Pergamon Press.

Felner, R.D., Lease, A.M. and Philips, R.S.C. (1990) 'Social competence and the language of adequacy as a subject matter for psychology: A quadripartite trilevel framework', in Gullotta, T.P., Adams, G.R. and Montemayor, R. (eds) *Developing Social Competency in Adolescence*, Thousand Oaks, CA, Sage.

Finkelhor, D. (1984) *Child Sexual Abuse: New Theory and Research*, New York, The Free Press.

Finkelhor, D. (1986) 'Abusers: special topics', in Finkelhor, D., Araji, S., Baron, L., Browne, A., Peters, S.D. and Wyatt, G.E., *A Sourcebook on Child Sexual Abuse*, Beverly Hills, CA, Sage.

Finkelhor, D. (1988) 'The trauma of child sexual abuse', in Wyatt, G.E. and Powell, G.J. (eds) *Lasting Effects of Child Sexual Abuse*, Beverly Hills, CA, Sage.

Finkelhor, D. and Brown, A. (1985) 'The traumatic impact of child abuse: a conceptualisation', *American Journal of Orthopsychiatry*, 55(4), 530–541.

Finkelhor, D., Araji, S., Baron, L., Browne, A., Peters, S.D. and Wyatt, G. (1986) *A Sourcebook on Child Sexual Abuse*, Beverly Hills, CA, Sage.

Fisher, D. and Thornton, D. (1993) 'Assessing risk of reoffending in sexual offenders', *Journal of Mental Health*, 2, 105–117.

Fisher, W.A. and Barak, A. (1989) 'Sex education as a corrective: immunizing against possible effects of pornography', in Zillman, D. and Bryant, J. (eds) *Pornography: Research Advances and Policy Considerations* (pp. 289–320). Hillsdale, NJ, Lawrence Erlbaum.

Fishman, H.C. (1988) *Treating Troubled Adolescents: a Family Therapy Approach*, London, Unwin Hyman.

Fitzpatrick, C. and Fitzgerald, E. (1991) 'Sibling sexual abuse: family characteristics', *ACCP Newsletter*, 3(6), 10–13.

Fransella, F. and Bannister, D. (1977) *A Manual for Repertory Grid Technique*, London, Academic Press.

Freckleton, J.R. (1987) *The Trial of the Expert: a Study of Expert Evidence and Forensic Experts*, Melbourne, Oxford University Press.

Freedman, B.J., Rosenthal, L., Donahoe, C.P., Schlundt, D.G. and McFall, R.M. (1978) 'A socio-behavioural analysis of skill deficits in delinquent and nondelinquent adolescent boys', *Journal of Consulting and Clinical Psychology*, 46, 1448–1462.

Freeman-Longo, R. and Pithers, W.D. (1992) *A Structured Approach to Preventing Relapse: A Guide for Sex Offenders*. Orwell, VT, The Safer Society Program.

Friedman, S. and Harrison, G. (1984) 'Sexual histories, attitudes and behaviour of schizophrenic and "normal" women', *Archives of Sexual Behaviour*, 13(6), 555–567.

Frydenberg, E. and Lewis, R. (1993) *Adolescent Coping Scale*, Melbourne, Australian Council for Educational Research.

Furnham, A. (1983) 'Research in social skills training: a critique', in Ellis, R. and Whittington, D. (eds) *New Directions in Social Skills Training*, London, Croom Helm.

Garland, R.J. and Dougher, M.J. (1991) 'Motivational intervention in the treatment of sex offenders', in Miller, W.R. and Rollnick, S. (eds) *Motivational Interviewing: Preparing People to Change Addictive Behavior* (pp. 303–313). New York: Guilford Press.

Garlick, Y. (1991) 'Intimacy failure, loneliness and the attribution of blame in sexual offending', *Prison Service Psychology Conference Proceedings*, Home Office, HM Prison Service.

Gay, P. (1988) *Freud: A Life for Our Time*, London, Papermac.

George, K.D. and Behrendt, A.E. (1985) 'Research priorities in sex education'. Special issue: *Sex Education: Past, Present, Future* of the *Journal of Sex Education and Therapy*, 11(1), 56–60.

Gil, E. and Johnson, T.C. (1993) *Sexualised Children: Assessment and Treatment of Sexualised Children and Children Who Molest*, Rockville, MD, Launch Press.

Glass, C., Gottman, J. and Schmurak, S. (1976) 'Response acquisition and cognitive self-statement modification approaches to dating skills training', *Journal of Counseling Psychology*, 23, 520–526.

Glick, B. and Goldstein, A.P. (1987) 'Aggression replacement training', *Journal of Counselling and Development*, 65, 356–367.

Goldstein, A.P. and Keller, H. (1987) *Aggressive Behaviour: Assessment and Intervention*, New York, Pergamon Press.

Gonsiorek, J.C., Bera, W.H. and LeTourneau, D. (1994) *Male Sexual Abuse: a Trilogy of Intervention Strategies*, London, Sage.

Graham, F. (1993) 'Treatment of sexually abusive adolescents', *Division of Criminological and Legal Psychology*, 17(2), 82–86. BPSS.

Graham, F. (1995) *Assessing Risk in Sexually Abusive Young People*, Newcastle, Kolvin Unit. The Derwent Initiative.

Green, D. and Yeo, P. (1982) 'Attitude change and social skills training: Potential techniques', *Behavioural Psychology* 10, 79–86.

Gresham, F.M. (1985) 'Utility of cognitive–behavioural procedures for social skills training with children: a critical review', *Journal of Abnormal Psychology*, 13, 411–423.

Groth, A.N. (1977) 'The adolescent sexual offender and his prey', *Journal of Offender Therapy and Comparative Criminology*, 21, 249–254.

Groth, A.N. (1978) 'Patterns of sexual assault against children and adolescents', in Burgess, A.W., Groth, A.N., Holmstrom, L.L. and Sgroi, S.M. (eds) *Sexual Assault of Children and Adolescents*, Toronto, Lexington Books.

Groth, A.N. and Loredo, C.M. (1981) 'Juvenile sex offenders: guidelines for assessments', *International Journal of Offender Therapy and Comparative Criminology*, 25, 31–39.

Gudjonsson, G.H. (1990) 'The psychologist as an expert witness', in Bluglass, R. and Bowden, P. (eds) *Principles and Practice of Forensic Psychiatry*, London, Churchill Livingstone.

Guerra, N.C., and Slaby, R.C. (1990) 'Cognitive mediators of aggression in adolescent offenders: 2. Intervention', *Developmental Psychology*, 26, 269–277.

Hacker, S.S. (1986) 'Telling it like it is: a challenge to the field of sex education', *Journal of Sex Education and Therapy*, 12(1), 13–17.

Hains, A.A., Herrman, L.P., Baker, K.N. and Graber, S. (1986) 'The development of a psycho-educational group program for adolescent sex offenders', *Journal of Offender Counseling, Services and Rehabilitation*, 11(1), 63–76.

Hanson, R.K. and Scott, H. (1995) 'Assessing perspective-taking among sexual offenders, non sexual criminals and non offenders', *Sexual Abuse: A Journal of Research and Treatment*, 7(4).

Hare, R.D. (1990) *The Psychopathy Checklist*, Odessa, FL, Psychological Assessment Resources.

Harrell, A.V. and Wirtz, P.W. (1994) *Adolescent Drinking Index*, Odessa, FL, Psychological Assessment Resources.

Harter, S.G. (1988) 'Causes, correlates and the functional role of global self-worth: a life span perspective', in Kolligian, J. and Sternberg, R. (eds) *Perceptions of Competence and Incompetence across the Life-Span*, New Haven, CT, Yale University Press.

Hayes, S.C., Brownwell, K.D. and Barlow, D.H. (1983) 'Heterosocial skills training and covert sensitization: Effects on social skills and sexual arousal in sexual deviants', *Behavior Research and Therapy*, 21, 283–292.

Hayman, C.R., Stewart, W.F., Lewis, F.R. and Grant, M. (1968) 'Sexual assault on women and children in the District of Columbia', *Public Health Reports*, 83(12), 1021–1028.

Hazel, J.S., Schumaker, J.B., Sherman, J.A. and Sheldon-Wildgen, J. (1982) 'Social skills training with court-adjudicated delinquents', *Child and Youth Services*, 117–137.

Herbert, M. (1991) *Clinical Child Psychology*, Chichester, John Wiley.

Higgins, J.P. and Thies, A.P. (1981) 'Social effectiveness and problem-solving thinking of reformatory inmates', *Journal of Offender Counseling, Services and Rehabilitation*, 5, 93–98.

Hildebran, D. and Pithers, W. (1992) 'Relapse prevention', in O'Donohue, W. and Greer, J. (eds) *The Sexual Abuse of Children: Clinical Issues* (pp. 365–393), Hillsdale, NJ, Lawrence Erlbaum.

HM Inspectorate of Probation (1991) *The Work of the Probation Service with Sex Offenders: Report of a Thematic Inspection*, London, HMSO.

Hobbs, N. (ed.) (1975) *Issues in the Classification of Children*, San Francisco, Jossey Bass.

Hoghughi, M. (1978) *Troubled and Troublesome: Working with Severely Disordered Children*, London, Burnett Books/Andre Deutsch.

Hoghughi, M.S. (1983) *The Delinquent: Directions for Social Control*, London, Hutchinson.

Hoghughi, M.S., Lyons, J., Muckley, A. and Swainston, M. (1988) *Treating Problem Children: Methods and Practice*, London, Sage.

Hoghughi, M. (1992) *Assessing Child and Adolescent Disorders*, London, Sage.

Hoghughi, M. (1993) *Youth at the Margins*, Aycliffe, Centre for Adolescent Studies.

Hoghughi, M.S. (1996) *Adolescent Crime: Surviving at the Margins*, Oxford, Bowerdean Publishing.

Hoghughi, M.S. and Richardson, G. (1990a) 'Sexually abusing adolescents', *Community Care*, 837, 22–24.

Hoghughi, M.S. and Richardson, G. (1990b) 'Abusing adolescents and legal sanctions', *Community Care*, 838, 21–23.

Hollin, C.R. (1989) *Psychology and Crime: Introduction to Criminological Psychology*, London, Routledge.

Hollin, C.R. (1990) *Cognitive-Behavioural Interventions with Young Offenders*, New York, Pergamon Press.

Home Office (1988) *British Crime Survey*, London, HMSO.

Home Office (1994) *Criminal Statistics in England and Wales 1993 and Supplementary Tables 1993*, Vol. 1, London, HMSO.

Horn, J.L., Wanberg, K.W. and Foster, F.M. (1990) *Alcohol Use Inventory*, Minneapolis, National Computer Systems.

Horne, L., Glasgow, D., Cox, A. and Calam, R. (1991) 'Sexual abuse of children by children', *The Journal of Child Law*, 3(4), 147–151.

Howells, K. (1981) 'Adult sexual interest in children: considerations relevant to theories of aetiology', in Cook, M. and Howells, K. (eds) *Adult Sexual Interest in Children*, London, Academic Press.

Hsu, L.K.G. and Starzynski, J. (1990) 'Adolescent rapists and adolescent child sexual assaulters', *International Journal of Offender Therapy and Comparative Criminology*, 34, 23–30.

Hughes, J.N. (1988) *Cognitive Behaviour Therapy with Children in Schools*, New York, Pergamon Press.

Hughes, J.N. and Hall, R.J. (1987) 'A proposed model for the assessment of children's social competence', *Professional School Psychology*, 2, 247–260.

Hursch, C.J. (1977) *The Trouble with Rape*, Chicago, Nelson-Hall.

Jackson, S. (1988) 'Self-characterisation: Dimensions and meaning', in Fransella, F. and Thomas, L. (eds) *Experimenting with Personal Construct Psychology*, London, Routledge and Kegan Paul.

Jesness, C.F. (1971). *Manual for the Jesness Behaviour Checklist*, Palo Alto, CA, Consulting Psychologists Press.

Johnson, P.R. (1981) 'Sex and the developmentally handicapped adult: a comparison of teaching methods', *British Journal of Subnormality*, 52, 8–17.

Kahn, T.J. (1990) *Pathways: A Guided Workbook for Youth Beginning Treatment*, Orwell, VT, The Safer Society Press.

Kahn, T.J. and Chambers, H.J. (1991) 'Assessing reoffence risk with juvenile sexual offenders', *Child Welfare League of America*, 70(3), May–June, 333–345.

Kahn, T.J. and Lafond, M.A. (1988) 'Treatment of the adolescent sex offender', *Child and Adolescent Social Work Journal*, 5(2), 135–148.

Kanfer, F.H. (1970) 'Self regulation: research, issues and speculations', in Neuringer, C. and Michael, J.L. (eds) *Behavior Modification in Clinical Psychology*, New York, Appleton Century Crofts.

Kaplan, M.S., Becker, J.V. and Tenke, C.E. (1991) 'Assessment of sexual knowledge and attitudes in an adolescent sex offender population', *Journal of Sex Education and Therapy*, 17(3), 217–255.

Kavoussi, R.J., Kaplan, M. and Becker, J.V. (1988) 'Psychiatric diagnoses in adolescent sex offenders', *Journal of the American Academy of Child and Adolescent Psychiatry*, 27, 241–243.

Kelly, G.A. (1955) *The Psychology of Personal Constructs*, New York, Norton.

Kendall, P.C. (1991) *Child and Adolescent Therapy: Cognitive-behavioural Procedures*, New York, Guilford Press.

Kendall, P.C. and Braswell, L. (1985) *Cognitive-behavioral Therapy for Impulsive Children*, New York, Guilford Press.

Kimmel, D.C. and Weiner, I.B. (1985) *Adolescence: A Developmental Transaction*, Hillsdale, NJ, Lawrence Erlbaum.

Kirby, D. (1984). *Sexuality Education: An Evaluation of Programs and their Effects*, Santa Cruz, CA, Network Publications.

Kirby, D. (1985) 'The effects of selected sexuality education programs: towards a more realistic view', *Journal of Sex Education and Therapy*, 11(1), 28–37.

Kirby, D., Alter, J. and Scales, P. (1979) *An Analysis of US Sex Education Programs and Evaluation Methods* (Report No. DC–2021–79–KD–FR). Atlanta, GA, US Department of Health, Education and Welfare.

Klein, M. and Gordon, S. (1992) 'Sex education', in Walker, C.E. and Roberts, M.C. (eds) *Handbook of Clinical Child Psychology*, 2nd edn (pp. 933–949). New York, Wiley.

Knight, R.A. (1992) 'The generation and corroboration of a taxonomic model for child molesters', in O'Donohue, W. and Greer, J.H. (eds) *The Sexual Abuse of Children: Theory, Research and Therapy* (pp. 24–70), Hillsdale, NJ, Lawrence Erlbaum.

Knight, R.A. and Prentky, RA. (1990) 'Classifying sexual offenders: the development and corroboration of taxonomic models', in Marshall, W.L., Laws, D.R. and Barbaree, H.E. (eds) *Handbook of Sexual Assault: Issues, Theories and Treatment of the Offender* (pp. 27–52), New York, Plenum Press.

Knight, R.A. and Prentky, R.A. (1993) 'Exploring characteristics for classifying juvenile sex offenders', in Barbaree, H.E., Marshall, W.L. and Hudson, S.M. (eds) *The Juvenile Sex Offender*, New York, Guilford Press.

Knight, R.A., Carter, D.L., and Prentky, R.A. (1989) 'A system for the classification of child molesters: reliability and application', *Journal of Interpersonal Violence*, 4, 3–23.

Knopp, F.H. (1985) *The Youthful Sex Offender: The Rationale and Goals of Early Intervention and Treatment*, New York, Safer Society Press.

Koss, M.P. and Dinero, T.E. (1987) 'Predictors of sexual aggression among a national sample of male college students'. Paper presented at the New York Academy of Sciences Conference on Human Sexual Aggression: Current Perspectives, New York.

Krasner, W., Meyer, L.C. and Carroll, N.E. (1976) *Victims of Rape*, Washington, DC, Government Printing Office.

Kuhn, T.S. (1970) *The Structure of Scientific Revolutions*, Chicago, University of Chicago Press.

La Gaipa, J.J. and Wood, H.D. (1981) 'Friendship in disturbed adolescents', in Duck, S.W. and Gilmour, R. (eds) *Personal Relationships in Disorder*, London, Academic Press.

Lane, S. and Zamora, P. (1984) 'A method for treating the adolescent sex offender', in Mathias, R., Demuro, P. and Allinson, R. (eds) *Violent Juvenile Offenders*, San Francisco, National Council on Crime and Delinquency.

Lange, A. (1986) *Rational-emotive Therapy: A Treatment Manual*, Tampa, FL, Florida Mental Health Institute.

Lanyon, R.I. (1991) 'Theories of Sex Offending', in Hollin, C.R. and Howells, K. (eds) *Clinical Approaches to Sex Offenders and Their Victims*, Chichester, John Wiley.

Laws, D.R. (1985) 'Fantasy alternation: procedural considerations', *Journal of Behaviour Therapy and Experimental Psychiatry*, 16, 39–44.

Laws, D.R. (ed.) (1989) *Relapse Prevention with Sex Offenders*, New York, Guilford Press.

Laws, D.R. and Marshall, W.L. (1990) 'A conditioning theory of the etiology and maintenance of deviant sexual preference and behavior', in Marshall, W.L.,

Laws, D.R. and Barbaree, H.E. (eds) *Handbook of Sexual Assault: Issues, Theories and Treatment of the Offender*, New York, Plenum Press.

Laws, D.R. and.Marshall, W.L. (1991) 'Masturbatory reconditioning with sexual deviates: an evaluative review', *Advances in Behavior Research and Therapy*, 13, 13–25.

Laws, D.R. and O'Neil, J.A. (1981) 'Variations on masturbatory conditioning', *Behavioural Psychotherapy*, 9, 111–136.

Lewis, D.O., Shankok, S. and Pincus, J.H. (1979) 'Juvenile male sexual assaulters', *American Journal of Psychiatry*, 136, 1194–1196.

Liberman, R.P., DeRisi, W.J. and Mueser, K.T. (1989) *Social Skills Training for Psychiatric Patients*, New York, Pergamon Press.

Lipton, D.N., McDonel, E.C. and McFall, R.M. (1987) 'Heterosocial perception in rapists', *Journal of Consulting and Clinical Psychology*, 55, 17–21.

Loeber, R. (1990) 'Development and risk factors in juvenile anti-social behaviour and delinquency', *Clinical Psychology Review*, 10, 1–41.

Loeber, R. and Dishion, T. (1983) 'Early predictors of male delinquency: a review', *Psychological Bulletin*, 94, 68–99.

Longo, R.E. and Groth, A.N. (1983) 'Juvenile sex offences in the histories of adult rapists and child molesters', *International Journal of Offender Therapy and Comparative Criminology*, 27, 150–153.

Loss, P. and Ross, J. (1988) *Risk Assessment Interviewing Protocol for Adolescent Sex Offenders*, Mystic, CT, Ross, Loss and Associates.

Luborsky, L., McClellan, A.T., Woody, G.E., O'Brien, C.P. and Averbach, A. (1985) 'Therapist success and its determinants', *Archives of General Psychiatry*, 42, 602–611.

McCarthy, M. and Thompson, D. (1992) *Sex and the Three Rs: Rights, Responsibilities and Risks*, Brighton, Pavilion Publishing.

Macdonald, J.M. (1971) *Rape Offenders and their Victims*, Springfield, IL, Charles C. Thomas.

McDougall, C. Barnett, R.M., Ashurst, B., and Willis, B. (1987) 'Cognitive control of anger', in McGurk, B.J., Thornton, D.M. and Williams, M. (eds) *Applying Psychology to Imprisonment: Theory and Practice*, London, HMSO.

McFall, R.M. (1982) 'A review and reformulation of the concept of social skills', *Behavioural Assessment* 4, 1–33.

McFall, R.M. (1990) 'The enhancement of social skills: an information-processing analysis', in Marshall, W.L., Laws, D.R. and Barbaree, H.E. (eds) *Handbook of Sexual Assault: Issues, Theories and Treatment of the Offender*, New York, Plenum Press.

McGuire, J. and Priestley, P. (1985) *Offending Behaviour: Skills and Stratagems for Going Straight*, London, Batsford.

McGuire, R.J., Carlisle, J.M. and Young, B.G. (1965) 'Sexual deviations as conditioned behaviour: a hypothesis', *Behaviour Research and Therapy*, 2, 185–190.

McGurk, B.J. and Newell, T.C. (1981) 'Social skills training with a sex offender', *The Psychological Record*, 31, 277–283.

Mackinnon, K. (1987) 'A feminist/political approach: pleasure under patriarchy', in Green, H. and' O'Donohue, W. (eds) *Theories of Human Sexuality*, New York, Plenum Press.

MacLeod, M. and Saraga, E. (1991) 'Clearing a path through the undergrowth: a feminist reading of recent literature on child sexual abuse', in *Social Work and Social Welfare*, Milton Keynes, Open University Press.

Malamuth, N.M. (1986) 'Predictors of naturalistic sexual aggression', *Journal of Personality and Social Psychology*, 50, 953–962.

Maletzky, B.M. (1991) *Treating the Sexual Offender*, Newbury Park, CA, Sage.

Marlatt, G.A. and Gordon, J.R. (eds) (1985) *Relapse Prevention: Maintenance Strategies in the Treatment of Addictive Behaviors*, New York, Guilford Press.

Marques, J.K. and Nelson, C. (1989) 'Elements of high-risk situations for sex offenders', in Laws, D.R. (ed.) *Relapse Prevention with Sex Offenders*, New York, Guilford Press.

Marques, J., Nelson, C., West, M.A. and Day, D.M. (1994) 'The relationship between treatment goals and recidivism among child molesters', *Behaviour Research and Therapy*, 32, 577–588.

Marsh, L.F., Connell, P. and Olson, E. (1988) *Breaking the Cycle: Adolescent Sexual Treatment Manual*, Beaverton, OR, St Mary's Home for Boys.

Marshall, W.L. (1979) 'Satiation therapy: a procedure for reducing deviant sexual arousal', *Journal of Applied Behaviour Analysis*, 12, 377–389.

Marshall, W.L. (1989) 'Intimacy, loneliness and sexual offending', *Behaviour Research and Therapy*, 27, 491–503.

Marshall, W.L. (1989) 'Pornography and sex offenders', in Zillman, D. and Bryant, J. (eds) *Pornography: Research Advances and Policy Considerations* (pp. 185–214). Hillsdale, NJ, Lawrence Erlbaum.

Marshall, W.L. and Barbaree, H.E. (1990) 'Outcome of comprehensive cognitive behavioural treatment programmes', in Marshall, W.L., Laws, D.R. and Barbaree, H.E. (eds) *Handbook of Sexual Assault: Issues, Theories and Treatment of the Offender*, New York, Plenum Press.

Marshall, W.L. and Eccles, A. (1991) 'Issues in clinical practice with sex offenders', *Journal of Interpersonal Violence*, 6(1) 68–93.

Marshall, W.L. and Eccles, A. (1993) 'Pavlovian conditioning processes in adolescent sex offenders', in Barbaree, H.E., Marshall, W.L. and Hudson, S.M. *The Juvenile Sex Offender*, New York, Guilford Press.

Marshall, W.L., Barbaree, H.E. and Christophe, D. (1986) 'Sexual offenders against female children: sexual preferences for age of victims and type of behavior', *Canadian Journal of Behavioral Science*, 18, 424–439.

Marshall, W.L., Barbaree, H.E. and Butt, J. (1988) 'Sexual offenders against male children: sexual preferences', *Behaviour Research and Therapy*, 26, 499–511.

Marshall, W.L., Laws, D.R. and Barbaree, H.E. (eds) (1990) *Handbook of Sexual Assault: Issues, Theories and Treatment of the Offender*, New York, Plenum Press.

Marshall, W.L., Barbaree, H.E. and Eccles, A. (1991a) 'Early onset and deviant sexuality in child molesters', *Journal of Interpersonal Violence*, 6(3) 323–336.

Marshall, W.L., Jones, R., Ward, T., Johnston, P. and Barbaree, H.E. (1991b) 'Treatment outcome with sex offenders', *Clinical Psychology Review*, 11, 465–475.

Marshall, W.L., Hudson, S.M. and Ward, T. (1992a) 'Sexual deviance', in Wilson, P.H. (ed.) *Principles and Practice of Relapse Prevention*, New York, Guilford Press.

Marshall, W.L., Hudson, S.M. and Hodkinson, S. (1993) 'The importance of attachment bonds in development of juvenile sex offending', in Barbaree,

H.E., Marshall, W.L. and Hudson, S.M. (eds) *The Juvenile Sex Offender*, New York, Guilford Press.

Marshall, W.L., Barbaree, H.E. and Fernandez, Y.M. (1995) 'Some aspects of social competency in sexual offenders', *Sexual Abuse: A Journal of Research and Treatment*, 7(2), 113–129.

Masson, H. (1995) 'Children and adolescents who sexually abuse other children: responses to an emerging problem' (interim report). Unpublished manuscript.

Matson, J.L. Esveldt-Dawson, K. and Kazdin, A. (1983) 'Evaluating social skills with youngsters', *Journal of Clinical Child Psychology*, 12, 174–180.

Mazur, T. and Michael, P.M. (1992) 'Outpatient treatment for adolescents with sexually inappropriate behaviour: program description and six-month follow-up', *Journal of Offender Rehabilitation* 18(3/4), 191–203.

Meehl, P.E. (1954) *Clinical versus Statistical Prediction*, Minneapolis, University of Minnesota Press.

Meehl, P.E. (1986) 'Causes and effects of my disturbing little book', *Journal of Personality Assessment*, 50, 370–375.

Meichenbaum, D.H. (1977) *Cognitive-behaviour Modification: An Integrative Approach*, New York, Plenum Press.

Meichenbaum, D.H. and Goodman, J. (1971) 'Training impulsive children to talk to themselves: a means of developing self control', *Journal of Abnormal Psychology*, 77, 115–126.

Miller, W.R. and Rollnick, S. (1991) *Motivational Interviewing: Preparing People to Change Addictive Behavior*, New York, Guilford Press.

Millon, T. (1993) *Millon Adolescent Clinical Inventory*, Minneapolis, National Computer Systems.

Mischel, W. (1968) *Personality and Assessment*, New York, Wiley.

Moffitt, T.E. (1993) 'The neuropsychology of conduct disorder', *Development and Psychopathology*, 5, 135–151.

Monahan, J. (1984) 'The prediction of violent behaviour: towards a second generation of theory and policy', *American Journal of Psychiatry*, 141, 10–15.

Monahan, J. (1988) 'Risk assessment of violence among the mentally disordered: Generating useful knowledge', *International Journal of Law and Psychiatry*, 11, 249–257.

Moos, R.H. (1993) *Coping Responses Inventory – CRI Youth Forum*, Odessa, FL, Psychological Assessment Resources.

Morris, R.W. (1991) 'Limitations of quantitative methods for research on values in sexuality education', *Canadian Journal of Education*, 16(1), 82–92.

Morrison, T. (1992) 'Managing sex offenders: the challenge for managers', *Probation Journal*, September.

Morrison, T. and Print, B. (1995) *Adolescent Sexual Abusers: An Overview*, Hull, NOTA Training Sub-Committee.

Mulvey, E.P., Arthur, M.W. and Reppucci, N.D. (1993) 'The prevention and treatment of juvenile delinquency: a review of the research', *Clinical Psychology Review*, 13, 133–167.

Mulvihill, D., Tumin, M. and Curtis, L. (1969) *Crimes of Violence: A Staff Report Submitted to the National Commission on the Causes and Prevention of Violence* (Vol. 2), Washington, DC, Government Printing Office.

Murphy, W.D. (1990) 'Assessment and modification of cognitive distortions in sex offenders', in Marshall, W.L., Laws, D.R. and Barbaree, H.E. (eds)

Handbook of Sexual Assault: Issues, Theories and Treatment of the Offender, New York, Plenum Press.

Murphy, W.D., Coleman, E.M. and Haynes, M.R. (1986) 'Factors related to coercive sexual behaviour in a nonclinical sample of males', *Violence and Victims*, 1, 255–278.

Murphy, W.D., Haynes, M.R. and Page, I.J. (1992) 'Adolescent sex offenders', in O'Donohue, W. and Greer, J.H. (eds) *The Sexual Abuse of Children*, Vol. 2, Hillsdale, NJ, Lawrence Erlbaum.

NACRO (1991) *Seizing the Initiative. Final Report of the DHSS Intermediate Treatment Initiative to Divert Juvenile Offenders from Care and Custody*, London, NACRO.

Nangle, D.W. and Hansen, D.J. (1993) 'Relations between social skills and high-risk sexual interactions among adolescents', *Behaviour Modification*, 17(2), 113–135.

National Adolescent Perpetrator Network (1988) *Preliminary Report of the National Task Force on Juvenile Sexual Offending*, Juvenile and Family Court Journal 39, 12.

National Children's Home (1990) *Survey of Treatment Facilities for Abused Children and of Treatment Facilities for Young Sexual Abusers of Children*, London, National Children's Home.

National Children's Home (1992) *Report of the Committee of Enquiry into Children and Young People who Sexually Abuse Other Children*, London, Central Office.

Needs, A. (1988a) 'Psychological investigation of offending behaviour', in Fransella, F. and Thomas, L. (eds) *Experimenting with Personal Construct Psychology*, London: Routledge and Kegan Paul.

Needs, A. (1988b) *The Subjective Context of Social Difficulty*, Unpublished DPhil Thesis, University of York.

Nichols, H.R. and Molinder, I. (1984) *Multiphasic Sex Inventory*, Tacoma, WA, Nichols and Molinder.

NOTA (1993) *Good Practice in the Inter-agency Management of Sex Offenders Who Assault Children*, Liverpool NOTA/NSPCC.

NOTA (1994) Policy and ethics sub-committee, 'Working with adults and adolescents who exhibit sexually abusive behaviour: the use of sexually salient and pornographic materials'. David Whiting Publishing Services.

Novaco, R.W. (1975) *Anger Control: The Development and Evaluation of an Experimental Treatment*, Lexington, MA, DC Heath.

Novaco, R.W. (1991) *Reactions to Provocation*, Irvine, University of California Press.

Nowicki, S. and Strickland, B. (1973) 'Internal/external locus of control scale', *Journal of Counselling and Clinical Psychology*, 40 (1), 148–154.

O'Brien, M.J. (1989) 'Characteristics of male adolescent sibling incest offenders: preliminary findings', *The Safer Society Program*, Orwell, VT.

O'Brien, M.J. (1991) 'Taking sibling incest seriously', in Patton, M.Q. (ed.) *Family Sexual Abuse: Frontline Research and Evaluation*, Beverly Hills, CA, Sage.

O'Brien, M.J. and Bera, W. (1986) 'Adolescent sexual offenders: a descriptive typology', *A News Letter of the National Family Life Education Network*, 1, 1–5.

O'Callaghan, D. and Print, B. (1994) 'Adolescent sexual abusers: research, assessment and treatment', in Morrison, T., Erooga, M. and Beckett, R. (eds) *Sexual Offending against Children*, London, Routledge.

O'Donohue, W. and Letourneau, E. (1993) 'A brief group treatment for the modification of denial in child sexual abusers: outcome and follow-up', *Child Abuse and Neglect*, 17, 299–304.

Offer, D., Ostrov, E. and Howard, K.I. (1982) *The Offer Self-Image Questionnaire for Adolescents*, Chicago, Michael Reese Hospital and Medical Center.

Orford, J. (1985) *Excessive Appetites. A Psychological View of Addictions*, Chichester, John Wiley.

Oster, G.D., Caro, J.E., Eagen, D.R. and Lillo, M.A. (1988) *Assessing Adolescents*, London, Pergamon.

Perkins, D. (1991) 'Clinical work with sex offenders in secure settings', in Hollin, C.R. and Howells, K. (eds) *Clinical Approaches to Sex Offenders and their Victims* (pp. 151–177), Chichester, John Wiley.

Perry, G. and Orchard, J. (1992) *Assessment and Treatment of Adolescent Sex Offenders*, Sarasota, FL, Professional Resource Press.

Pierce, L.H. and Pierce, R.L. (1990) 'Adolescent sibling incest perpetrators', in Horton, L., Johnson, B., Roundy, L. and Williams, D. (eds) *The Incest Perpetrator: A Family Member No One Wants to Treat*, Beverly Hills, CA, Sage.

Pithers, W.D. (1990) 'Relapse prevention with sexual aggressors: method for maintaining therapeutic gain and enhancing external supervision', in Marshall, W.L., Laws, D.R. and Barbaree, H.E. (eds) *Handbook of Sexual Assault: Issues, Theories, and Treatment of the Offender*, New York, Plenum Press.

Pithers, W.D., Marques, J.K., Gibat, C.C. and Marlatt, G.A. (1983) 'Relapse prevention with sexual aggressives: a self-control model of treatment and the maintenance of change', in Greer, J.G. and Stuart, I.R. (eds) *The Sexual Aggressor: Current Perspectives on Treatment*, New York, Van Nostrand Reinhold.

Pithers, W.D., Kashima, K.M., Cumming, G.F. and Beal, L.S. (1988) 'Relapse prevention: a method of enhancing maintenance of change in sex offenders', in Salter, A.C. (ed.) *Treating Child Sex Offenders and Victims: A Practical Guide*, Newbury Park, Sage.

Pollock, N., McBain, I. and Webster, C.D. (1989) 'Clinical decision making and the assessment of dangerousness', in Howells, K. and Hollin, C.R. (eds) *Clinical Approaches to Violence*, Chichester, John Wiley.

Quinsey, V.L. and Earls, C.M. (1990) 'The modification of sexual preferences', in Marshall, W.L., Laws, D.R. and Barbaree, H.E. (eds) *Handbook of Sexual Assault: Issues, Theories and Treatment of the Offender*, New York, Plenum Press.

Quinsey, V.L. and Marshall, W.L. (1983) 'Procedures for reducing inappropriate sexual arousal: an evaluation review', in Greer, J.G. and Stuart, l.R. (eds) *The Sexual Aggressor: Current Perspectives on Treatment*, New York, Van Nostrand Reinhold.

Radley, A.R. (1974) 'The effect of role enactment upon construed alternatives', *British Journal of Medical Psychology*, 47 313–320.

Rapaport, K. and Burkhart, B.R. (1984) 'Personality and attitudinal characteristics of sexually coercive college males', *Journal of Abnormal Psychology*, 93, 216–221.

Rathus, S.A. (1973) 'A 30 item schedule for assessing assertive behaviour', *Behavioral Therapy*, 4, 398–406.

Reid, F. (1979) 'Personal constructs and social competence', in Stringer, P. and Bannister, D. (eds) *Constructs of Sociability and Individuality*, London, Academic Press.

Reynolds, W.M. (1987) *Suicide Ideation Questionnaire*, Odessa, FL, Psychological Assessment Resources.

Rice, F.P. (1987) *The Adolescent: Development, Relationships, and Culture* (5th edn), Needham Heights, MA, Allyn and Bacon.

Richardson, G., Graham, F., Bhate, S.R. and Kelly, T.P. (1995a) 'A British sample of sexually abusive adolescents: abuser and abuse characteristics', *Criminal Behaviour and Mental Health*, 5, 187–208.

Richardson, G., Kelly, T.P., Bhate, S.R. and Graham, F. (1995b) 'Group differences in abuser and abuse characteristics in a British sample of sexually abusive adolescents', *Sexual Abuse: A Journal of Research and Treatment*, 9(3), 239–257.

Rierdan, J. (1980) 'Word associations of socially isolated adolescents', *Journal of Abnormal Psychology*, 89, 98–100.

Rimm, D., Hill, G., Brown, N. and Stuart, J. (1974) 'Group assertive training in the treatment of expression of inappropriate anger', *Psychological Reports*, 34, 791–798.

Rodriguez, R., Nietzel, M. and Berzins, J. (1980) 'Sex role orientation and assertiveness among female college students', *Behavior Therapy*, 11, 353–367.

Rogers, C.R. (1959) 'A theory of therapy, personality and interpersonal relationships as developed in client centred framework', in Koch, S. (ed.) *Psychology: The Study of a Science, Vol. 3, Formulations of the Person and the Social Context*, New York, McGraw Hill.

Rosenberg, M. (1965) *Society and the Adolescent Self-Image*, Princeton, N.J., Princeton University Press.

Ross, J. and Loss, P. (1991) 'Assessment of the juvenile sex offender', in Ryan, G.D. and Lane, S.L. (eds) *Juvenile Sexual Offending: Causes, Consequences and Correction*, Lexington, MA, Lexington Books.

Ross, R.R. and Fabiano, E.A. (1985) *Time to Think: a Cognitive Model of Delinquency Prevention and Offender Rehabilitation*, Johnson City, TN, Institute of Social Sciences and Arts.

Rouleau, J.L., Abel, G.G., Mittelman, M.S., Becker, J.V. and Cunningham-Rathner, J. (1986) 'Effectiveness of each component of a treatment program for non-incarcerated pedophiles'. Paper presented at the NIMH-sponsored Conference on Sex Offenders, Tampa, FL.

Royal Belfast Hospital For Sick Children, Queen's University (1990) *Child Sexual Abuse in Northern Ireland: a Research Study of Incidence*, Belfast, Greystone Press.

Russell, D. (1984) *The Secret Trauma: Incest in the Lives of Girls and Women*, New York, Basic Books.

Russell, D., Peplau, L.A. and Ferguson, M.L. (1978) 'Developing a measure of loneliness', *Journal of Personality Assessment*, 42, 290–294.

Russell, D., Peplau, L.A. and Cutrona, C.E. (1980) 'The revised UCLA loneliness scale: Concurrent and discriminant validity evidence', *Journal of Personality and Social Psychology*, 39 472–480.

Ryan, G.D. (1987) 'Juvenile sex offenders: development and correction', *Child Abuse and Neglect*, 11, 385–395.

Ryan, G. (1989) 'Victim to Victimiser', *Journal of Interpersonal Violence*, 4 (September), 325–341.

Ryan, G.D. and Lane, S.L. (eds) (1991a) *Juvenile Sexual Offending: Causes, Consequences and Correction*, Lexington, MA, Lexington Books.

Ryan, G.D. and Lane, S.L. (1991b) *Integrating Theory and Method in Juvenile Sexual Offending*, Lexington, MA, Lexington Books.

Ryan, G., Lane, S.R., Davis, J.M. and Isaac, C.B. (1987) 'Juvenile sex offenders: development and corrections', *Child Abuse and Neglect*, 2, 385–395.

Salter, A.C. (1988) *Treating Child Sex Offenders and Victims: A Practical Guide* Newbury Park, CA, Sage.

Samson, D.M. and McDonnell, A. (1990) 'Functional analysis and challenging behaviour', *Behavioural Psychotherapy*, 18, 259–271.

Sapp, A.D. and Vaughn, M.S. (1990) 'Juvenile sex offender treatment at state-operated correctional institutions', *International Journal of Offender Therapy and Comparative Criminology*, 34(2), 131–146.

Sarafino, E.P. (1979) 'An estimate of nationwide incidence of sexual offences against children', *Child Welfare*, 587(2), 127–134.

Saunders, E.B. and Awad, G.A. (1988) 'Assessment, management and treatment planning for male adolescent sexual offenders', *American Journal of Orthopsychiatry*, 58(4), 571–574.

Saunders, E.B., Awad, G.A. and White, G. (1986) 'Male adolescent sexual offenders: the offender and the offense' (Special Issue: Canadian Academy of Child Psychiatry: A Canadian Perspective), *Canadian Journal of Psychiatry*, 31, 542–549.

Scavo, R. and Buchanan, B.D. (1989) 'Group therapy for male adolescent sex offenders: a model for residential treatment', *Residential Treatment for Children and Youth*, 7(2), 59–74.

Schlank, A.M. (1995) 'The utility of the MMPI and the MSI for identifying a sexual offender typology', *Sexual Abuse: A Journal of Research and Treatment*, 7(3) 185–194.

Schofield, M. (1965) *The Sexual Behaviour of Young People*, London, Longman.

Schonfeld, L., Oeters, R. and Dolente, A. (1993) *Substance Abuse Relapse Assessment*, Odessa, FL, Psychological Assessment Resources.

Scott, P.D. (1977) 'Assessing dangerousness in criminals', *British Journal of Psychiatry*, 131, 127–142.

Segal, Z.V. and Marshall, W.L. (1985) 'Heterosexual social skills in a population of rapists and child molesters', *Journal of Consulting and Clinical Psychology*, 53(1) 55–63.

Segal, Z.V. and Stermac, L.E. (1990) 'The role of cognition in sexual assault', in Marshall, W.L., Laws, D.R. and Barbaree, H.E. (eds) *Handbook of Sexual Assault: Issues, Theories and Treatment of the Offender*, New York, Plenum Press.

Shoor, M., Speed, M.H. and Bartelt, C. (1966) 'Syndrome of the adolescent child molester', *American Journal of Psychiatry*, 122, 783–789.

Shure, M.B. and Spivack, G. (1978) *Problem-solving Techniques in Childrearing*, San Francisco, Jossey Bass.

Skuse, D. (1995) 'Family dynamics of abusive adolescents'. Paper presented at the Annual Conference of British Paediatric Association, York.

Smets, A. and Cebula, M. (1987) 'A group treatment for adolescent sex offenders: five steps towards resolution', *Child Abuse and Neglect*, 11, 247–254.

Smith, W.R. (1988) 'Delinquency and abuse among juvenile sexual offenders', *Journal of Interpersonal Violence* 3(4), 400–413.

Smith, W.R. and Monastersky, C. (1986) 'Assessing juvenile sexual offenders' risk for reoffending', *Criminal Justice and Behaviour*, 13, 115–140.

Snyder, J.J. and White, M.J. (1979) 'The use of cognitive self-instruction in the treatment of behaviorally disturbed adolescents', *Behavior Therapy*, 10 227–235.

Sorensen, R.C. (1973) *Adolescent Sexuality in Contemporary America*, New York, New World.

Spence, S. (1978) *Social Skills Training with Children and Adolescents*, Windsor, Berks, NFER.

Spence, S. (1980) *Social Skills Training with Children and Adolescents*, London, NFER.

Spence, J.T. and Helmreich, R.L. (1972) 'The Attitudes Toward Women scale: an objective instrument to measure attitudes towards the rights and roles of women in contemporary society', *Psychological Documents*, 2(153).

Spielberger, C.D. (1991) *State-Trait Anger Expression Inventory: Revised Research Edition*, Odessa, FL, Psychological Assessment Resources.

Spivack, G. and Shure, M.B. (1974) *Social Adjustment of Young Children: A Cognitive Approach to Problems*, San Francisco, Jossey Bass.

Steen, C. and Monnettee, B. (1989) *Treating Adolescent Sex Offenders in the Community*, Illinois, C. Thomas Publications.

Stermac, L.E. and Quinsey, V.L. (1986) 'Social competence among rapists', *Behavioral Assessment*, 8, 171–185.

Stermac, L.E. and Sheridan, P. (1993) 'The developmentally disabled adolescent sex offender', in Barbaree, H.E., Marshall, W.L. and Hudson, S.M. *The Juvenile Sex Offender*, New York, The Guilford Press.

Stewart, V. and Stewart, A. (1981) *Business Applications of Repertory Grid*, London, McGraw-Hill.

Striar, S.L. and Ensor, P.G. (1986) 'Therapeutic responses to adolescent psychiatric patients' sexual expression: beyond a restriction/permission stance' (Special Issue: Adolescent Sexualities: Overviews and Principles of Intervention), *Journal of Social Work and Human Sexuality*, 5(1), 51–69.

Summit, R.C. (1988) 'Hidden victims, hidden in pain – societal avoidance of child sexual abuse', in Wyatt, G.E. and Powell, G.J. (eds) *Lasting Effects of Child Sexual Abuse*, Newbury Park, CA, Sage.

Svalastoga, K. (1962) 'Rape and social structures', *Pacific Sociological Review*, 5, 48–53.

Taylor, J.L., Pearce, G., Roy, N.S. and Williams, K.L. (1997) 'The Sexual Information, Reasoning and Attitudes Test (SIRAT)'. Unpublished paper, Dept of Psychology, Northgate Hospital, Morpeth.

Thomas, J. (1991) 'The adolescent sex offender's family in treatment', in Ryan, G. and Lane, S. (eds) *Juvenile Sexual Offending: Causes, Consequences and Correction*, Lexington, MA, Lexington Books.

Tingle, D., Barnard, G.W., Robbins, L., Newman, G. and Hutchinson, D. (1986) 'Childhood and adolescent characteristics of pedophiles and rapists', *International Journal of Law and Psychiatry*, 9, 103–116.

Toch, H. (1969) *Violent Men*, Chicago, Illinois, Aldine.

Trower, P. (1984) 'A radical critique and reformulation: From organism to agent', in Trower, P. (ed.) *Radical Approaches to Social Skills Training*, London, Croom Helm.

Tschudi, F. (1977) 'Loaded and honest questions: a construct theory view of symptoms and therapy', in Bannister, D. (ed.) *New Perspectives in Personal Construct Theory*, London, Academic Press.

Twentyman, G.T. and Zimering, R.T. (1979) 'Behavioral training of social skills: a critical review', in Hersen, M., Eisler, R.M. and Miller, P.M. (eds) *Progress in Behavior Modification*, Vol. 7, New York, Academic Press.

Ussher, J. and Dewberry, C. (1995) 'The nature and long term effects of childhood sexual abuse: a survey of adult survivors in Britain', *British Journal of Clinical Psychology*, 34, 177–192.

Van Ness, S.R. (1984) 'Rape as instrumental violence: a study of youth offenders', *Journal of Offender Counseling, Services and Rehabilitation*, 9, 16–170.

Vander Hey, B. (1992) 'Theories of incest', in O'Donohue, D. and Greer, J.H. (eds) *The Sexual Abuse of Children* Vol. 2, Hillsdale, NJ, Lawrence Erlbaum.

Vinogradov, S., Dishotsky, N., Doty, A.K. and Tinkelberg, J.R. (1988) 'Patterns of behavior in adolescent rape', *American Journal of Orthopsychiatry*, 58, 179–187.

Vizard, E., Monck, E. and Misch, P. (1995) 'Child and adolescent sex abuse perpetrators: a review of the research literature', *Journal of Child Psychology and Psychiatry*, 36, 731–756.

Vizard, E., Wynick, S., Jawkes, C., Woods, J. and Jenkins, J. (1996) 'Juvenile sexual offenders: assessment issues', *British Journal of Psychiatry*, 168, 259–262.

Ward, T., Hudson, M. and Siegert, R.J. (1995) 'A critical comment on Pithers' relapse prevention model', *Sexual Abuse: A Journal of Research and Treatment*, 7(2), 167–175.

Warner, N. (1992) *Choosing with Care* – The Report of the Committee of Enquiry into the Selection, Development and Management of Staff in Children's Homes. London, HMSO.

Wasserman, J. and Kappel, S. (1985) *Adolescent Sex Offenders in Vermont*, Burlington, Vermont Department of Health.

Watson, D. and Friend, R. (1969) 'Assessment of social-evaluative anxiety', *Journal of Consulting and Clinical Psychology*, 33, 445–457.

Wechsler, D. (1992) *Wechsler Intelligence Scale for Children – III UK*, Sidcup, Kent, Psychological Corporation.

Weinrott, M.R. (1994) 'A new clinical package for arousal control of adolescent offenders', Paper presented at ATSA Annual Conference, San Francisco.

Weinrott, M.R. and Saylor, M. (1991) 'Self-report of crimes committed by sex offenders', *Journal of Interpersonal Violence*, 6(3), 286–300.

Weissberg, M. (1982) *Dangerous Secrets: Maladaptive Responses to Stress*, New York, W.W. Norton.

West, D. (1987) *Sexual Crimes and Confrontations* (Cambridge Studies in Criminology), Aldershot, Gower.

West, D.J. (1991) 'The effects of sex offences', in Hollin, C.R. and Howells, K. (eds) *Clinical Approaches to Sex Offenders and Their Victims*, Chichester, John Wiley.

Whalley, L.J. and McGuire, R.J. (1978) 'Measuring sexual attitudes', *Acta Psychiatrica Scandinavia*, 58, 299–314.

White, J.W. and Koss, M.P. (1993) 'Adolescent sexual aggression within heterosexual relationships: prevalence, characteristics and cause', in Barbaree, H.E., Marshall, W.L. and Hudson, S.M. (eds) *The Juvenile Sex Offender*, New York, Guilford Press.

Williams, S. (1991) 'Sex education' (Special Issue: Challenging Behaviour), *Australia and New Zealand Journal of Developmental Disabilities*, 17(2), 217–219.

Wilson, G. (1978) *Wilson Sex Fantasy Questionnaire*, London, J.M. Dent and Sons.

Winter, D. (1992) 'A personal construct view of social skills training', in Maitland, P. and Brennan, D. (eds) *Personal Construct Theory, Deviancy and Social Work*, Inner London Probation Service/Centre for Personal Construct Psychology (Revised 2nd Edition).

Wish, J.R., McCombs, K.F. and Edmonson, B. (1980) *The Socio-Sexual Knowledge and Attitude Test: Instruction Manual and Stimulus Picture Book*, Wood Dale, IL, Stoetling.

Wolf, S.C. (1984) 'A multi-factorial model of deviant sexuality'. Paper presented at the 3rd International Conference on Victimology, Lisbon, Portugal.

Wright, K.J.T. (1970) 'Exploring the uniqueness of common complaints', *British Journal of Medical Psychology*, 43, 221–232.

Wright, R. (1980) 'Rape and physical violence', in West, D.J. (ed.) *Sex Offenders in the Criminal Justice System*, Cambridge, Institute of Criminology.

Yates, A. (1982) 'Children eroticized by incest', *American Journal of Psychiatry*, 139, 482–485.

Yochelson, S. and Samenow, S.E. (1977) *The Criminal Personality, Vol. 1: A Profile for Change*, New York, Jason Aronsen.

Zimpfer, D.G. (1992), 'Group work with juvenile delinquents', *Journal for Specialists in Group Work*, 17(2), 116–126.

Index

Compiled by Meg Davies (Registered Indexer)